MW00456983

"This excellent book is of vital importan[ce]
concepts of shamanism from traditional C[...]
looked within Western spirituality. David [...]
by his speaking and working with, as w[...]
having indispensable first-hand experience of these unbroken traditions. It provides
the reader with great insight into the true beliefs of authentic, traditional shamanism.
A must-have for anyone's collection."
— **Aminaa Batmunkh**, traditional Mongol shaman, Mother Tree Shamanism

"David Shi, a leading shamanic practitioner, has written a comprehensive exploratory
book on hearing the ancestral call, spirit flight, and trance states for communion
with the divine. Shi demonstrates incisive knowledge and a deep understanding of
North Asian shamanic traditions. A long-awaited and important resource on the subject, *Spirit Voices* is a masterfully written, engrossing read."
— **Benebell Wen**, author of *The Tao of Craft* and *I Ching, The Oracle*

"From blood to scholarship, David Shi is aligned with making sure spiritual traditions
remain both intact and accessible for the North Asian diaspora. An important book
and voice for Asian Americans and those interested in a strong perspective of North
Asian traditions."
— **Chaweon Koo**, author of *Spell Bound: A New
Witch's Guide to Crafting the Future*

"*Spirit Voices* is a very valuable addition to the study and understanding of authentic
shamanism for today's reader. David Shi provides a powerful glimpse into the rich
and fascinating world of traditional shamanism in a book of exceptional importance.
The author's breadth of knowledge and experience shine out brightly in this accessible
book. Shi provides an invaluable and clearly written overview of a complex topic,
bringing exceptional insight to a subject often shrouded in mystery. This is a most
valuable read for anyone seeking to understand more about these ancient traditions."
— **Nicholas Breeze Wood**, editor of *Sacred Hoop Magazine*

"David Shi is a blessing, sharing his knowledge and rich resources on North Asian
shamanism. Speaking as a Korean shaman, I admire how David is able to share the
meanings of our traditional practices, revealing the power and magic of our beliefs on
connecting with ancestral spirits and land spirits, and the calling of spirits. He includes
the deep symbolism within the practices of shamanism, providing access to those looking to understand the roots of our shamanism, connecting us deeper to our spirits."
— **Jennifer Kim**, teaching artist, practicing mudang, and consultant
on Muism, Korea's ancient and enduring indigenous religion

"An invaluable voice on the modern spiritual landscape, David Shi has authored a work
that is deeply informative and powerful, handed to the seeker with great wisdom as well
as great kindness. His curiosity about the spirit world and its history along with his gen-
erosity in sharing his own wisdom is unparalleled. No matter the seeker's faith or background, they will find crucial pieces in *Spirit Voices* to aid their own spiritual journey.
Shi's work should be a must-read for anyone on the magickal or spiritual path."
— **Courtney Weber**, author of *Hekate: Goddess of Witches*

"David Shi's *Spirit Voices* is a comprehensive survey of Northern Asiatic shamanism, a topic broad in both scope and depth. Delivered in a concise and comprehensible style, *Spirit Voices* skillfully leads the reader to a deeper and more complete understanding of shamanism. Woven throughout this exploration of history, hardy research, and cultural context are *telingus*—moments of David's personal narrative— and invitations to join him, if only briefly, on his path. And, in these moments of walking with the author, there is a chance to reflect upon the paths we each walk. An important part of this reflection is David's careful, sensitive, and sometimes frank discussion about the importance of culture, ontology, cosmology, and the vital need for a lineage of teachers and teachings. David's care for and deep connection to the people and concepts he is writing about is plain. *Spirit Voices* is a strong addition to the library for any serious student of shamanism."

—**Ron Teeples**, Pathfinder Counseling and Communications

"The word 'shaman' is of North Asian origin, and yet, so many people associate it with an assortment of spiritual and cultural practices that have roots in other places. While the hunger for grounded and earth-honoring spirituality is strong and urgent, there is a dearth of culturally specific and accessible knowledge available in English on the topic of North Asian indigenous spirituality. David Shi's contribution to bridging this gap is presented with humility, clarity, and respect, offering a picture of the similarities and differences found throughout the shamanic traditions of North Asia. I particularly recommend *Spirit Voices* for those with ancestral ties to this part of the world."

—**Laura Perlin**, ritualist and student of Sakha (Yakut) traditions

"I first saw David Shi speak many, many years ago at the amazing Catland bookshop in Brooklyn. It was my first exposure to North Asian magic and religion. Prior to that, I had only seen shamanism in a watered-down version, stripped of its cultural context. Almost as soon as David began to speak, I felt things begin to slide into place. When his first book, *North Asian Magic,* came out, I devoured it, loving every bit. Perhaps more than any other book, it helped me weave my own fledgling practice of trance journey, at that time largely self-taught and spirit-led, into a more coherent and strongly rooted system of magic.

When I learned of David's next book, *Spirit Voices,* I eagerly wrote to our shared editor to request to read an early review copy. I'm so glad I did! *Spirit Voices* is very well organized, walking beginners step by step on a tour through many specific styles of North Asian practice. If that were the whole book, I would have been satisfied. However, the last section of the book, with chapters on shamanic tools, divination, folk magic, and ceremonies, is a treasure trove of magical inspiration. I expect to return to it time and time again. I recommend this book to you with my whole heart. May it inspire you to be the magicians our time needs."

—**Sara Mastros**, author of *The Big Book of Magical Incense*

SPIRIT VOICES

The Mysteries and Magic of
North Asian Shamanism

DAVID SHI

WEISER BOOKS

This edition first published in 2023 by Weiser Books, an imprint of
Red Wheel/Weiser, LLC
With offices at:
65 Parker Street, Suite 7
Newburyport, MA 01950
www.redwheelweiser.com

ISBN: 978-1-57863-792-8

Library of Congress Control Number: 2023930512

Cover design by Sky Peck Design
Interior by Steve Amarillo / Urban Design LLC
Typeset in Sabon and Interstate

Printed in the United States of America

IBI

10 9 8 7 6 5 4 3 2 1

*To my grandparents, especially to my grandmother
Suyun Jiang, who passed away in 2022.*

Contents

Contents

Preface:
The Journey to This Book

As an Asian American growing up in New Jersey, I had little interest in exploring my ancestral culture or heritage. Why would I pursue an identity that had already made me a target of mockery, insensitive jokes, condescension, and even bullying? Like many other Asian Americans in their teenage years, I wanted to assimilate into Western values and lifestyle, and tone down or distance myself from my Asian roots. But my spirits had other plans.

My family had told me we were Manchus (mixed with Han Chinese blood), but that, for all intents and purposes, Manchus were now "Chinese" and thus no different from the Han. In fact, most Manchus in China today identify themselves as Chinese both politically and nationally, and would at most identify themselves with Dongbei/Northeast Chinese culture. My family was no exception. Although they knew we had Manchu roots, they did not place much importance on it.

Then, in 2009, I started having dreams of my Manchu ancestors. They told me to study about them to learn about Manchu history, culture, and identity. Manchus were known to take their dream divination seriously, so this message awoke in me a passion to explore just who these mysterious ancestors were. Those who knew me between 2009 and 2013 referred to me as the "Manchu guy," someone who proudly identified himself as Manchu, a race and culture that many had either never heard of or believed to be long dead. I became an expert on Manchu history and culture, and their legacy in China. I even voiced controversial opinions about the Qing Dynasty and the short-lived Japanese puppet state of Manchukuo.

When I was in middle and high school, I became interested in witchcraft and Neopaganism, although my interest waned somewhat when I was in college. In 2012, I began interacting with New York's Pagan community, attending public rituals, workshops, and classes, and connecting with many members and even some leading figures of New York's witchcraft community. I also studied both African American Hoodoo and Nordic rune practices to expand my magical knowledge. Initially, I wanted to use magic and witchcraft to improve the results of my own studies and hard work, but I soon realized that I had a deep hunger for magical practice. Even my own ancestors encouraged me to continue studying magic, with an emphasis on the folk magic of other cultures.

In 2014, my ancestral dreams returned, telling me to explore the shamanic traditions of my Manchu heritage. In this, I had very little success. Most researchers only mentioned Manchu shamanism in passing, often in a footnote and frequently in broad generalizations. I was frustrated.

But my dreams continued. In them, my ancestors told me to observe and study the shamanism of the Manchus' neighbors in order to better understand Manchu shamanism itself. This at least gave me a starting point. To the south of Manchuria were the Han Chinese, who had strong animistic spiritual and magical beliefs, although these were not specifically shamanic. To the east were the Koreans, who still maintained a shamanic tradition known as *Mugyo Mudang*. To the north were the Siberians, including the Tungus (the Amur, the Evenk, and the Oroqen), as well as the Buryat Mongols. To the west were the Mongols, who appeared to have the strongest living shamanic traditions.

Thanks to the late Buryat American shaman Sarangerel, the traditions of the Siberian Buryat Mongols were perhaps the most accessible. Her works still remain one of the few English-language resources written by a traditional shaman that give information on actual shamanic tools and techniques. Most others, written by academic researchers and anthropologists, give only a detached view of these traditions. Yet, the more I studied, the more I realized that I could not rely on written sources to further my knowledge. I had to engage with a traditional shamanic community, one not corrupted by Western New Age beliefs or the core shamanism practice developed by Michael Harner that was widely practiced in the United States.

One day, during a Google search, I accidentally slipped into a light trance (something that had frequently happened ever since I was young), and my spirits guided me to look up specific words. Through this spirit-led search, I stumbled onto *Sacred Hoop* magazine, which focuses on global shamanic and animistic practices, with a special emphasis on Mongolian, Siberian, Himalayan, and Native American traditions. When I connected with its editor, Nicholas Breeze Wood, I discovered a large community of scholars, practitioners, and even traditional shamans among North Asian and other cultures.

For a long time, this community was accessible only online, most of its members based across Asia and Europe, with only a few scattered across the Americas. Thus my spiritual community in the United States consisted primarily of practitioners of Western witchcraft, and Hoodoo and rootwork, which often overlapped. Even though my understanding of traditional North Asian shamanism was only in its earliest stages, I wanted to build bridges to these other spiritual communities so that at least the American communities could understand my own spiritual heritage. In 2016, these attempts culminated in my first book, *North Asian Magic: Spellcraft from Manchuria, Mongolia, and Siberia*, which focused on North Asian folk magic.

I was persuaded to write this book because there were very few works dedicated to Asian folk magic as a whole, let alone the traditions of North Asia. The book consisted of research ranging from Sarangerel's work, to academic research papers, to historical commentary on the Qing Dynasty. It also included interviews with a Tuvan American shaman, as well as stories I collected from my relatives who still believed in spirits and shamanism. Yet, although the book did introduce North Asian folk magic into the Hoodoo and witchcraft communities, it did not address the different traditions and regional practices of North Asian spirituality or discuss how the fluidity across these traditions was affected by regional differences.

In 2016, my employer-company offered me the opportunity to work in Hong Kong to develop our corporate-services business. Since this aligned well with the will of my spirits, I packed my bags and went. Living in Hong Kong was difficult for me, and I learned first hand the consequences of neglecting local land spirits. Although I strongly believe that any magical or spiritual practice involves local land spirits, I attempted to engage my spirituality and magical practice before giving them offerings.

Hong Kong's tumultuous history has created an environment that is home to many restless spirits and ghosts. But many spiritual traditions there are centered on family spaces (driving ghosts out of homes), businesses (hiring feng shui masters to design optimal environments), and personal enlightenment (primarily through local Buddhist beliefs). As a result, public areas are often plagued by many restless spirits who are particularly fickle and cantankerous. Within my first two months in Hong Kong, I experienced a wide range of difficulties—both in my health and in my finances—before I realized that I had not given proper offerings to the land spirits there (they particularly enjoy fish powder, rice, and herbal teas). Once I did so, many of these problems subsided.

Living in Asia allowed me to explore the many different forms of spirituality found there, and I came to understand the enormous diversity of the region. My travels took me to Buddhist temples and Shinto shrines in Japan, mosques and Hindu temples in Indonesia, Buddhist and folk temples in Hong Kong and Taiwan, and Buddhist temples in Korea. In Korea, I had the chance to visit local Mudang shamans. While visiting Manchuria, I reconnected with relatives and learned about the *Tiaodashen* shamanism practiced by the Han Chinese settler-descendants there.

Most significantly, I traveled to Mongolia twice.

My first trip was organized by a Khalkha shaman. On this trip, I met with several local Khalkha and Darkhad shamans and visited the large Buddhist monastery at Amarbayasgalant. On my second trip, a Darkhad shaman (now a close friend) took me to the remote Darkhad Valley, where I met with elders who are some of the most powerful shamans in Mongolia. I also traveled to the taiga, coniferous permafrost forests near the Russian-Mongolian border. These are very remote regions that cannot be reached except in specialized vehicles and on horseback. Here, the spiritual energy was extremely intense, often causing me to experience headaches, fuzzy focus, and mood swings.

It was during this second trip that my friend and her elders determined that I indeed did have a shamanic spirit, and that I was destined to be a shaman. Despite our friendship, I was limited in the ceremonies in which I could participate. Manchus and Darkhad Mongols were bitter enemies during the Qing Dynasty, so there was a risk that I could be hurt if I participated in some ceremonies or, worse yet, initiated with them.

When I told the Darkhad elders about the dreams I had from my ancestors and their message to explore neighboring shamanic traditions, they knew that Mongol and Siberian shamanism would be most relevant for me, and they were happy to teach me some of their concepts and practices. But they were very clear that, in order to be properly initiated, I would have to find a specific teacher within a specific group of Manchus or Inner Mongols in China to be properly taught and initiated. They were confident that I would find this person within five years, but warned that, if I didn't initiate by age thirty-five, my spirit sickness might return with more serious symptoms. Despite these apparent limitations, however, they were extremely generous with me, sharing their knowledge and closed teachings, and even providing me with several new tools after determining that some of my own were unsuitable.

In early 2019, not long after returning to the United States, I took another huge step forward on my journey. I became acquainted with Jan Van Ysslestyne, whose book *Spirits from the Edge of the World* (Pathfinder Counseling, 2018) describes in detail the beliefs and shamanic practices of the Ulchi-Nanai, a people who are part of the Amur tribes. As such, they are the direct northern neighbors of the Manchu and speak almost the same language, which Van Ysslestyne also spoke fluently. Although still not exactly the tradition that I was meant to follow, learning about Ulchi spiritual and shamanic practices elevated my own practices greatly.

I knew, both logically and intuitively, that the tradition I was meant to practice lay somewhere between the traditions of the Ulchi and those of the Darkhad. Through her work, many aspects of Manchu shamanism that I had researched earlier began to make more sense. Sadly, Van Ysslestyne passed away in June 2021. Her enormously important work had a huge impact on this book. I wish she could have read it.

In March 2020, when a worldwide pandemic hit, I accepted that I would be forced to suspend my spiritual journey and I trusted my spirits to guide me when the time was right. To my pleasant surprise, the opposite proved true when my Darkhad friend decided to hold classes on the teachings of Darkhad shamanism for a select group of students through an organization called Mother Tree Shamanism Teachings, which is still active today. Although we have been in active communication to make sure that this book does not disclose more than is appropriate, these teachings are certainly a pivotal component of my writing. Before her passing, Van Ysslestyne also offered a self-study program on Ulchi shamanism through her website, Pathfinder Counseling. This class, along with her book, greatly expanded my perception of shamanic practice in North Asia and showed me how truly diverse it is.

In August 2020, my friend, author and editor Judika Illes, asked me to consider writing a book on my studies and research. In fact, Judika had been contacting me every year since we had met five years before to write another book, but, given my lack of knowledge and experience, I had felt wholly unqualified and declined. By this time, however, I had learned a lot about the shamanic traditions of many different North Asian cultures and had discovered both their many similarities and their important differences. And I realized that now, after five years of research and travel, this was something I could write about. Most published materials on shamanism dive deeply into one tradition or another, and they are often very academic and inaccessible to most. Even in my own research, I frequently had difficulty distinguishing between traditions, as experts in one field tend to speak (often incorrectly) for other groups as well. Thus it took me a long time to understand the subtle and unique aspects of each tradition.

As I considered writing this book, I realized that this is exactly the type of resource I wish I had had available to me many years ago—a clear and accessible guide that explores the many different North Asian shamanic traditions. Moreover, I knew that the next stage in my life's journey would take me in a very specific direction and focus on a specific tradition. So it was now or never. I hope this book serves as a resource for Asian Americans like me, as well as many others, who hunger for ancestral spiritual connection. Although it may not address the traditions of all Asian Americans, I hope that my own journey and research can serve as an inspiration to others who are geographically separated from their ancestral lands and help them to celebrate and practice their spiritual heritage. It flows in our blood! For those not of Asian heritage, I hope you can glean insights from this book that can enrich your own spiritual journey.

As you read this book, remember that the purpose of shamanism can be summed up in two words: *coexistence* and *balance*—coexistence with our spirits and our communities, and the balance that must be preserved between all of us and within ourselves. I wish nothing but blessings, wisdom, and peace upon you as you discover these ancient traditions.

CHAPTER 1

The Roots of Shamanism

Shamanism is one of the most misunderstood words in the West. To most people in the United States, it conjures up images of Native American, South American, and even African spiritualities. For others, it suggests fantasy gaming and comic books. Today, the term is used carelessly in mass marketing for products ranging from "shamanic" yoga or reiki, to "shamanic shampoo." Yet very few understand what the word actually means, where it comes from, or the family of traditions it truly represents.

Most resources acknowledge that the word *shaman* comes from the Tungus-Evenk people of Siberia. In fact, the word shaman (*saman*) is used by nearly all Tungus tribes. Dutch explorer Nicolaes Witsen produced the earliest known depiction of a Siberian shaman in the late 17th century. Around that time and into the 18th century, Russian explorers, hunters, and traders traveled into the region and interacted with the Siberian peoples. Russian and Dutch researchers, the first Westerners to interact with North Asian peoples, used the word to describe the spiritual practices of all indigenous Siberian cultures. The Russian usage of the word then spread to France, where the word is rendered as *chaman*, and from there to both Spain and Britain, which then controlled the largest colonial empires in the world. As these empires expanded, the word began to refer to all indigenous spiritual elders. This is why it is used so widely around the world today.

The Etymological Roots of Shamanism

Western anthropologists and linguists have posited that, since the Tungus root *sa* means "to know," *saman* (shaman) must mean "one who knows." While this is certainly possible, in the Tungus languages, the entire word *saman* implies "to heat up" or "to become excited." In some tribes, it relates to fire, boiling, or even fury. And in fact, this metaphor describes the role of a shaman more accurately than merely "one who knows."

A long-debunked theory that still frequently appears online is that the word *shaman* derives from the Sanskrit word *sramane*, which means "ascetic" or "Buddhist monk." While there are many shamanic practices across North Asia that do indicate extensive Buddhist influences (sometimes even working with Buddhist spirits), in fact no relation exists between the roots of Vedic Buddhism and those of North Asian shamanism. Not only has there never been ancient direct contact between the Tungus peoples and Vedic Indians, none of the cultures that lie between Vedic India and Tungus lands use the word *saman* or shaman for spiritual purposes. I suspect this "theory" stems from Western researchers and ceremonialists seeking to identify a potential Indo-European origin for shamanism in both name and practice, perhaps in a colonialist attempt to attribute Siberian spiritual traditions to the same roots as pre-Christian European beliefs.

So what does the word "shamanism" actually mean? The best definition I've seen to date comes from shamanic researcher Nicholas Breeze Wood, who defines it thus:

A shaman is someone chosen by the spirits [typically at or before birth] and who can go into a controlled and repeatable deliberate trance state, during which they A) experience "spirit flight," where they go to the spirit worlds and meet spirits, who they either fight with, negotiate with, or trick, in order to create change in this physical world, or B) are often taken over/possessed by the spirits (normally ancestral shaman spirits, or local land spirits) while in this physical world—the spirits using the shaman's voice and body to heal, or give advice to members of the shaman's community.

Without the spirits and their blessing, a shaman cannot exist or function. Without the trance state, it is not shamanism.[1]

This definition holds true not only for the Tungus tribes, but also for sister traditions among other cultures, especially those of North Asia.

The Cultural Roots of Shamanism

Shamanism is believed to have originated in North Asia—some say in modern-day Khentii province in northeastern Mongolia, some say around the Lake Baikal region in southern Siberia. Yet others locate its origins in the Altai region of Siberia bordering Mongolia and Kazakhstan. Researchers typically agree that, contrary to popular belief, shamanism as a practice arose roughly 10,000 years ago and is therefore a fairly recent practice.[2] By comparison, Native American tribes migrated to the Americas from Asia between 15,000 and 20,000 years ago. Although their spiritual and animistic beliefs are similar to those of North Asia, however, the majority of Native American tribes left before shamanism first developed there.

The first written account of shamanism comes from China around 2,000 years ago. It describes the practices of their northern neighbors with whom they were frequently at war—likely the Hunnu/Xiongnu people, a confederation of nomadic tribes that frequently raided Chinese villages and are believed to have later migrated westward toward Europe as the Huns. Reports by Chinese visitors to Hunnu lands talk about shamans in trance possession offering sacrifices to spirits, the sky, and the earth.[3] This region birthed a shamanic tradition that has spread to neighboring peoples through migration, intermarriage, and other forms of direct contact. Although each group practiced within a different cultural framework, the traditions that sprang from this area stretch east toward Korea and to the Ainu in Hokkaido and the Inuit in

North America, and west toward the Hungarians and the Saami people in Scandinavia. Even the shamanic traditions of Tibetan and Himalayan areas may be traceable back to these same roots. It is unclear, however, if the shamanic traditions of southeastern Asia, including those of the Hmong and of Pacific tribes, are also related to this family.

Shamanism vs. Animism

When most Westerners speak about shamanism, they are more than likely referring to animism, the belief that everything embodies spirits—mountains, rivers, plants, and rocks, and even "modern entities" like furniture, electricity, and technological gadgets. Even viruses and bacteria, which were formerly envisioned as disease spirits. And because everything is innately animated by spirits, we can interact with these spirits to affect change in our physical world and in our lives.

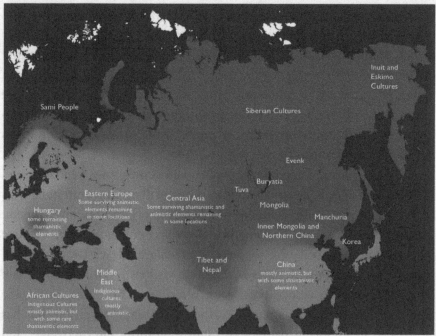

Figure 1. This map lists the broad distribution of shamanic cultural traditions across Asia, as well as neighboring non-shamanic animistic cultural traditions.

Just about every culture in the world has practiced some form of animistic spirituality at some point in its history. In North America, the fastest-growing movements of animistic spirituality today appear to be Neopaganism and witchcraft, which are based on reconstructions of pre-Christian European beliefs, and African traditional religions, which include practices like Hoodoo and Conjure, as well as formalized religions like Vodou, Lucumi, and Candomblé. These traditions reflect attempts to create new belief systems based on records of ancient practices, and on existing practices that have endured and traveled from their original lands, albeit with some "New World" adaptations.

Although these are all legitimate spiritual traditions, most of them are not, strictly speaking, shamanism as defined here. While several tribes and cultural communities in Africa and South America have developed traditions that may be considered shamanic (or at least something close to it), the vast majority of true shamanic traditions sprang from North Asia. Some are offended by my claim that their traditions are not shamanic and seem to equate that with my saying they are somehow not legitimate. But just because a spiritual tradition is not shamanic does not mean that it is any less legitimate or powerful. It simply means that shamanism encompasses very specific practices and beliefs that are not a part of those spiritualities, just as those traditions include practices and beliefs that are not a part of North Asian shamanism.

Others object to the use of the word "animism" to refer to these traditions, claiming that the word neglects the importance of essential spiritual elders who guide these communities, connect them with spirits, and help them maintain balance. And I agree. We need a better term that honors the importance of elders in these spiritual traditions. I'm just not convinced that "shamanism" is the right word.

The foundation of any true shamanic tradition is the spirits, who determine what we do and how we do it. In true shamanism, the word "spirits" refers specifically to shamanic spirits who engage with their human counterparts. These are usually ancestral shaman spirits—past shamans who are part of a person's ancestry. Occasionally, however, these may also include land spirits who are perhaps attached to a family lineage and/or guardians of ancestral lines. These shamanic spirits decide which people become shamans at birth, and they stay with those people for life to help them answer their shamanic calling.

When the time is right, these spirits manifest signs that indicate that a shaman is ready to be initiated. Once initiated, shamans go through a rigorous lifelong training process under the tutelage of both their shamanic spirits and their human teachers and elders. We will discuss these signs and other steps that ultimately lead to initiation later in this chapter.

Trance States

Shamans, like spiritual elders in many traditions, are spiritual healers and occasionally also leaders in traditional societies. As we have seen above, however, the methodologies of shamanism are quite unique. The defining trait of a shaman is that he or she can go into deliberate, controlled, and repeatable trance states at will. This means that, whenever shamans need to conduct spiritual workings through trance, they can achieve a trance state at a moment's notice. Although a ceremonial setting and assistants are immensely helpful, they are technically not required. While newly initiated shamans may sometimes slip into trance states accidentally, experienced shamans have full control over when they are in trance and when they are not. I myself accidentally slip into unintentional trance states fairly often. But when I need to perform a simple working, I can easily achieve a light trance as well.

Shamans induce trance using a specially prepared instrument—most commonly, a drum made from specific materials and activated so that it becomes enlivened. Other items like staffs or walking sticks and blacksmith-forged jaw harps can also be activated and used to induce trance, and these items may vary between tribes (see chapter 8).

When shamans induce trance, they call to their spirits, asking them to come. One of my favorite metaphors of shamanism is that every person is like a pool of water, capable of engaging in spiritual activity. As a person works with spirits and energy, the water heats up (remember that the connotation for the word *shaman* is "to heat up"). As shamans go deeper into the trance state, the water gets hotter, and they achieve the climactic trance state the moment the water boils, which is when the spirits finally arrive. At this point, shamans lose control of their bodies, and the spirits can possess them or carry their souls on what is known as "spirit flight." When I was in Mongolia, I was in the presence of elder shamans who induced trance by calling to their spirits several times. The first time I experienced the energy of the increasing trance state (and of the arriving spirit), I was so over-whelmed that I nearly collapsed and passed out on the spot.

Spirit Flight

The defining work of shamans occurs when they deliberately induce trance states to engage in either spirit flight or spirit possession. In most North Asian tribes, spirit possession is far more common, as it takes less of an energetic toll on the body. However, some tribes (notably in the Siberian taiga) perform spirit flight just as often, or even more frequently. The shamans of the Tungus tribes in the Amur River Valley (the Ulchi and the Nanai) and the Evenk in the taiga are all examples of cultures where spirit flight is performed more often than it is by their counterparts among the Mongol, Turkic, and even Tungus-Manchu peoples (see chapter 7). Because the North Asian peoples first encoun-tered by European researchers were from the taiga, and much later the Amur River Valley, spirit flight became more recognized in Western academic circles. Thus it is not a coincidence that Western-style core shamanism engages heavily in "shamanic journeying," which is loosely based on the spirit flight of Evenki shamans.

If you ask traditional North Asian shamans about spirit flight, you may not get a clear, direct, or honest answer. Some may deny that they ever do this work, even if they do. Shamans tend to be a bit tight-lipped on this topic, and not without reason. Spirit flight is one of the most dangerous aspects of a shaman's work. Most Westerners who practice core shamanism use guided meditation to journey to the spirit world, primarily to gain insight and clarity. This is *never* the reason that traditional shamans engage in spirit flight. If they are simply look-ing for answers, they use divination and/or engage in spirit possession to ask the spirits directly. When traditional shamans fly to the spirit world, they have a clear and singular purpose, like finding part of a lost soul or engaging directly with hostile spirits on their own turf. In these instances, they may be forced to negotiate, bribe, trick, or even fight spirits directly.

Even when performed successfully, spirit flight entails many addi-tional risks during both the journey to the destination in the spirit world and the journey back. Shamans may be attacked or delayed by wandering spirits. They may encounter obstacles like mountains, cliffs, lakes, or even oceans in the spirit world. They may even be tricked or trapped by spirits. There are also stories in which shamans have encountered their own ancestors, who either demand that they stay with them or beg them to take their souls back to the physical world. Some shamans even report being asked to perform tasks for their living relatives after returning to the physical world. And sometimes, there is great risk that a shaman's soul may never return to the physical world.

Given these risks, shamanic cultures often stress that only initi-ated shamans with years of experience should attempt to perform spirit flight—and only when necessary—because it demands that they have strong relationships with their spirits. In many traditional stories and legends, shamans' souls encounter obstacles so great and so over-whelming that they might have perished or remained stuck if not for the aid of their shamanic spirits, who are able to guide them and even rescue their souls while in the spirit world.

Shamans engage in spirit flight in many different ways. In some cases, their souls climb up and down the World Tree, which connects the spiritual worlds to the physical world; the paths of the world tree connect the "three worlds" (see chapter 2). In other traditions, sha-mans' souls fly directly out of their bodies to their desired destina-tion. In traditions where this is a common practice, a shaman's coat or armor may contain specially prepared feathers that are often attached to the headdress, but sometimes to the coat itself (see chapter 8).

In almost all traditions, shamanic spirits play a crucial role in facilitating spirit flight, serving as escorts who guide shamans' souls into the spirit worlds. Sometimes shamans' souls ride directly on one of these spirits for the journey. Sometimes they reside in a shaman's drum, or jaw harp, or other tool used to call them. In many of the tribes of the Siberian taiga, shamans' souls ride on a deer spirit who is summoned by a drum typically made of specially prepared deerskin.

Although spirit flight often entails traveling to destinations in the spirit world, this is not always the case. In some Tungus traditions, shamans may fly their souls to another part of the physical world. In Amur River traditions, they may fly them to distant planets and stars. Among the Ulchi, it is quite common for shamans to fly the souls of newborn children to Venus so that they can be safeguarded from spiritual pollution and risks.[4] The late Ulchi shaman Nadia Duvan once remarked that, while traveling in the Pacific Northwest of the United States, everywhere she went she saw the same two birds perched nearby staring at her. When she returned to her native village in southeastern Siberia, she discovered that the birds were two of her elders who, worried for her safety in a foreign land, had flown their souls out in the form of birds to check on her. The two shamans were able to describe the landscapes, houses, people, and everything they had seen in quite accurate detail, despite never having left the Amur River Valley.[5]

Spirit Possession

In most North Asian shamanic traditions, spirit possession, and not spirit flight, is the most common practice. One key milestone in initiations is reached when shamans are fully possessed by their spirits for the first time. As with spirit flight, shamans use one of their instruments (drum, jaw harp, bells, staffs, etc.) to induce trance and call their spirits. As the trance intensifies and the shamans "heat up," the moment of full trance occurs when the summoned spirits enter and fully possesses them.

Once possessed, the shamans may tremble slightly or start singing and dancing. They may even exhibit erratic breathing, as the spirits are not used to being in a state where physical breathing is necessary.

The first full breath that spirit-possessed shamans take is usually an indication that the possession has stabilized; this breath often comes in the form of a sound or loud exhalation. It's not unusual for shamans to make animal noises like wolf howls or bird chirps to signify the stabilized breath. One Korean Mudang shaman told me that, in her tradition, this breath often takes the form of yawning.

Once shamans are fully possessed by their spirits, they usually begin singing and/or dancing. While a few shamanic songs have been recorded, these are typically unique to each shaman and spirit. They are not learned from elders or teachers, but from the spirits directly. Spirit-possessed shamans sing in what seems like a free-form style, but these songs are stored in their memories and then used to call upon specific spirits. For this reason, shamanic songs are normally kept secret, as, in the wrong hands, they can be abused by enemies or by misguided, if well-intentioned, individuals.

Shamanic dancing serves multiple purposes. While certainly meant to entertain ceremony attendees, these dances may be used to call and entertain spirits (land spirits or even higher powers), highlighting the way in which shamans and their spirits act as bridges between the human and the spirit worlds. Moreover, shamans often wear empowered and activated implements containing jingle cones and bells that are meant to rattle and frighten away harmful spirits or entities. This is why a shaman's garb is often referred to as "armor."

Traditional North Asian shamans rely on a combination of divination and spirit possession for answers. Shamans may employ possession to find answers to questions when the results of divination are vague and they want to ask the spirits directly for more clarity. While practitioners in Western core shamanism typically journey into the spirit world to find answers and insights, traditional North Asian shamans rely on a combination of divination and spirit possession for answers. If they diagnose a potential issue, they typically use the session to try to rectify the condition. This is considered especially powerful, as the spirit uses the shaman's body to perform spiritual and magical healing, channeling the energy and methods of ages past into the present. If the techniques used are unable to correct the condition, shamans perform a later session—employing a heavier dedicated ceremony that may include spirit flight. These intense ceremonies are known to last for days, and even up to a week or longer depending on the issue being addressed, which could include a harmful spirit attachment, like a life-threatening disease that is not responding to medical treatment, or soul loss in which a strong hostile spirit has taken a soul part and is unwilling to release it.

In shamanic possession ceremonies, attendees approach the spirit-possessed shamans who quickly divine clients' conditions by tossing their drumbeaters to the ground then beating the drum over the kneel-ing clients' heads and backs to cleanse and purify them. They then use the drumbeater again to divine whether the cleansing was sufficient. In his book *Sky Shamans of Mongolia* (North Atlantic Books, 2016), shamanic researcher Kevin Turner describes how his chronic back pain was cured during one of his visits to a Buryat shaman who underwent possession and correctly diagnosed his condition. While in possession, she used her spirit whip to strike at various parts of his back before striking very hard at the central point of the pain. After that session, his chronic back pain disappeared.[6]

When my grandmother was a little girl in a northern Manchurian village bordering Inner Mongolia, she witnessed possessed shamans dipping their hands into pots of boiling oil and was amazed that their hands never burned or blistered. She described them using their hands (while covered in boiling oil) to miraculously heal attendees.

Shamanic Calling

One defining feature of shamanism is that shamans must be chosen by the spirits. Not everyone can be a shaman; you can't just study to become one. Shamans are chosen by spirits at birth, if not earlier. In almost every case, they have ancestors who were also shamans. Moreover, most of a shaman's spirits are ancestors who were also shamans.

And the reverse is true as well. Those chosen by the spirits to become shamans cannot reject that calling. To be a shaman is to dedicate your life to serve the spirits, and those chosen have no choice but to answer the call. At most, they may delay, but the call must be answered within their lifetime. There are numerous stories of individuals who did not want to become shamans and tried to refuse or reject their calling. In these cases, unfortunately, this refusal results in worsening shamanic sickness— sometimes physical or mental illnesses that may be healed by an initiation, and sometimes even physical injury. There have even been people who have lost their lives, as their constant refusal angered the spirits so much that they punished them beyond what their bodies could endure.

Does this mean that only people of North Asian descent can become shamans in North Asian traditions? Yes and no. One almost certainly must have blood that traces back to North Asian cultures (with shamanic ancestry). Some Europeans today have been called by North Asian shamanic spirits, because they retain some blood link to these cultures from generations past, though this is not common. Most North Asian cultures were nomadic and ranged across broad regions. The Mongol Empire founded by Chinggis (Genghis) Khan was the largest continuous land empire in history. Its genetic imprint may thus very well have circled the globe several times within the past 500 years. Moreover, individuals from other traditions may become shamans if their ancestors were spiritual elders who encouraged them to become elders as well and engage in spirit possession and spirit flight. However, these ancestors might force them to practice their own ancestral traditions and not North Asian ones.

There are many signs, especially among children and infants, that *may* indicate a shamanic calling, just as there are signs associated with being called to witchcraft in the West. Physical signs include marks on the body, like birthmarks. Occasionally, an extra finger or toe may also be a sign. Indications for a newborn may include being born with a caul, which many Western traditions also recognize as a mark of potential spiritual power. In cultures with heavier Buddhist influence, being born with the umbilical cord wrapped around the body is often taken as a sign as well, because of the cord's resemblance to Buddhist *mala* (prayer) beads. Epileptic fits may also be considered an indication of spiritual power.

Generally, however, personality and behavioral signs are much more common than physical signs. Behavioral signs can manifest in the urge to wander into woods and forests for long periods, having imaginary childhood friends, and general eccentricity. Someone with a shamanic calling may also experience glimpses of the future, a sense of déjà vu, or other psychic abilities. Other indications may manifest through dreams in which messages are conveyed by the spirits. This was the case for me.

All these are merely signs, however, and they do not necessarily indicate that a person is chosen to be a shaman. Once someone reaches an appropriate age, the spirits may induce stronger signs that adversely affect the person's physical, mental, or psychological health. This "pre-shamanic" state is known by several specific names—for example, *sagaasha* (cocoon) or *ongodtengertei* (one who has *ongod tenger*, or shamanic spirits) in Mongolian. This period is often very dangerous and shamans-to-be may be vulnerable; they may even suffer serious physical ailments that require hospitalization. They may experience hallucinations or paranoia, or may be diagnosed with mental disorders because they see visions or hear spirit voices. In extreme cases, individuals may disappear in the forest for long periods of time (weeks or months) and reappear in town naked, as in some Ulchi stories.[7]

The only way to know for sure if you have been called by the spirits is to visit an experienced shaman. Medical doctors may not be able to diagnose the cause of problems that may in fact be a shamanic or spirit sickness. In this case, only an experienced shaman will be able to tell if you are cursed or have been called by the spirits to become a shaman. It is important to note, however, that while these physical and psychological symptoms *may* be signs of spiritual sickness from a shamanic calling, this is not always the case. If you suffer from these or similar symptoms, please consult a medical professional first before seeking out a shaman or spiritual elder.

Shamanic Initiation

Those identified and recognized by an experienced shaman as having been chosen by shamanic spirits must find a suitable teacher and begin training and preparing for their eventual initiation. For those who grow up on their ancestral lands within their own cultural community, these teachers are often the shamans who recognized them (or one of their colleagues) and are therefore not hard to identify. In today's global society, in which more and more people are born and raised outside of their ancestral lands, this process can be more challenging. Some say that, if those recognized as having shamanic spirits don't have good karma, they may never find their teachers. Because the spirits will continue to induce the signs of calling via shamanic sickness, however, they will ultimately live harsh, unfulfilled "half-lives." I am currently in this stage. I have been recognized by both Darkhad Mongolian shamans and Korean Mudang shamans as having shamanic spirits, but I am still searching for my teacher.

Why is it so important for those called to be shamans to find the right teachers, as opposed to simply initiating and training under the shamans who identified them? There are many complicated reasons for this, but the most important is the compatibility of ancestral spirits. For those born within a shamanic culture, this is not a problem. But for those born into a different culture, several issues may arise.

In the best-case scenario, the ancestors of these "pre-shamans" may not recognize the practices of these teachers' spirits. Thus, while they may try to help, aspiring shamans may ultimately be unable to perform as effectively using their teachers' practices. In other words, they will not be as powerful as they could be under teachers with compatible shamanic spirits. In the worst-case scenario, these spirits may be from a culture that is still considered to be an enemy of the students' culture—and vice versa. If this is the case, the students' initiation and training may anger the spirits, who may try to hurt or kill the students or even their teachers. Good teachers will often recognize if this is the case and refuse to initiate or train students for reasons of safety, even if they are recognized and have a good relationship with the teachers.

In cultures that perform formal initiation ceremonies, it is incumbent upon teachers to perform the ceremonies properly. There is a dangerous rise today in the number of initiation ceremonies performed quickly or carelessly by "New Age" teachers, even within traditional shamanic cultures. And this has resulted in repercussions that include harm, as well as accidents and even premature death.

Every North Asian culture has different initiation practices and structures. While some cultures, like the Turkic Siberians and the Darkhad Mongols, have a single-stage ceremony and emphasize ongoing learning and even renewal ceremonies, other cultures like the Buryats have multiple initiation stages that take place throughout the shaman's lifetime. In both cases, however, shamanic training is a lifelong process, because shamans are expected to learn throughout their time on earth.

Although here I have placed special emphasis on human teachers, all North Asian cultures believe that initiation and the ongoing learning process are primarily conducted by the spirits. Human teachers are required to prepare for and perform the steps for the physical ceremonies and to teach young shamans how to connect with their spirits properly, but it is the spirits who teach them insight, wisdom, and sacred practices. Sometimes young shamans act as apprentices to older shamans, as in the Darkhad Mongol tradition, helping them with their mundane needs and responsibilities in return for instruction. In other cultures, like the Amur Ulchi tribe, there is no formal apprentice relationship, but rather multiple human teachers who serve as guides and mentors for young shamans in their beginning stages of "self-initiation" and "self-learning." Multiple Ulchi shamans may perform "road-opening" ceremonies and sing for young shamans so that their initiation process can be as smooth as possible. Nonetheless, it is important to remember that shamanism is not a set of official teachings. Shamans are chosen by the spirits. No one can "learn" to be a shaman.

The First Shamans

Shamans are almost always chosen from families that have ancestors who were also shamans. So who were the first shamans and how were they chosen if they didn't have shamanic ancestors? There are two ways to answer this question—one anthropological and one mythological.

Anthropologically speaking, shamanism was a specific practice that came into being through thousands of years of continuous spiritual work. In this sense, there is no such thing as a "first shaman," as shamanism was developed through multiple generations. Perhaps, at some point, someone learned about spirits and then, several generations later, that person (now an ancestor) spoke to a descendant in dreams. Then several generations after that, other descendants learned to induce trance in order to speak directly to their ancestors. Another generation may have honed the ability to enter a trance state enough to be able to induce possession. And this went on until shamanism as we know it came into existence.

The mythological explanation is a bit more complex, as every tribe has different stories of the "first shaman." In nearly every case, however, the first shaman wasn't even human, but rather a spirit who came down and took on physical form, or a child born of a union between a spirit and a human. In these stories, a spirit usually comes down to instruct the people in shamanism to remedy a great imbalance in the world—raging warfare, pollution of the land, disrespect to the spirits, or simply widespread suffering. In Manchu belief, the Eagle Mother nurses the first shaman by feeding her divine essence/food, and then trains her in shamanism to help humans and keep peace following the cataclysmic war between heaven and the demons.

The word *shaman* or *saman* is actually a masculine word. In the original Tungus language, male shamans were referred to by this term, but, in fact, the word for a male shaman is extremely diverse among North Asian cultures, appearing as *böö* or *böge* among Mongols, as *kam* or *gam* among the Turkic Tuvan and Altai tribes, as *khamma* or *ayun* among the Turkic Yakuts, as *baksy* among the Kyrgyz people, and as *tadibey* among the Samoyed.

On the other hand, the word for a female shaman is derived from the same root across almost all these cultures. Female shamans are referred to as *udugan* or *odogan* in the Tungus languages. Similarly, the word is udgan in Mongolia, odigon among Siberian Buryats, and *udagan* among Turkic Yakuts. Other variations across North Asia include *utagan, utygan, utügan, ubakan, idugan,* and *iduan.* These words are likely based on the root word Etugen, the Earth Goddess in Mongolic and Turkic mythology.

Since the words for a female shaman are so similar compared to the widely disparate words for a male shaman, it is fair to assume that they come from a single source and are therefore much older than the words for a male shaman. This, in turn, implies that the first shamans were women, and that male shamans appeared much later in history. Most likely, the word "shaman" is so ubiquitous in the West simply because Western researchers studied and spoke only to male shamans and did not bother to study or speak to their female counterparts. If it were not for patriarchy, we would very likely be talking about u*daganism* rather than shamanism.

CHAPTER 2

North Asian Cosmology

The most common criticism I hear of Western core and contemporary shamanism is that they don't possess a cosmology. They don't have a framework that maps them to an understanding of the physical and spiritual worlds. Instead, practitioners are encouraged to explore and map out these realms themselves via shamanic journeywork. This lack of cosmology can easily be understood as the result of shamanic practices that have been taken out of their cultural context.

Core shamanism purposefully removes cultural contexts from its practices to make the techniques more accessible to Western audiences. But critics of this approach argue that shamanic practices are implicitly rooted in their cultural frameworks. In almost all forms of traditional shamanism, shamanic (helping) spirits are usually ancestors who were themselves shamans; they therefore operate within their respective traditions and it is impossible to ask them to work outside that framework, just as it is impossible to ask people to step outside of their own cultural context. Even the land spirits of different areas operate within their own cultural framework, the most basic of which is whether a particular offering is appropriate—for instance, if it has never been offered before in that context or if it has been abused by that offering in some way, as in the case of alcohol.

This is one of the reasons why shamanism is such a regional practice. It is entirely possible that what is acceptable spiritual practice in one culture and area is unacceptable in another. Therefore, this begs the question of whether it is appropriate, or even possible, to remove a shamanic technique from its cultural context and disseminate it to a global audience. Although cosmologies vary across the tribes of North Asia, practices there remain largely similar and often share many of the same cosmological foundations. In this chapter, we will explore some elements of these cosmologies and examine how the physical and spiritual worlds are viewed across North Asia.

Creation Myths

Nearly every culture in the world has a creation myth. In North Asia, these myths tend to focus more on the creation of humans, or even of specific plants and animals, as opposed to Western myths that attempt to give different explanations of how the entire world or universe came into being. In North Asia, there tends to be broad agreement about how the universe first came to be.

In most of these myths, spiritual existence preceded the physical world of form and matter. Originally, there was only the realm of energy, from which a single consciousness was born. This consciousness, the first spirit, created other subordinate spirits, but remained the powerful master of them all. Nobody knows how long this realm of spirits has existed, because it is dimensionless and exists outside of time.

Then, in a sudden instant, a violent, cataclysmic, explosive separation occurred, creating fire across the universe. A world of form separated itself from the spiritual plane and eventually gave birth to the world of physical existence. The world of physical existence became the Middle World; the original spiritual plane of existence on one side of the Middle World became the Upper World, and the original spiritual plane of existence on the other side became the Lower World. The primordial master spirit became Lord of the Upper World—known as *Munkh Kokh Tenger/Tenger Etseg* to the Turkic and Mongol people, *Buga* to the Evenk, and *Abka/Ba Enduri* to the southern Tungus.

The Middle World was originally to consist only of water, the first form of physical existence—although after studying scientific theories, some shamans today hypothesize that the first form of existence in the Middle World may have been intangible gases that condensed into water. Either way, water (and liquid in general) remains the softest and most malleable form of existence, and therefore the essence closest to the spirit worlds.

Over time, land formed from this watery essence, although many cultures differ in their account of how land appeared. In some stories, the Earth Mother simply came into existence when the Middle World separated and created land. In pre-Manchu Jurchen belief, the matriarchal sky goddess, Abka Hehe (later reimagined as the male lord of heaven, Abka Enduri), created the Earth Mother, Banamu Hehe, along with the Light Mother, Ulden Hehe. Banamu Hehe then created land and life, while Ulden Hehe created the sun, stars, and celestial bodies.[1] In several Siberian and Tungus beliefs, the land was pulled from within the water by mythical beasts and animals—sometimes by a bird like a swan, sometimes by a fish like a salmon or sturgeon, and sometimes by a frog or a tortoise.[2] In tribes where this legend persists, the animal is always one that either lives in water or can travel between land and water. These animals are believed to be able to travel across the three worlds as well.[3]

A unique aspect of all North Asian shamanic cultures is the belief that humankind descends from animals. They also believe that each tribe or culture descended from different animals, so they usually emphasize the origins of their own people in their respective creation myths. The Mongols believe that they descended from the union between a blue wolf and a red deer, so sometimes Mongols poetically refer to themselves as "people of the wolf and deer." Different groups of Buryat Mongols believe they descended from the swan, the bull, or even the cod.[4] Many Turkic tribes similarly believe that they descended from a wolf. Notably, the Ashina clan that ruled the Gokturk empires believes that their first ancestor was one of ten sons born to a gray she-wolf, sometimes imagined as a lupine season goddess. Multiple Turkic, Mongolic, and Tungusic tribes in Siberia claim the bear as their ancestor.[5]

The Amur tribes all have different origin stories as well. Some believe they are descended from the Siberian tiger. Another legend says that divine frogs fell from heaven to earth and became the first people. Among Manchus, the Aisin-Gioro clan believes that their first ancestor was born after the heavenly maiden, Fekulen, who was bathing in Heaven Lake on Changbaishan mountain, ate a red date that was dropped on her clothes by a magpie. After eating the date, she became pregnant with the first ancestor, Bukuri Yongson, who is considered to descend from Fekulen and the magpie. This story likely related at first only to this clan, which identified itself with the magpie totem. But after the Jurchen unification, it was forced upon other Manchu clans (see chapter 7). These mythological stories are likely metaphors used to describe either spirits or groups of people who worshiped or identified with those animals's traits, and do not literally refer to physical animals giving biological birth to humans.

The Three Worlds

Now let's take a closer look at these three worlds and the role they played in the cosmological framework of North Asian shamanism.

The Upper World

The Upper World is referred to by all North Asian peoples as the heavens. It is the seat of power for the lord and master of the Upper World (and all three worlds). Nearly every North Asian culture believes that the Upper World consists of multiple layers. Mongols, who sometimes refer to it as the Eternal Blue Sky, believe that the heavens consist of ninety-nine *tengers,* or realms, each with its own spirit or lord also referred to as tengers. Of these, fifty-five are believed to be the heroic, yet gentle and beneficial, western white tengers, and forty-four are believed to be the wrathful, vengeful, and powerful eastern black tengers (see chapter 3).[6] The black tengers are not considered evil, but rather are dark spirits who use their wrath to battle evil spirits, protect from harm, and act as agents of vengeance to restore balance. They are therefore locked in humanity's struggles against every kind of evil.[7]

Among the Evenk, the Upper World, known as *Uga Buga*, consists of three levels. The top level is managed by the highest sky spirit, *Buga*, who doesn't concern himself with the physical world. The third level is managed by *Enekan Buga*, the grandmother sky spirit to whom Evenks primarily pray when petitioning heaven. The Turkic Yakut believe that heaven consists of nine levels. According to Bulgakova's *Nanai Shamanic Culture in Indigenous Discourse*, there is no agreement on the structure of heaven among the Amur tribes, even between individual shamans, primarily because these shamans rarely interact with each other culturally, let alone confer and reconcile their experiences. As a result, even the reports of shamanic field researchers conflict. Some say the Amur believe there are three levels of heaven; some report nine levels; some just describe a "Manchurian city" that contains many sub-areas.

In most North Asian cultures, shamans travel to the Upper World either by flying their souls there or by riding a spirit animal that can carry them there. For this reason, the shamanic vestments of almost all these cultures incorporate sacred feathers and display bird or animal motifs, all of which give the shamans the ability to fly (see chapter 8).

The Middle World

The Middle World has been called by many names across North Asian cultures. The Evenki refer to it as *Dulin Buga*; the Oroqen call it *Berye*; the Amur call it *Duentey*. Mongols euphemistically refer to it as the Sunny World, as it receives light from the heavens. Whatever name it goes by, however, the Middle World is understood by all to encompass the physical realm and the overlapping spiritual realms, and includes all the physical and spiritual beings that inhabit them.

The Middle World is ruled by the Earth Mother, who also rules over all the earth/land spirits and gives physical form to all beings. The land spirits are the only spirits who are indigenous to the Middle World. While curses from spirits of the Upper and Lower Worlds (the spirit worlds) usually result in spiritual, mental, or psychological effects like bad luck, money problems, or attracting enemies, land-spirit curses usually result in physical effects like disease and injury.[8] Sometimes ancestral spirits can act as land spirits if their souls were enshrined or housed in a physical landmark like a mountain or a lake.

Land spirits are particularly important for shamanic practice. While they can act directly as shamanic spirits, they are also needed to connect ancestral spirits to shamans and other people. Because they are indigenous to the physical world, they serve as a bridge between shamans and ancestors, and ancestral spirits often ride them to connect with physical beings.

Animals and animal spirits also dwell in the Middle World. Like human souls, animal souls often come from the heavens, although, from a karmic perspective, the souls of animals are hierarchically lower than those of humans. Land spirits can take animal forms when working with humans, and certain Middle World gods can also take on animal aspects.

It is said that the Middle World faces the Upper World during the day and the Lower World at night. For this reason, shamanic and spiritual ceremonies performed at night require extra levels of protection.

The Lower World

The Lower World is the realm about which we know the least. Among Tungus tribes, it is sometimes called *Buni* (land of the dead), although sometimes the term refers only to a section of it. Almost all North Asian tribes agree that the Lower World is dark, as the Middle World takes all the light from the heavens and blocks it from reaching the lower realm. However, while some Amur shamans agree about the perpetual darkness, others disagree and say that the Lower World is opposite to the Middle World. Thus, when it is night in the Middle World, it is daytime in the Lower World. Likewise, when it is winter in the Middle World, it is summer in the Lower World.

Most North Asian cultures believe that the Lower World is ruled by a distinct lord and master spirit. Many Turkic and Mongol tribes call this spirit *Erlik Khan*, while Manchus and Daur Mongols call him *Ilmun* and *Irmu Khan* respectively. The Yakuts call him *Ulu Toyon*. The Evenks consider *Khargi* to be the highest spirit of this world, but he rules only the portion of it that is home to demons and evil spirits. By contrast, the Amur do not believe the Lower World has a master, but believe that *Temu*, the lord of the waters of the Middle World, has dominion over the deceased souls that go to the Lower World. Black Darkhad shamans believe that their ancestral shamanic spirits inhabit the dark spiritual world and reside physically in the Upper World, but have powers within the Lower World.[9]

Different North Asian cultures have different beliefs about whether their spirits come from the Upper or Lower Worlds. The Buryats, having been influenced by the Buddhist worldview, see the Lower World as equivalent to the Buddhist hell. They believe that the dead go to an intermediate place between the Middle and Lower Worlds.[10] Many Tungusic cultures believe that a significant portion of the Lower World is a watery or river-like area that connects to the Middle World and is extremely difficult for spirits and shamans (other than the most powerful) to cross.[11] The Amur and Oroqen believe it is very bad luck to talk about the Lower World and will not discuss it if possible (hence limiting our understanding of how they view it).

Unless absolutely necessary, shamans avoid travel to this world if possible, with the exception of the few who specialize in psychopomp work (see chapter 4).

The Importance of Fire

Fire is extremely important in almost every North Asian shamanic tradition. When the Middle World separated violently from the Upper and Lower Worlds, the resulting explosion created fire. As in many Western traditions, fire is the essence of life, so much so that some of the primordial gods and spirits of life appeared as gods with a fiery aspect. Fire is also one of the central ways in which physical beings connect with spirits. In this sense, North Asian shamanism can be seen as a form of fire worship, as fires are necessary for almost all of its formal rituals and ceremonies (see chapter 9).

The elevated importance of fire in North Asian shamanism may have been due to some level of influence from Persian Zoroastrianism, in which fire is the ultimate purifier that can cleanse all spiritual pollutions and negativity. In the ancient Mongol Empire, any visitor to the great khan had to pass through a gate with fires burning on each side in order to be spiritually cleansed before entering the khan's presence. Objects can also be cleansed by passing them through fire. Fire can even remove good spirits, which is why spiritual objects and tools must never pass directly through fire. Lighting sacred herbs or heating iron gives them cleansing properties as well.

Fire spirits play a particularly important role in North Asian shamanism, as they are the protectors of bloodlines. Because of this, blood families are also extremely important, as they share the same household fire. If a bloodline has a strong fire, the family is protected and harmonious. If a bloodline's fire is weak, the family is vulnerable to dangers, quarrels, and conflicts that could potentially destroy the household (and thereby harm individual family members). Every family has its own protector fire spirit, which resides in the family hearth. In nomadic dwellings, the hearth is the center of the yurt where the fire pit (now stove and chimney) resides. In modern dwellings, this can be the kitchen, the fireplace, or a fireproof plate or container where spiritual fires are lit. Fire ceremonies not only carry offerings to the spirits, but also strengthen the household fire. This boosts protection and energy, and brings good karma to the household by helping the family.

Many Asian (including East and Southeast) cultures share a belief that offerings are best given to spirits through fire and smoke. Therefore, incense and herb smudges are central to all Asian practices. In fact, smoke is one of the best basic offerings to give, and smoke from sacred herbs can double as both spiritual cleansing and as an offering. While food offerings can be thrown to the sky or left out in nature, the best way to give them is to burn them. Liquid offerings can also be presented to the fire. Many people are familiar with the Chinese tradition of burning paper offerings, like spirit money, as gifts to the ancestors. In much of North Asia, shamans conduct fire ceremonies in which offerings are placed or poured directly into the fire. If the offerings are not flammable, they are poured to the side of the fire plate or container but must never be poured directly into it. In chapter 9, I give an example of how to perform such a fire ceremony.

The TriPartite Soul

Almost all North Asian peoples believe the human soul consists of three parts. Although some groups believe there are more than three, they all believe there are at least three. However, there are two competing schools of thought regarding the nature of these three souls, and these are illustrated by the two main shamanic traditions of Mongolia.

For Darkhad black shamans, the soul consists of bone, flesh, and consciousness (see chapter 4 for an explanation of black, white, and yellow shamanism). While bone and flesh are physical traits, they each have a soul component as well. According to Purev:

Every person has three souls. Two of them are mortal, but the remaining one is immortal . . . They include the female spirit of flesh and blood, the male spirit of bones, and lastly the Heaven spirit. After a person's death, the mortal spirits will remain in the body for three years . . . [after which] the mortal spirits disappear and finally the immortal spirit will rise up.[12]

When a shaman dies, the immortal portion of his or her soul, consciousness, is typically interred in a "spirit house" that acts as a shrine for the shaman's soul (see chapter 8).

Because these three souls are intimately connected, damage to one affects the others. This is why bonesetters are especially vital, as they can treat broken bones and chiropractic conditions physically, but are also trained to heal the bone soul simultaneously, as well as any resulting damage to the consciousness. Khorchins are known to have some of the strongest bonesetters, some of whom can trace their lineage back to those who personally treated Chinggis Khan.[13] The Darkhad perspective of the three souls is parallel to that of the Buryats, apart from the soul's reincarnation cycle.

Buryat yellow shamanism identifies the three souls as the *ami*, the *suld*, and the *suns*, each of which is connected to one of the three worlds in the Buddhist perspective. In this tradition, the ami is the Upper World soul and the "breath of life." Before and after death, the ami takes the form of a bird that sits on the Upper World branches of the World Tree (see chapter 1). The suns (not to be confused with the English word "suns") is the Lower World soul that is sent to the Middle World by Erlik Khan when a person is born. It is said that, while the ami provides the breath that sparks life, the suns provides emotional traits.

The ami and the suns correlate to the mortal souls in Darkhad black shamanism. But in Buryat yellow shamanism, the ami and the suns reincarnate through multiple lifetimes. In this tradition, memories of past lives come primarily from the suns and secondarily from the ami. A person's last breath is their ami, which flies back to the Upper World on its own.[14] The suns usually finds its way (typically via a body of water) back to the Lower World, lest it become a ghost stuck in the Middle World. Shamans with psychopomp abilities can help guide lost suns souls back to the Lower World (see chapter 4).[15] The suld lives only one lifetime and remains on earth after a person dies. Buryats similarly enshrine the sulds of past shamans in spirit houses and believe that, eventually, they will join the family of nature spirits. Although they are less influenced by Buddhist beliefs, the Daur have a similar perspective of the souls, referring to the upper soul as the *ami*, the middle soul as the *suld* or *suli*, and the lower soul as the *sumus*.[16]

These two perspectives regarding the three souls that are described through a Mongol lens reflect largely the same beliefs, although they contain small differences in detail, and they permeate the beliefs of most North Asian tribes. The Tungusic and Manchu peoples believe that the first soul is the life soul (like the ami breath of life), which disappears when a person dies. The second soul is the floating soul, which carries personality like the suns soul, but also comprises intuitive abilities. The third soul is the spiritual or true soul, which stays on earth and can be invoked as an ancestral spirit.[17]

Guiding a soul part to the Lower World in yellow shamanism bears similarities to Tungus beliefs in which psychopomp shamans guide souls to the Lower World realm of the dead, and this may be due to cross-cultural influences between the Tungus and the Buryats. The Turkic Yakuts view the three souls as the earth soul (*teng*), the air soul (*sunei* or *sur*), and the mother soul (*kut*), which returns to the realm of Aiyy after death.[18] This bears similarities to both perspectives discussed above, since the earth soul is believed to dissipate into the earth after death (as in Mongol black shamanism), but the mother soul returns to Aiyy (as in Buryat yellow shamanism, where the ami returns to Umay in the Upper World). This suggests that this may be due to a Tungusic rather than Buddhist influence, as Yakuts were not influenced by Buddhism.

We'll examiine the cultural and historical differences between these various traditions in chapters 5, 6, and 7.

The Soul's Power

Because human souls are conscious forms of energy that sustain human life, they have varying degrees of strength and power. Mongolians refer to this power as *hiimori,* which translates as "windhorse" and refers to a person's potential and ability to accomplish all sorts of tasks. Those with strong hiimori think more analytically and are more creative. They have stronger psychic and spiritual powers, and enjoy more charisma, success, and luck. In short, hiimori represents a person's ability to perform any task successfully. According to Sarangerel: "Windhorse is the ability to perceive things beyond physical reality and the ability to use spiritual power to manifest what a person focuses attention on."[19] Those with weak hiimori tend to have less energy, may struggle with focus, and suffer from exhaustion, frequent accidents, poor employment, and difficult financial situations. In general, they are not able to perform at the same physical, mental, and spiritual levels as others.

Those whose hiimori is weak are also at risk of soul loss. When the soul is weak, it becomes unstable and can easily be knocked out of the body by harmful energy, pollution, or trauma. A person with strong hiimori has greater resistance to the effects of negative energy or trauma. Therefore, weak hiimori can be a sign of potential soul loss and may require a shaman or other spiritual elder to perform a soul calling or soul-retrieval ritual (see chapter 9). The best way to strengthen the soul and increase hiimori is to perform "merits."[20] Merits entail giving offerings and prayers to the spirits, but also performing acts of service and kindness for others, as well as taking care of nature. Performing many merits over a long period helps build accumulate blessings and good karma, and strengthens the soul.

In Northern Tungusic beliefs, there is a comparable relationship between the souls (*omi*), and energy and power (*musun*). Among the Evenks, musun, which likely corresponds to hiimori, is a specific moving power or energy that is connected with a shaman's ability to work with kind spirits, while *eru* is a negative energy that can generate disease, failure, and disaster.[21] Everything that is born, moves, and changes in the world has musun. When creating spiritual tools or spirit containers (see chapter 8), shamans imbue them with musun, which then activates the object with omi, or soul. Everything that exhibits signs of reasonable behavior possesses an omi.[22]

The Evenki view of omi is like the Buryat view of the ami, in that both descend from the Upper World, suggesting that there may have been cross-cultural influences. Although it is implied that Evenks believe in multiple souls, the omi soul is unfortunately the only soul that has been explained in detail to outsiders, possibly due to the importance of omi in Tungusic shamanic belief. But this may also be due to information being intentionally withheld.

Tengerism

Across most North Asian peoples, shamanism was practiced through a sky-based spirituality known as *Tengerism* (sometimes spelled *Tengrism*), which may first have been practiced by Turkic peoples before it spread to other groups, most notably Mongols and Siberians (see chapter 5).

According to Tengerist belief, the highest power in the universe is *Tenger* or *Tengri*, which means "sky" or "heaven" in most North Asian languages. Tenger is the chief sky god, considered to be the supreme being and creator of everything. Tenger—also sometimes known as *Gok* (Blue) *Tengri* or *Tenger Etseg* (Sky Father)—holds dominion over other gods, most notably *Etugen*, the Earth Mother, who is also considered to be one of the supreme beings second only to Tenger (see chapter 3). Many other gods and deities—including those of natural forces and the elements, as well as those of the sun, the moon, the stars, the clouds, water, fire, air, rain, storms, thunder and lightning, and other creator gods—are also subordinate to Tenger. And under these gods, there are numerous spirits who range from nature (land and water) spirits, to elevated ancestors who have entered the realms of the tengers, to other spiritual entities and minor deities who are ruled by the higher gods.

All these spirits are extremely diverse and may be inclined either to help or to harm, or even to stay neutral in human affairs. Generally, the tengers are divided into the gentle and heroic white tengers, and the wrathful black tengers. Please note that white and black do not mean good and evil, but simply refer to the temperament and powers of the tengers.

While Tengerism is sometimes considered to be the religion of shamanism, it is actually a very broad spiritual and philosophical system. Just as there are many different lineages, practices, and identities that fall under the rubric of Buddhism, Tengerism is a similarly diverse philosophy of universal being of which shamanism is only a part. We'll examine how these beliefs developed across North Asian cultures and how they influenced the shamanism of the Turkic, Mongolic, and Tungusic cultures in chapters 5, 6, and 7.

Astrology

Eastern astrology is intimately connected with and inseparable from shamanism. Before any spiritual or shamanic work begins (including divination), the names and astrological information of both worker and client must be announced. This allows the spirits to identify all participants properly, as these are the primary forms of spiritual identification. When complicated shamanic work is performed, it is essential to identify astrologically auspicious days for the rituals, otherwise the spirits may be angered or harmful spirits may be attracted. Astrological information is also used to determine personal attributes that indicate how additional work should be performed if necessary.

Generally, Mongols and Turkic Siberians follow Tibetan astrology, while the Tungusic peoples follow the Chinese astrology also followed by most eastern and southeastern Asian cultures like the Korean, the Vietnamese, and the Japanese. Although Chinese and Tibetan astrology are very similar, there are several important differences, most notably their calendars and their astrological associations. Tibetan astrology was heavily influenced by Indian astrology, which primarily affects its medical aspects. Tibetan and Chinese astrology recognize different dates for the lunar year and consider different days to be astrologically auspicious or dangerous. Mongolians and Tibetans share similar astrological beliefs because of their shared nomadic lifestyles, frequent cross-cultural influences, and similar geographic elevations.

Eastern astrology and its calculations are a topic that could take up an entire book, so for our purposes here, we will discuss only its most basic concepts and how you can use them to research your own astrological information and its relevance to North Asian spirituality.

If you want to dabble in Eastern astrology at its most basic level, you must identify the animal that corresponds to your birth year—the rat, the ox, the tiger, the rabbit, the dragon, the snake, the horse, the sheep, the monkey, the rooster, the dog, or the pig (see Figure 2). Each lunar year corresponds to one of these twelve animals and those born in each year will thus exhibit different attributes, different strengths and weaknesses, and different relationships with the other animals. Because these animal designations are based on the Eastern lunisolar calendar, your birth animal is the animal of the year in which your birthday falls if you were born after the lunar New Year (typically between mid-January and mid-February). Those born in January and February of the Western calendar must verify whether their birth animal is that of the new lunar year or the previous one. As an example, 2021 is the Year of the Ox. However, if you were born on January 2, 2021, then your birth animal is the rat, the birth animal for 2020 (a Year of the Rat), as the lunar New Year for 2021 had not yet occurred.

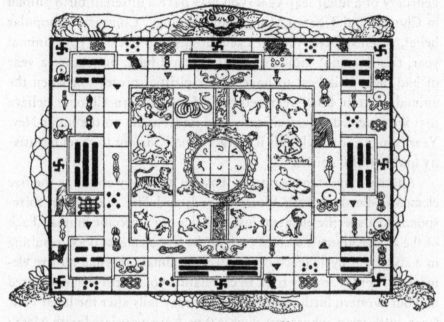

THE MYSTIC TABLET.[13]

Figure 2. The Mystic Tablet, showing the twelve zodiacal animals of Eastern astrology, the nine karmic squares, and the trigram directional map on the back of a giant mythical turtle. Drawn by an anonymous Tibetan artist.

One note of caution, however: all forms of Eastern astrology do not necessarily share the same date for the New Year. This is due to different calculations for the leap year, when the lunar calendar adjusts to the seasons (making the calendar lunisolar). Eastern calendars have twelve lunar months (moon cycles) per year. But in a leap year, they typically have thirteen months, as twelve moon cycles do not account for the four seasons exactly. In the Chinese calendar, the lunar New Year is the second New Moon after the winter solstice. In the Tibetan/

Mongolian calendar, the lunar New Year is the New Moon after two fully completed moon cycles following the winter solstice.

If the first New Moon appears soon after the solstice, the dates for the lunar New Year in the two calendars fall one month apart. For this reason, if your birthday happens to fall in January or February of a lunar leap year, you may have a different birth animal in Chinese and Tibetan/Mongolian astrology. Contrary to popular belief, when the twelve-year cycle brings you back to your animal year, this does not indicate a year of good luck, but rather a year of bad luck. It is best to have extra spiritual protection when the animal of your birth year returns. Many modern Chinese believe that wearing red (or specifically, red underwear) on the lunar New Year brings good luck, but it is traditionally meant to repel negativity and harmful spirits.

Another important feature of Eastern astrology concerns the five elements—Earth, Metal, Water, Wood, and Fire. Each year corresponds to a specific element, just as it does to a specific animal. Each of the twelve animals crosses each of the five elements once, resulting in a sixty-year cycle (each of the twelve animals crossing all five elements). There is an easy trick to calculating your birth element, based on your Western birth year. If your birthday falls after the lunar New Year, birth years whose last digit is 0 or 1 are associated with Metal; last digits of 2 or 3 are associated with Water; last digits of 4 or 5 are associated with Wood; last digits of 6 or 7 are associated with Fire; last digits of 8 or 9 are associated with Earth. So those born in 1990 have Metal as their element; those born in 2005 have Wood as their element; those born in 1977 have Fire as their element. Although each of the twelve animals has its own fixed element, the rotating elements that each animal crosses better determine individual traits. You can find the individual traits of each element online.

As a rule, each element is best matched with the elements that fall before and after it. Of the remaining two, one is its friend and the other its enemy (with some exceptions between specific elements). Ironically, this means that every relationship between opposite elements will simultaneously be a "friend" for one and an "enemy" for the other, indicating that one side will usually dominate in that relationship. For any shamanic ceremony or divination, the client's birth name, birth element, and birth animal are required. The birth name must be the name the person was given at birth, as that is the name that is identified to the spirits. If you want to change your name for the purposes of spiritual work, a name ceremony must be performed—or re-performed for those born into cultures that conduct name ceremonies at birth.

Other astrological factors worth mentioning, although not required, are the nine magic squares (Tibetan, *mewa*; Mongolian, *menge*; Chinese, *luo shu*) and the trigrams (Tibetan, *parkha*; Mongolian, *suudal*; Chinese, *bagua*). The nine squares represent nine categories of karmic patterns or relations that develop from lifetime to lifetime. Although everyone has unique karma, all karma can be classified into nine different patterns, each of which is also associated with a year and with its own element. We won't go into the specifics of how to calculate the nine squares for each person (which can also be found online), but the calculation can be confusing for some. Just understand that each number or square carries personality traits, strengths and weaknesses, and physical and spiritual sensitivities.

The trigrams are another feature of shamanic practice that, although not strictly astrological (in the sense of a person's characteristics), use astrological information to calculate the changing directional and geographic significance for each person each year. They can be used for divination (similar to the I Ching), for arranging home furnishing and layout (as in feng shui), and for determining ideal directions in which to travel. For shamanic purposes, they are typically used to determine the ideal directions in which to conduct ceremonies (e.g., blessings vs curses), give offerings, and dispose of spiritual waste.

Not every North Asian group uses astrology to the same extent. Some use only the birth animal and the element; some delve deeper into the magic squares and trigrams. In Mongolia, shamans almost always consult astrological calendars that are compiled into almanacs by Tibetan Buddhist astrologer-monks to determine what is auspicious or inauspicious for specific days. While there is no need for you to become a master of Eastern astrology, any study of North Asian spiritual traditions requires that you have at least a basic understanding of this tool to practice safely.

Pollutions and Curses

The biggest difference between pollutions and curses is that pollutions consist of negative and harmful energies that we experience in life due to chance encounters, making unsafe choices, or carelessly engaging in activities that cause pollution. Curses, on the other hand, are harmful energies that are intentionally sent by other people or spirits. Pollutions can be caused in many ways, including but not limited to gossip, visiting haunted areas or the sites of death, or interacting with someone who has pollution.[23] In some cases, pollutions can be sent accidentally by someone who bears resentment—similar to the Evil Eye—and they can cause many problems if not removed quickly.

In the case of both pollutions and curses, if the harmful energy is not treated or removed quickly, it can potentially weaken both a person's soul and the family fire. Pollutions can also activate diseases and illnesses that may have lain dormant in the body—for instance, if a person or bloodline carries the spirits of inactive viruses, cancer, etc. Moreover, harmful energies can affect the physical, mental, and spiritual components of a person's life. When pollution builds up, it can block or muddle connections to the spirits and gods. In some cases, an accumulation of harmful energies can also attract the attention of harmful or parasitic spirits.

Because of these risks, it is extremely important to perform regular spiritual cleansing. In both traditional and modern societies, people often seek the help of spiritual professionals when things are going wrong in their lives. In most circumstances, this is due to a buildup of harmful energies. Because life is messy and full of conflicts, it is impossible to avoid these energies entirely. And in most cases, a little bit of pollution may not create a noticeable effect, especially if a person's soul power or hiimori is already strong. But if the pollution is not removed, it can fester over time and attract other forms of pollution. In fact, regular spiritual hygiene is just as important as physical cleanliness. Experienced shamans can often "smell" the buildup of spiritual pollution, which must be removed regularly through spiritual cleansing techniques.

Harmful energies and pollutions are in no way a concept unique to North Asian spiritual traditions, but it would be irresponsible of me not to address them here. In chapter 9, we'll discuss some of the spiritual cleansing techniques used among North Asian cultures. I also encourage you to explore spiritual cleansing techniques in your own culture.

Reincarnation and the Afterlife

According to Purev, black shamanic traditions did not originally believe in reincarnation. Before the influence of Buddhism, Mongols believed that "humans and animals alike are born, have a period in the Sunny World and then, when they die, the soul remains forever in Darkness."[24] Yet today, just about every North Asian culture believes in some form of reincarnation. This is largely attributed to the influence of Buddhism, even among cultures where such influence is more limited, like that of the Darkhad Mongols or northern Tungusic tribes.

Mongolic and Turkic Siberian peoples were directly influenced by Buddhism, which seeped into their respective worldviews on life after death. The Manchu were influenced by both Buddhism and Chinese folk beliefs (which were also influenced by Buddhism). Although the Amur and northern Tungusics had extremely little contact with Buddhism, it is possible that they were influenced by Chinese (and therefore indirectly Buddhist) beliefs, given the heavy levels of historical interaction—so much so that Chinese artifacts and even beliefs (like astrology) expanded into these regions. Nor is it impossible that these groups developed the concept of reincarnation organically.

Although almost all North Asian tribes now believe in reincarnation, many of them have different views regarding the process. The groups most influenced by Buddhism believe that reincarnation is dictated by karma. While shamanic traditions don't necessarily believe people's end goal should be to clear their souls' karma and reach enlightenment, they agree that karma ultimately influences the state of each soul's rebirth. For the black shamans of the Darkhad Mongols, the immortal consciousness soul continues to reincarnate as dictated by karmic law, even when it has finished with physical life and passed into the spirit world. The Buryat Mongols believe that the ami and suns reincarnate based on accumulated karma from past lives. Interestingly, they believe that the ami soul reincarnates only through the same bloodline, while the suns soul can reincarnate across different bloodlines (and potentially across different races).[25]

It is unknown if the original Manchu tradition included a belief in reincarnation of the true soul and/or floating soul, but since the Manchus were heavily converted to Tibetan and Chinese Buddhism during the Qing Dynasty, they largely adopted the Buddhist view on reincarnation. Some of the Amur tribes believe that souls live three lives in the physical world, and then three additional lives in the spirit world.[26] Across North Asia, it is widely believed that those chosen by spirits to be shamans live their final lifetime in the physical world, as after death they must become shamanic spirits for future shamans. If shamans commit atrocities during their lifetime, they face the karmic consequences in the spirit world.

Belief in karmic law is ingrained in most Asian cultures, and North Asian shamanic cultures are no exception. Many Westerners interpret karma simply as the belief that "what goes around, comes around," but it's not that simple. Karma is not limited to our current lifetimes. Something we have done in a past life may have a karmic effect in a future life and not in the present. Moreover, we do not suffer only from our own soul's karma. We are just as much subject to our community's karma. We bear the karmic burdens of our ancestors because we share the same bloodline and family. We bear the karmic burdens of our village, our city, and our race and ethnicity. We bear the karmic burdens of our country as well. In fact, we each bear a small degree of karma from the entire human race.

Several of my friends in Mongolia believe that because the ancient Mongol Empire committed numerous atrocities against many cultures and peoples, Mongols today are paying the karmic price. Once the center of the largest contiguous land empire in the world, Mongolia today is divided, much of its indigenous land controlled by other countries. The country today is politically weak and socioeconomically disadvantaged on the world stage. From a shamanic perspective, the best we can do today is to live a life of merits, being good people, living a life of balance, and showing compassion and service to others. This will not only help our own karma, but also heal the karmic burdens and traumas of our ancestors and pave the way to a better life for our descendants.

CHAPTER 3

Shamanic Gods
and Spirits

In this chapter, we'll explore the gods and spirits who populate the North Asian pantheons. We'll discuss how they illustrate the spiritual worldview of North Asian cultures and see how they differ across North Asian shamanic traditions.

Of course, this catalog won't include every single spirit or deity recognized in North Asia, as that would require an entire book. Instead, it includes those that I consider to be the most important historically and mythologically. I have grouped these spirits based on type and included a notation that indicates under which North Asian group they fall—TUR for Turkic; MON for Mongolic; and TUN for Tungusic. Sometimes these spirits may belong to more than one tradition; sometimes they may belong to all three. For more information on these specific shamanic traditions, see chapters 5 (Turkic), 6 (Mongolic), and 7 (Tungusic).

In general, I have listed spirits within each group from the most to the least powerful, but in some cases I have organized them by cultural family. In general, the first entries in each group refer to specific spirits, while those that follow refer to groups of spirits.

Upper World Spirits

As we saw in the last chapter, the Upper World is referred to by all North Asian peoples as the heavens, and the gods and spirits who inhabit that realm are among the most powerful. The Upper World is the seat of power for the lord and master of the three worlds—the Lord of the Heavens, the Sky Father.

Sky Father: The main deity in every North Asian spirituality. Known as *Tenger, Tenger Etseg,* or *Tengri* to the Mongols and Tuvans, *Aiyy Toyon* to the Yakut, *Abka Enduri* to the Manchu, *Buga* to the Evenk, and *Ba Enduri* to the Amur. The Sky Father is so supreme that he does not interfere with or concern himself with human matters, which are relegated to lesser spirits and deities. He is one of the few, or perhaps the only, spirits who predates the separation of the three worlds. (TUR, MON, TUN)

Kayra: In ancient Turkic mythology, either the son of or an embodiment of the Sky Father. Sometimes referred to as *Kara-Khan* (Black King), he is the lord above the dual gods *Ulgen* and *Erlik*. In Tatar legend, the water goddess *Ak Ana* convinced him to create the three worlds. (TUR)

Ulgen: A Turco-Mongolic deity also thought to be a world creator, specifically of the land, the atmosphere, the stars, rainbows, humans, animals, and everything good. Thought to be the son of either *Tengri* or *Kayra*, he is the enemy of *Erlik* (god of darkness and the Lower World). In ancient times, he was considered the patron of shamans and accepted white horses as his sacrifices. Also known as *Bai-Ulgen*. (TUR, MON)

Abka Hehe: In pre-Manchu Jurchen belief, the supreme master of heaven (Sky Woman). She created *Banamu Hehe* (Earth Woman) and *Ulden Hehe* (Light Woman). Not much is known about Abka Hehe, since after Jurchen unification the Manchus worshipped *Abka Enduri*, the Sky Father. Ancient Jurchen cultures may thus have been matriarchal. Our knowledge of these female deities comes primarily from the Manchu creation myth "War in Heaven."[1] (TUN)

Enekan Buga: In Evenki belief, the second supreme heavenly being after *Buga*. Because Buga is above the affairs of humans, people make their prayers to Enekan Buga. Known in English as Heavenly Grandmother, this sky goddess oversaw all life and was the main provider of blessings and luck. All ancestral shamanic spirits ultimately serve *Seveki*, who in turn serves her. (TUN)

Seveki: Creator of all living things and manager of life, notably in the taiga. This deity can manifest in male, female, or even animal form (reindeer or elk) and grants luck in hunting. Many shaman drums and rock paintings in the taiga forest carry images of Enekan Buga and/or Seveki.[2] (TUN)

Khan Khormasta: Sometimes known as *Qormusta Tengri*, he is likely derived from Ahura Mazda, the creator and highest deity in Zoroastrianism. For Buryat Mongols, he is one of the leaders of the ninety-nine tengers (mainly the fifty-five western tengers) and is sometimes also seen as leader of thirty-three additional deities (see chapter 2). Buryats believe he is the father of *Abai Gesar*, an important folk hero from Tibetan Buddhism.[3] (MON)

Big Dipper: An important constellation for most North Asian peoples. Turkics and Mongols see it as supremely powerful and able to change luck and guard destiny.[4] The Tungus (notably the Amur) see it as a stage on shamans' journeys to the Upper World, as the pole star contains a portal that opens to other realms. Sometimes described as seven women with hammers, sometimes as seven fairies.[5] The Manchus believe that the seven stars are star-fairies, one of which (*Fekulen*) gave birth to the Imperial Aisin-Gioro clan. In multiple cultures, it is symbolized by a swastika, as it forms that shape as it rotates around the North Star (see Figure 2 on page 33). (TUR, MON, TUN)

Orion: Sometimes seen as the organizer of the world among Amur tribes, and as the heavenly first ancestor and/or shaman among the Ulchi. More significant for the Tungus than for Turkics or Mongols. Also known as *Khadai*, hunters often pray to her for luck.[6] (TUN)

Sun/Moon spirits: Although both spiritual entities, the sun and moon don't appear frequently in shamanic spiritual workings and are employed primarily in an astrological context. Nor are they always tied to a specific gender. The Turkics simultaneously acknowledge a sun god (*Koyash*), a sun goddess (*Gun Ana*), and a moon god (*Ay Dede*).[7] The Amur portray the sun as either male or female and, in one story, describe the moon as a young man chasing his female lover (the sun) across the sky.[8] (TUR, MON, TUN)

Dragons: Symbol of might and power in almost all North Asian cultures. They are related to the *nagas* or *lus savdag* land spirits and appear in serpentine form, although typically grander and more powerful. They reside in the heavens. The Tungus often portray the Sky Father as a dragon; the Amur believe that *Ba Enduri* often takes the form of a dragon; the Manchus adopted the Blue Dragon (symbolizing *Abka Enduri*) as the official flag of the Qing Dynasty. (TUR, MON, TUN)

Weather spirits: Clouds make up both the physical and spiritual form of the weather spirits, which act as a direct reflection of the sky spirits' disposition. For this reason, most North Asian peoples fear thunderstorms, because they indicate that the gods are angry. When thunder and lightning appear, Mongols believe that Tenger is angry. Chinggis Khan used his weather shamans to cast thunderstorms on his enemies. The Ulchi believe thunder and lightning indicate that thunder spirit *Agdi* is angry or that the cloud spirits are arguing with each other. Thus they advise that it is best to stay away from windows during a thunderstorm. The Ulchi believe that rainbows after a thunderstorm show Agdi's soul. Sometimes, Amur shamans ride clouds on their journey to the heavens, similar to the way in which Chinese Taoist deities travel.[9] (TUR, MON, TUN)

Tengers: Sky spirits in Mongol and most Turkic traditions. Although Mongols today use the word to refer to any higher power, its original meaning was any spirit from the heavens, as well as the realms of heaven themselves. White tengers are generally benevolent, divine, and gentle. Black tengers are not evil, but rather dark spirits who can unleash fierce vengeance, punishment, and even war and disease on those who incur their wrath. (TUR, MON)

Sky vampires: see below.

Middle World Spirits

The Middle World is understood in all North Asian cultures to encompass the physical realm. It is ruled by the Earth Mother, who also rules over all the earth and land spirits and gives physical form to all beings.

Earth Mother: Often depicted as a beautiful voluptuous woman. All living beings and land spirits are subordinate to her. Although the Amur recognize Na Adja as the earth mother, they believe the land is co-ruled by the tiger and bear spirits, while the waters are ruled by Temu.[10] Known as *Etugen/Itugen Ekhe* or *Gazar Eej* to Turkics and Mongols, and *Banamu Hehe* to the Manchu. The Evenk do not appear to have an Earth Mother figure, but believe *Enekan Buga* manages all living things in a similar manner. While Tenger determines fates of peoples and nations, natural forces yield to Etugen. Although not necessarily attending to each individual, she is the one who gives humans their physical bodies. As a rule, all prayer rituals first address the Sky Father, and then the Earth Mother to show the proper respect. (TUR, MON, TUN)

Umay: Fertility goddess among Turkics and Mongols, sometimes analogous to and/or a different incarnation of the Earth Mother. The Turkic root *umay* used to mean "placenta," "afterbirth," or "womb." In Buryat belief, Umay cares for ami souls and assigns them to new life born in the physical world.[11] Sometimes equated with the fire goddess *Golomt Eej*, another incarnation of Umay. As the fire goddess, she is also the protector of life. Among Yakuts, she is known as *Ajyyhyt/Aisyt*, who serves an identical function.[12] (TUR, MON)

Fodo Mama: Manchu goddess of fertility, life, and the hearth, also known as Grandmother Willow. Worshipped primarily through domestic rites and believed to be a progenitor goddess, she is equated with the Manchu goddess *Omosi Mama*, although Omosi Mama dwells in the Lower World, while Fodo Mama dwells in a sacred cave in the Changbai Mountains. Given the Jianzhou Jurchens' worship of the Changbai Mountains, she was likely the Jianzhou equivalent of Omosi Mama.[13] (TUN)

Uha Loson: Chief of the *lus* water spirits in Buryat Mongol belief, he resides in Lake Baikal and is father to the warrior goddess *Alma Mergen*, who Buryats believe is the wife of *Abai Gesar*. When Buryats address the *lus savdag* spirits, they address him first as King of the Lus.[14] (MON)

Temu: Master spirit of all bodies of water among the Amur tribes, specifically ruling over the watery portions of the Middle World. He also has dominion over deceased souls, as they can reach the Lower World only via bodies of water. Temu sometimes appears as an old man, an old woman, an old couple, or an aquatic animal.[15] (TUN)

Auli Burkhan: Mountain spirit who takes the form of a fox and is primarily invoked by *bariyachi* (midwives) to divine for pregnant women about their unborn children (primarily gender). Those who take the path of bariyachi draw their powers almost entirely from Auli Burkhan (see chapter 4).[16] (MON)

Lus savdag: Two types of land spirits. Lus are water spirits; savdag, or "earth lords," are mountain spirits. Because waters and mountains are connected, they are often referred to together. Their domains frequently overlap, and they both travel and exist below ground as well as in the atmosphere. As spirits who are indigenous to the Middle World, they play a key role in connecting ancestral shamanic spirits to shamans. Because they are very vain and materialistic, prayers to them must include compliments, and offerings must be given frequently. If someone offends a lus savdag, their family may suffer severe consequences. If they are angered, it is difficult but possible for a shaman to placate the spirit. Thus people are advised never to throw milk, blood, excrement, dirt, hair, wool, or trash into bodies of water. As lus are guardians of the earth's treasures, precious stones (lapis lazuli, pearls, etc.), rare metals (gold, silver, etc.), and crystals are some of the best offerings for placating them.[17] (TUR, MON, TUN)

Animal spirits: Prominent in Tungusic shamanic cultures. Tungusic shamans employ both ancestral shamans and animal spirits as shamanic spirits. Many Mongol shamans believe that these animal spirits are either manifestations of lus savdag or companion spirit animals of ancestral shamans. Mongol shamans believe that Tungus shamans with animal spirits are fortified by *nagas* (lus savdag); the Tungus believe shamans with animal spirits are more powerful. These spirits often appear as cobras and vipers, as reindeer (among the Evenk), as tigers and leopards (among the Amur), and as wolves, foxes, bears, boars, birds, weasels, frogs and toads, and marmots or gray rats. Since so many Tungusic shamans have animal spirits, Manchus sometimes refer to initiations as "discovering your animals." Manchus believe that all shamans descended from the heavenly eagle spirit's daughter, who was the first shaman. (TUN)

Kuljamu: An ancient race, said to be over eight feet tall with conical heads, who inhabit the mountains. They are referred to as physical beings who live in stone houses, wear clothes, and use tools. They have immense spiritual power, appearing and acting as semidivine spirits. They are incredibly important to Amur shamanic traditions, protecting and soothing children, watching over travelers and homes, and blessing hunters and journeys. When displeased, they can bring death and bad luck upon a household, or even steal or demand to be given children.[18] Ulchi shamans have said that the kuljamu physically visited and had direct contact with their villages many generations ago, but still work with them through spirit dolls.[19] It is possible they are related to the *savdag* earth lords in Mongolian belief, possibly as a subgroup or a cousin race.[20] (TUN)

General Middle World spirits: As North Asian shamanic cultures are all animistic, they believe that everything in nature has a spirit. The spirits listed here are the key Middle World spirits, but there also many other spirits who may or may not be worshipped or worked with by shamans. These spirits may be beneficial, harmful, or neutral to humans, and they generally don't bother them. They are called *iye* by Central Asian Turkics, *ichchi* by Yakuts, *ezen* by Mongols, *weceku* by Manchus, *omi* or *saiven* by Evenks, and *sava* or *saven* by Amurs. *Omi* can also mean "soul" and the terms *sava, saven,* and *weceku* are used primarily to refer to shamanic spirits. Depending on the context, however, they can also refer generally to the spirits all around us. (TUR, MON, TUN)

Demonic Spirits and Ghosts

Khargi: In Evenki belief, he is the Lord of Khergu, the realm of demons in the Lower World, who seeks to undo his brother Seveki's creations and bring grief to the world. In legend, he appears as a human with a terrible green-fanged head in place of his right hand, and a claw in place of his left. Some stories depict him with stumps for legs, a completely bald head, and a hairy torso. Sometimes he is described as one-legged.[21] Folk legends have him sticking his human-headed right arm above ground to frighten people and capturing them with his claw, then drinking their blood and causing them to fall ill and die if they are not healed by a shaman. But if a person is not frightened, Khargi can't touch them. (TUN)

Yeruri: The supreme demon in Manchu belief. Originally the nine-headed, eight-limbed goddess *Oochin* created by Abka Hehe and Ulden Hehe to assist Banamu Hehe in creating and managing life. When she sought to learn everything and plotted against Banamu Hehe, the goddess tried to punish her by burying her under mountains. She transformed the mountains into horns and became the male demon *Yeruri,* who launched a war against the three goddesses, but was ultimately defeated and trapped within the earth or the Lower World (depending on the legend). He occasionally emerges to spread disease and conflict, and to give orders to his demon minions. It is interesting to note that Oochin was originally female, but became male after transforming into a demon.[22] (TUN)

Ad: Demonic spirit who usually afflicts children, causing spiritual sickness, bad temper, mood swings, and spiritual and emotional imbalances that can lead to addiction or obsession later in life. The *lus savdag* also have their own Ad spirits that they can send to cause wounds and illnesses to the skin, flesh, and organs.[23] (MON)

Chotgor: Spirits who have become stuck due to unresolved trauma, resentment, or unfinished business. They are classified as demonic because of their hostility to humans and other living beings. In black shamanism, they are consciousness souls who cannot move on. In yellow shamanism, they are suns souls who cannot find their way back to the Lower World.[24] These ghosts are known as *iyuers* to Yakuts, and *shurkul* to the Daur. They can haunt specific buildings or people, or places like forests, mountains, graves, and tombs. While it is generally a good idea to avoid the harmful energy of these places, the greatest risk is becoming the target of a chotgor. When chotgors attach themselves to people, they can cause great harm, sometimes by pretending to be helpful spirits. Incompetent shamans can confuse them with shamanic spirits or even guardian angels, although good shamans can naturally sense if a person's "spirit" is not actually an ancestral shamanic or land spirit. Undergoing initiation or performing ceremonies with a chotgor can create serious complications for the body and soul for both shaman and client. (TUR, MON)

Ari/Arenk: The names *ari* in Manchu and *arenk* in Evenk refer to ghosts and restless spirits and are likely other names for the chotgor. While not always the case, *ari* and *arenk* generally refer to spirits who are stuck in mountain forests. My maternal grandmother tells of how she encountered one as a little girl while out in the mountains with a friend. The figure was wearing a long tattered robe and had pale gray skin, sunken eyes, and a blank expression. It didn't look at them directly but, my grandmother recognized it as a ghost and yelled to her friend to run back to the village, although my grandmother was fine after the encounter, within a week, her friend fell sick and died. (TUN)

Sky vampires: While most traditions tend to consider Upper World spirits as beneficial, there are some who are not—like sky vampires. Called *ebaha* or *busawu* by the Amur and *abkai ari* by Manchus, sky vampires appear as beautiful humans who fly about at night hunting humans both physically and in their dreams. Some stories claim they drink human blood to obtain its life essence, while others claim they kill people and take their souls. If they take a soul but leave the body intact, a shaman may be able to do battle and retrieve the soul. The best way to protect yourself against them when outside at night is to stay near a body of water, as water spirits repel them.[25] (TUN)

General demons: Almost all North Asian cultures believe that there are powerful demonic entities residing in the Lower World that are implacably hostile to humans and to life in general. Because these spirits are so powerful and feared, people often refuse to talk about them to researchers, who end up believing that these traditions don't have demons at all. In fact, many Turkic and Mongol shamanic sources refuse to disclose the existence of demons, although some have vaguely implied that such entities may exist, sometimes calling them simply "servants of Erlik Khan."[26] Our primary knowledge of their existence comes from Tungusic mythological references. In the Manchu "War in Heaven" story, many of the demons who served Yeruri retreated into the depths of the earth and/or the Lower World after he was defeated. Occasionally, however, they return to the Middle World to spread disease and misfortune. The Evenki believe that the servants of Khargi retreated in a similar way after he was defeated by Seveki and now reside in the Khergu region of the Lower World. In these mythological stories, fire is often acknowledged as the best way to repel demonic entities, as fire was brought down from the heavens to thwart the cold attacks of malign spirits. We'll talk about fire spirits later in this chapter.

Lower World Spirits

As we saw in the last chapter, almost all North Asian cultures agree that the Lower World is a realm of darkness, because the Middle World blocks all the light from the heavens and keeps it from reaching the lower realm. That does not mean, however, that the spirits who inhabit that realm are necessarily "evil" or hostile. In fact, some can be quite helpful to humans, and the most powerful of these is the Lord of the Lower World himself.

Lord of the Lower World: Known as *Erlik Khan* to Turkics and Mongols, *Ulu Toyon* or *Arsan Duolan* to Yakuts, and *Ilmun/Irmu Khan* to Manchus and Daurs, this spirit is known to both help and harm humans. Among Buryats and Yakuts, he is responsible for supplying humans with one of their three souls. The Yakuts also believe he gave humans fire and played a part in creating the physical world.[27] But he is also known to do harm for selfish or emotional reasons, as in the story of Nisan Shaman (see chapter 7). Many Central Asian Turkic beliefs depict him as the evil counterpart of *Ulgen*, whose hubris caused him to be banished to the Lower World, where he plots to spread misfortune, sickness, and death.[28] (TUR, MON, TUN)

Omosi Mama: Manchu goddess of life, identical to *Fodo Mama* in almost every way except that the latter resides in the Middle World. Omosi Mama also figures prominently in the Nisan shaman story. Translated literally as Grandchildren's Grandmother, she gives the spark of life to humans before they are born, either through providing a soul or by lighting the fire that initiates life, which is likely why Sarangerel attributes her to the Turco-Mongol Goddess *Umay*.[29] Sometimes she is combined with Fodo Mama through the title *Fere Fodo Omosi Mama*. Her worshippers often employ a sacred rope tied with knots and anklebones, usually tying it from the altar to the spirit tree or pole to represent her connecting the physical and spiritual worlds.[30] Although she is not a fire goddess, she has a fire aspect. She manages the hearth and is often petitioned to help strengthen each family's household fire or hearth spirit. (TUN)

Monggoldai Nakcu: The boatman who ferries souls across the Lower World river to the realm of the dead. He is called Mongolian Uncle by the Manchus, although why this is so is unclear. Daur Mongols refer to him as *Mongoldai Nagts.* (TUN)

Kudaai Bakhsi: Patron of blacksmiths and one of the preeminent powers of the Lower World, especially important to Yakut black shamans, who work closely with Lower World spirits. All properly made shamanic metal tools must be forged by a blacksmith who can imbue them with Kudaai Bakhsi's power and blessing. Because of this, it is said that a spiritually trained blacksmith can overpower any shaman, and shamans must maintain good relationships with blacksmiths to obtain powerful and high-quality tools. In Yakut legend, the first blacksmith was the older brother of the first shaman. (TUR)

Lower World animal spirits: In Tungus belief, which places great importance on animal spirits, the Lower World is host to many animal spirits who frequently travel between the Middle and Lower Worlds. These spirits typically include snakes, reptiles, amphibians, fish, and insects; almost all of them have a deep connection with water. They can serve as allies to shamans, especially when they need to engage with the Lower World or engage in healing. (TUN)

Other Lower World spirits: As with the Upper and Middle Worlds, the Lower World contains many spirits who are "neutral"—neither beneficial nor harmful to humans—as they largely don't interfere with the Middle World at all. In Yakut, they are known as *abaasy.* (TUR, MON, TUN)

Fire Spirits

When the Middle World separated violently from the Upper World, the resulting explosion created fire. Thus fire plays an important role in all North Asian cosmologies, as do spirits and gods of fiery aspect.

Golomt Eej: The Fire Mother, another aspect of *Umay*, who gives humans their Upper World soul and simultaneously lights each person's spark of life.[31] As a fire goddess, she rules over every family's hearth fire and is thereby petitioned for the strength and protection of the hearth (and thus of the family). She is the primary Buryat Mongol fire goddess. (MON)

Tuwayalha: Manchu fire goddess who appears as a flaming animal with tiger eyes and ears, a leopard head, and a badger body, with eagle claws and a lynx tail. She was originally the goddess *Chichitan*, wife of the thunder god. She became Tuwayalha after she stole fire from the heavens to give to humans.[32] (TUN)

Od Iyesi (Ana/Ata): Turkic fire goddess/god, Od Ana, is the equivalent of the Buryat *Golomt Eej* in Central Asia. *Od Ata* (Fire Father) is the spirit's male form. Together they are the leaders of all other fire spirits. (TUR)

Alaz: Another Turkic fire god, pictured as an old man with a torch. Alaz is the son of *Kayra*. (TUR)

Household and hearth fire spirits: Almost every North Asian tribe worships fire to some degree, and this veneration is centered on the hearth fire. As fire was necessary for survival in the frigid north, the health of the hearth fire was paramount to the household's safety and an important connection to the spirits. Among Mongols, this spirit was known as *Gallakhai* or *Golomt*, who typically appears as female. The Turkic peoples knew this spirit as *Od Iyesi* (see above), *Ocak Iyesi* (hearth spirit), or *Soba Iyesi* (stove spirit). The Amur refer to her as *Pujen* or *Fojia Mama*, who appears as an old woman and is a key spirit who connects a household to its ancestors.[33] (TUR, MON, TUN)

Other Spirits and Gods

In addition to the dizzying array of spirits and gods listed above, North Asian shamans venerated other deities that don't neatly fit into the above groups, but deserve exploration.

Damdin/Damjin Dorlig: Blacksmith god venerated by Buryat black shamans. He fulfilled a role similar to that of *Kudaai Bakhsi* for the Yakuts, in that metal tools used by shamans are consecrated and dedicated to him. There is no apparent connection, however, between the two, as Damdin Dorlig came to the Buryats from Tibet, where he is known as *Damchen Garwa Nakpo*.[34] (MON)

Tsagaan Obgon: Mongolian Buddhist deity known as White Grandfather or White Old Man who is very important to Buryat white shamans. He appears as a smiling old man with a long white beard and eyelashes, dressed in white robes and carrying a large wooden dragon staff (see Figure 3 on page 56). Although Buryat white shamans work with ancestral shamanic spirits, they also work with this god and even carry wooden dragon staffs as one of their main shamanic tools in reverence of him. He is also one of the main characters in the Mongolian *tsam* dance, a Buddhist dance originating from Tibet. (MON)

Dayan Deerh: Originally an important fertility god widely worshipped in Khovsgol Province in Mongolia. He was said to grant cattle and children to people and became a protector spirit, particularly for shamans. While he is still venerated by yellow shamans, black shamans largely rejected him. It is said that he became a protector of yellow shamanism because he welcomed the Buddhist traditions coming into Mongolia, including their influence on shamanism. Black shamanism, which resisted Buddhist influence fiercely, thus saw him as a traitor.[35] (MON)

Avgaldai: Bear spirit venerated by Buryat and Daur Mongols, commonly represented by a copper mask with animal hairs for eyebrows, moustache, and beard. Avgaldai is typically venerated during the triennial *ominan* ritual, which simultaneously venerates all spirits and initiates new shamans.[36] He is also kept as a protector in a spirit house and can remove spiritual pollutions from objects and the home. (MON)

Zar Zargaach: Mongolian spirit of protection, wisdom, and justice who is portrayed as either a man without legs or a porcupine. He helps bring wisdom and insight into legal matters and is therefore venerated by those in the legal profession. In folk magic that uses porcupine quills for protection, prayers are often made to him.[37] (MON)

Zol Zayaach: A pair of spirits depicted as a man and a woman standing side by side. They protect households while also bringing success and good fortune.[38] In the Forbidden City, the Manchu Imperial family also worshipped a pair of spirits known only as *Khatun* ("queen") *Noyan* ("lord") in Mongolian. These spirits were likely imported into the Qing court by one of the early Mongol queens or concubines, and they likely served the same purpose as Zol Zayaach for the Imperial family. (MON, TUN)

Ajige Ilha Mama and *Amba Ilha Mama:* Manchu flower goddesses ("small flower goddess" and "large flower goddess"). They were originally recognized as heavenly maidens who created flowers and colorful fragrant clouds in heaven. When the smallpox epidemic (known as Heavenly Flower sickness) struck the Manchus, those afflicted with the disease appealed to them for help.[39] (TUN)

Aodu Mama: Manchu war goddess, often depicted riding into battle on a horse or reindeer.[40] (TUN)

Chaohazhan-ye: Manchu hero deity among the Shikteri clan, likely a personification of the Changbai Mountain spirit.[41] Possibly related to *Mulihan*, a Manchu god worshipped in the Forbidden City who is also identified as the Changbai Mountain spirit. (TUN)

Forest Lord: In several North Asian cultures, the forests are home to a master spirit who oversees the animals who live there. Hunters must pray to this spirit to request luck and success before they hunt, stating that they are contributing sustenance to the tribe or village. The Buryats and Daurs refer to this spirit as *Bayan Ahaa* or *Bayan Hangai.*

Daur shamans open the hunt by firing a single arrow into the forest after the blessing ceremony. Buryat hunters typically carve the face of Bayan Ahaa into a birch tree and pray and leave offerings to it.[42] The Yakuts refer to this spirit as *Bai Baianai*. The Amur do not appear to have a name for the forest lord, but conduct similar rituals for luck and success before hunting. (TUR, MON, TUN)

Burkhan: In Mongolia, the term *burkhan* formerly referred to primordial nature spirits that could be engaged as allies only by the most powerful shamans. Today, the term typically refers to gods from other cultures and religions who are not easily defined or classified in Mongolian worldview. Most commonly, the term is used to refer to Buddhist spirits (Buddhas, Bodhisattvas, Arhats, etc.). Among Daur Mongols, the name (pronounced "Barkan" by the Daur) refers to all spirits and gods, but in common usage retains the original meaning of primordial nature spirits or great gods. (MON)

Figure 3. 1880 picture of a Mongolian Tsam Buddhist dance troupe, with Tsagaan Obgon seated at front right. Unknown Tibetan artist, prior to 1895.

Shamanic Spirits

Shamanic spirits, as the name suggests, are the most important spirits to shamans. The biggest difference between shamanic spirits and other spirits is that they specifically choose those who will become shamans and are thereafter tied to those shamans for life. As a spiritual practice that's meant to connect humanity with the spiritual world, shamanism is grounded in this shaman-spirit partnership. In most cases, shamanic spirits are ancestors who were also shamans. When shamans pass away, their souls become shamanic spirits who choose the next shamans from within the bloodline, and the cycle continues. Shamanic spirits can work with one or multiple generations of shamans until they fulfill their responsibility, then they move on to the next stage of spiritual life.

Daur Mongols have another type of shamanic spirit known as the *hojoor* who weren't shamans in life. Rather they were ancestral clan leaders who sometimes demanded that shamans work with them. In many cases, the hojoor are male and follow female shamans. Thus when a female shaman marries, that family must worship the hojoor as well.[43]

Occasionally, shamanic spirits are not ancestors, but rather land and nature spirits, animal spirits, or divine or semidivine beings. But even in these cases, they are still tied to a bloodline for multiple generations. Sarangerel describes shamanic spirits as "extra souls," and, in a way, this is true, as they are past shamans' souls that are tied to a shaman for life and will usually only work with the shaman(s) they choose.[44] By contrast, other spirits and gods are not dedicated to individual shamans and can be prayed to or worked with by anyone.

Although every North Asian group agrees on the nature of shamanic spirits, they disagree on where these spirits reside. Most Turkic and Mongol black shamans believe that ancestral shamanic spirits reside in the "dark world," which includes both the upper and lower spirit realms (usually the Upper World). Yellow shamans believe that they reside in the Middle World, as sulds that remain on earth. In this tradition, non-shaman ancestors reside in a plane between the Middle and Lower Worlds. The Evenk and Oroqen believe that ancestral shamanic spirits reside in the Upper World. Some groups, like the Amur, believe that they can reside in any of the three worlds.

It is important to remember here that shamanism in its original sense requires that shamans be chosen by shamanic spirits. And shamanic spirits exist only because ancestors carried a specific way of working with spirits into the spirit world. But shamanic lineage and practice can be broken when (despite shamanic sickness) future members of these bloodlines no longer work with or refuse to acknowledge these spirits. Without a human shaman with whom to work, they eventually fade away into the next stage of spiritual existence and shamanism ceases to exist within that bloodline or culture. (TUR, MON, TUN)

Ancestral Spirits

Even in families that don't have shamans or shamanic ancestors, people still typically pray to their ancestors for blessings, luck, and protection. In fact, it is generally believed that everyone is guarded by their ancestors. For this reason, non-shamans conduct regular spiritual practices that include worshipping and giving offerings to their ancestors, the local land spirits, and the household fire and hearth spirits. They also regularly perform spiritual cleansings to remove negative energy that could impact their lives or block their ancestors' assistance.

According to Van Ysslestyne, the Amur are cautious about praying to ancestors, especially if they are unsure whether they have physically reincarnated. If they have, praying to them or giving them offerings is not only useless, but could even indirectly harm the reborn child by forcing the shadows or remnants of a past life on him or her. For similar reasons, other North Asian peoples may address their ancestors as "ancestral spirits" rather than "ancestors," as this specifies ancestors who are now spirits who have finished their reincarnation cycles. (TUR, MON, TUN)

CHAPTER 4

Shamans and
Spiritual Workers

Shamanism is a regional practice. Not only are there different traditions across North Asia, there are also variations within the same tradition, as well as different types of shamans. In this chapter, we will explore some of the different types of shamans and other spiritual workers found within these lineages.

Black vs. White Shamans

Black shamanism is considered one of the the earliest forms of shamanism in the Turco-Mongolic world. As such, it experienced the fewest external influences from belief systems like Buddhism and retains many of the original shamanic beliefs and practices. This tradition is described as "black" because its ancestral shamanic spirits are thought to dwell in the "dark" spiritual world, as the spirit worlds were typically envisioned to be without sunlight. Prior to Buddhist influence, black shamanism did not draw distinctions between shamans. Anyone identified as having shamanic spirits underwent the same initiation and training. Although an initiation ceremony was required most of the time, there were no formalized initiation degrees, as there are in yellow shamanism.

Although all shamans naturally develop their own strengths and specializations, black shamans were all trained by elders in the same techniques and practices. The only clear distinctions made were those based on strength, power, and experience, and these were reflected in their armor (see chapter 8). Traditionally, every time these shamans performed a ceremony, their clients were expected to tie a prayer scarf onto their armor (or to give one to the shaman if armor was not worn). The most experienced and powerful shamans were thus easily recognized as those having more prayer scarves hanging from their armor.

Today, mainstream shamanism among the Turkic, Mongolic, and even some neighboring Tungusic traditions classifies shamans as either "black" or "white." Sometimes they are distinguished by their spirit types—Lower World vs Upper World or Middle World, traditional shamanic spirits vs deities, etc. Sometimes they are differentiated by the type of work they do—wrathful, dangerous, or harmful vs healing, blessing, or protective. Sometimes they are simply seen as being stronger or weaker.

Darkhad black shamanism, on the other hand, makes no clear distinction between the types of spirits their shamans have. All are dark, traditional shamanic spirits. Nor do they differentiate based on the type of work they are *able* to do. Rather, younger shamans of the Darkhad lineage like to use the terms "black" and "white" to distinguish the type of work they are *willing* or *unwilling* to do. Specifically, "white" or "white-in-black" shamans are those who prefer not to do wrathful or harmful work if they can avoid it, while "black" or "black-in-black" shamans are those who don't hesitate to perform wrathful or harmful work if desired or requested.

Yellow Shamans

Yellow shamanism developed in traditions that were significantly influenced by Buddhism, and the term is used primarily to refer to Siberian Buryat shamanism. It is known as "yellow" because the primary Buddhist tradition that spread to North Asia was the *Gelug-pa*

(Yellow Hat) school led by the Dalai Lama. While yellow shamanism still retains many aspects of original black shamanism, many of its practices and its spirits, and even its spiritual worldview, were significantly shaped by or drawn directly from Buddhist traditions.

Buryat black shamans, also known as "black-in-yellow" shamans, are a subgroup of shamans within yellow shamanism who retain the most pre-Buddhist practices. They are known for connecting with shamanic spirits from the Middle World and the dark Lower World, or from the forty-four black tengers in the Upper World (see chapter 2). Historically, Buryat black shamans were more involved in political affairs, often handling intertribal relations and performing war magic during times of conflict. Although they don't perform healing as often as white shamans do, they frequently battle with hostile spirits (sickness, attachments, etc.) and perform ceremonies that are more dangerous in nature, as they are more powerful than Buryat white shamans.

During the Buddhist persecutions, black shamans were specifically targeted and nearly eradicated by Buddhists and, later, by the Soviets. After the dissolution of the Soviet Union, Buryat black shamanic traditions were largely revived.

Buryat white shamans, also known as "white-in-yellow" shamans, are a subgroup within yellow shamanism that was extremely influenced by Buddhism, as many of them were forced to lead a double life as Buddhist monks when shamanism was under persecution. Although white shamans do work with ancestral shamanic spirits, they also work prominently with Mongolian Buddhist deities, notably Tsagaan Obgon (see chapter 3). Ceremonies performed by white shamans incorporate many Buddhist mantras, most notably "Om Mani Padme Hom." White shamans can be recognized by their use of a Buddhist bell rather than a drum to induce trance, although today, Buryat white shamans can be found using drums as well. Historically, white shamans dealt with matters within the community, like mediating conflicts and general healing, blessing, and protection ceremonies. They are considered weaker than black shamans.

Yellow-in-Yellow Shamans

During the Buddhist persecutions, many white shamans—considered by Buddhist authorities to be less evil then black shamans, who worked with more wrathful spirits—were coerced into giving up their shamanic practices and were initiated as Buddhist monks. Black shamans, by contrast, were generally imprisoned and executed. While these former white shamans lived their lives as Buddhist monks, many of them continued some form of shamanic practice at night. However, since they could no longer dress in shamanic armor, they practiced wearing Buddhist vestments and using Buddhist tools. Moreover, they worked almost exclusively with Tibetan Buddhist deities. Hence, these shaman-monks became known as "yellow" shamans.

Although these yellow shamans no longer exist, as Buryat white shamans today are no longer forced to become Buddhist monks, it is largely due to the historical influence of yellow-in-yellow shamans that Buryat white shamanic practice is now so heavily Buddhist.

Nine Degrees of Buryat Initiation

Buddhist influence is also clearly evident in the complicated initiation process used by Buryats. Known as the "nine shanar degrees," this tradition strongly emphasizes ceremonial stages of initiation. Each degree initiates shamans into a stronger level of shamanic practice and each brings with it different abilities and responsibilities. Sarangerel says that these nine degrees can be achieved through eighteen years of nonstop study and practice, but that, given their busy lives, most only make it to the sixth or seventh degree.

The nine degrees represent the nine branches of the World Tree (see chapter 1).[1] Based on their titles and descriptions, these degrees most likely refer to Buryat black shamans.[2]

1. First degree: *Manjilaitai Boo*; newly initiated student

2. Second degree: *Noitolhon Boo*; baptized shaman

3. Third degree: *Jodooto Boo*; fir-tree shaman

4. Fourth degree: *Shereete Boo*; altar shaman

5. Fifth degree: *Hesete Boo*; drum shaman

6. Sixth degree: *Horiboto Boo*; horse-staff shaman

7. Seventh degree: *Tengeriin Orgoito Boo*; heavenly armor shaman

8. Eighth degree: *Tengeriin Orgoito Buheli Boo*; complete heavenly armor shaman

9. Ninth degree: *Tengeriin Tabilgatai Zaarin Boo*; great shaman mandated by heaven

"Big" vs "Little" Shamans

The Amur tribes believe that everyone has the ability to perform some level of shamanic work. However, only a certain few can become "big shamans"—those who are chosen by spirits to perform shamanic work for others. These shamans go through shamanic sickness and the initiation process and live lives in spiritual service to the village and beyond. They are the bridge between the physical and spiritual worlds, standing with one foot in one world and one foot in the other.

"Little shamans," on the other hand, are all others who engage in shamanistic practices. They can perform small levels of shamanic work for themselves, like simple prayer rituals and ceremonies for good luck, protection, and cleansing. They must defer to big shamans, however, for more complicated work, which can include soul retrievals and negotiating or battling with harmful spirits or each other. Little shamans can only do work for themselves and their families, not for others. In many ways, they are comparable to shamanists, as they are trained only in the basic spiritual knowledge and practices that everyone is expected to know. They engage primarily in non-spiritual activity on a day-to-day basis.[3]

Psychopomps

Psychopomps are the most powerful among the big shamans. They are the ones who engage in death rituals—performing last rites and guiding lost souls and ghosts to the Lower World. They are even powerful enough to journey to the Lower World for soul retrieval or to engage with Lower World spirits.

Both the northern and southern Tungus tribes refer to these shamans as *kasa* shamans (see Figure 4). However, even kasa shamans prefer not to perform psychopomp rituals if possible, as the Lower World is a terrifying place that can overpower them if something goes wrong.[4] Even among Mongols, death rituals (or any ritual that uses items associated with death) are performed only by those who have received the necessary teachings and training, and even then, they avoid them when possible.

The Ulchi perform two types of psychopomp rituals. The first takes place a year after a person has passed. In it, kasa shamans journey to the Lower World to see whether the deceased has arrived, to learn how their journey went, and to give them a chance to pass messages to their living relatives. The second, which can be performed at any time, involves setting up a raised platform between two tall young trees, with metal spirit cones, bells, and wooden streamers tied on and between the trees. Shamans stand on the platform and begin shaking the trees and rattling the cones and bells, falling into trance and journeying to the Lower World. They then invite the deceased to possess them so that family members can ask and answer questions.[5] This somewhat resembles the *chaktu* ritual in Korean shamanism, in which shamans stand on a raised platform between two poles. Unlike the Korean ritual, however, Ulchi shamans do not stand on sharp blades.

Figure 4. Ulchi shaman Grandfather Misha Duvan (1903–1997) performing a kasa ritual in 1996. Photo courtesy of Pathfinder Counseling.

Wild vs Domestic Shamans

During the Qing Dynasty, Manchus had largely institutionalized their spirituality—so much so that spiritual activity was categorized as either "wild" or "domestic." Manchu spirit workers were thus classified as either "wild" shamans or "domestic" shamans. Only wild shamans are considered true shamans, as the rituals of domestic shamans do not incorporate any form of trance work. Domestic shamans are often clan leaders or significant women (for example, the Qing empress) whose roles are analogous to those of priests or ritualists. Domestic shamans primarily lead and conduct ceremonies and sacrifices to deities and gods (like the Sky Father), mostly within the Manchu pantheon. They have been known, however, to incorporate Buddhist and Chinese gods as well. When not leading ceremonies, they maintain the village clan altars, as well as the Imperial temples (*tangse*).

Although wild shamans can also perform sacrifices and offering ceremonies, they are primarily known for falling into trance states in which they undergo spirit possession or travel to the spirit worlds. They serve ancestral shamanic spirits and animal god spirits, rather than the deities to whom domestic shamans pray and make offerings. Manchu wild shamans fulfill the same role as shamans in the Turkic, Mongol, and other Tungus traditions. Generally, Manchus seek domestic shamans to perform ceremonies for blessing and protection, but they seek wild shamans who can perform healing when they fall sick. Wild shamans can also negotiate and battle with spirits, and may even be called on to perform war or curse magic. They can perform more "active" spirit work and intervention.

In some Manchu villages today, domestic and wild ceremonies are combined, but the separate roles of domestic shamans (who perform sacrifice ceremonies) and wild shamans (who undergo spirit possession on behalf of villagers) are still maintained. Manchu practices are possibly the only ones in which these spiritual responsibilities are separated into different roles. In most other North Asian cultures, shamans perform both domestic and wild ceremonies.

Shamans Fortified by Land Spirits

In most cases, shamans work only with their ancestral shamanic spirits, as the spirits of past shamans are the ones responsible for choosing the next shamans within their bloodline. Sometimes, however, shamans may also have a land spirit among their retinue of shamanic spirits. This happens when the land spirit is tied to the shaman's bloodline, either through past shamans who established a strong connection with the spirits of a particular place (perhaps ancestral spirit houses that are located there), or through curse spirits who have negotiated and agreed to curse *for* a bloodline instead of cursing the bloodline itself. Among the Turkic (Tuvan, Dukha) and Mongol peoples, these shamans are considered "fortified by the lus" (see chapter 3). Among the Tungus, shamans may have animal spirits in addition to ancestral shamanic spirits, which may be representations of land spirits. However, because the animals that break the bones of deceased shamans become their spiritual companions, these spirits are sometimes instead representations of ancestral shamanic spirits. As Manchu "wild" shamans almost always have animal spirits, I suspected I would as well; when I visited Darkhad shamans in Mongolia, they recognized me as fortified by land spirits.

Shamans who are fortified by land spirits are more powerful than those who have only ancestral shamanic spirits. All shamans understand that the extent of their power comes not from themselves but rather from the spirits. Thus they are only as strong as their strongest spirits. Shamans who carry both ancestral shamanic *and* land spirits are able to access powers and abilities from both. Land spirits possess powers that are not completely understandable to humans so shamans fortified by them have always been seen to be more powerful.

Although many shamans carry only ancestral spirits, few carry only land spirits. The most common cases I have encountered are among the Chinese *Tiaodashen* shamans in Manchuria, who inherited lineages from ancestral intermarriages between the Han and the Manchu. These shamans work only with animal spirits. While some of these animal spirits may represent ancestors (as noted above), it is also possible that they are simply land spirits and that the few rare shamans who work exclusively with them do not carry ancestral spirits at all.

Half-Shamans and Diviners

Across North Asia, there are spiritualists who are masters at divination, but not shamans as such. Among some groups—like the Ulchi and other Amur tribes—there is a class of shamans who do only divination. These are shamans who have not completed their training or received enough initiation songs from Amur elders, and who are thus only empowered to divine. Among the Ulchi, they are known as *isachula* or *nairigda*. Because they have not completed their training, they are known as "half-shamans."[6]

Although not directly stated anywhere, it is generally accepted that to become a good shaman, one must develop strong intuitive and psychic abilities. After all, without intuitive abilities, how can anyone expect to communicate effectively with their spirits? In traditional societies that maintain shamanic training, new shamans are expected to master their intuitive abilities either before initiation or soon after, before they move on to the next stage of spirit work. These skills are primarily honed through divination. In fact, divination is the cornerstone of all shamanic work, as shamans must use it to diagnose their clients' issues before they can conduct any ceremonies. Otherwise, an improper ceremony could lead to worsening conditions and even death—possibly for the shaman as well.

Every time I've asked a traditional shaman in Mongolia and even in Korea about my path, they would ask me to perform divination for them. They initially ask me to answer simple questions, and then move on to more difficult ones. Sometimes they even ask for information about issues in their own lives or in the lives of their family members and ask me to report on possible solutions from the spirits. Only after they have determined that the person has divination abilities do they even consider sharing some of their knowledge and techniques. If they are not impressed, they may remain tight-lipped and even suspicious about the person's intentions.

In his book *Sky Shamans of Mongolia*, Kevin Turner reported similar experiences in which shamans sometimes even acted abrasive and hostile until he was able to demonstrate his divination abilities, after which they became much friendlier.[7] While it is true that a person doesn't need to be a shaman or have shamanic spirits to perform divination, those with shamanic spirits usually prefer using techniques that non-shamans cannot use. We will explore some of these techniques in chapter 9.

The cornerstone of divination is astrology, as astrological information can be calculated for each person and then compared against information for the current or upcoming time period—usually a year, but sometimes months or even multiple years (see chapter 2).

Non-shamans can also divine based on signs in nature, or by tossing items and reading how they land—a practice called "sortilege." Knucklebones of sheep, reindeer, and pigs are most commonly used in this type of divination, though the Tungus have also been known to toss the bones of various other animals, and sometimes even pearls (see chapter 9). Nonetheless, because half-shamans still have shamanic spirits, they can glean more information through their spirits than those without shamanic spirits. While non-shamans can still receive information from their non-shamanic protector spirits, this is generally more difficult, as they have to rely more on their tools than on hearing directly from spirits.

Non-Shaman Roles

Although shamans are among the most common and well-known spiritual roles, they are certainly not the only spiritual authorities across North Asia. As we saw above, although all shamans can divine, it is often easier and more affordable to consult a non-shamanic diviner if you want only information and are not necessarily looking for a ceremony or spiritual intervention. Some of these non-shamanic spiritual roles are extremely helpful and even necessary for shamans to function. Other times, these roles involve specialties that require special mastery. While a good shaman is expected to have at least basic knowledge in all spiritual disciplines (in addition to their specialized shamanic work), sometimes a specialized mastery in a non-shamanic field is needed. This makes these other non-shamanic roles necessary in North Asian cultures.

Assistants

Shamanic assistants are in many ways crucial to the successful performance of shamans. In addition to assisting them in preparing for ceremonies and even handling administrative work, these assistants also play an active role while shamans are in ceremony. They read the shamans and their spirits and react quickly to new developments.

Sometimes this may involve only interpreting the spirits' words and relaying them to clients or the audience. Sometimes it involves determining whether the ceremony is going well or poorly and suggesting alternatives or new directions to shamans while they're in trance. If a spirit possessing a shaman is in a foul mood, it is up to the assistant to calm it and provide offerings.

In some cases, assistants may also conduct non-trance spirit work to support shamans who are in trance. Without them, shamans can be very vulnerable. Because trance possession and spirit flight can be so unpredictable, and because shamans relinquish control over their bodies while in trance, assistants are often needed to alleviate or to counter dangerous situations. In Turkic and Mongolic shamanic ceremonies, spirit-possessed shamans may start jumping and spinning, and assistants must keep them from falling, since it is said that if shamans in trance fall to the floor, they lose much of their power and the ceremony suffers.

Assistants are even more important among the Tungus cultures. In Amur tribes, shamans frequently conduct spirit flight, and it is the assistants' responsibility to make sure they don't go too far and to help pull them back if necessary. Among the Manchu, assistants are expected to drum and play instruments while shamans are in trance, mostly to act as support for their work, but sometimes also to call upon other spirits and gods to come to their aid. In Chinese Tiaodashen ceremonies in Manchuria, shamans cannot even undergo trance possession without assistants, who drum and sing to call down the spirits.

Today, the role of assistant is often filled by family members, other shamans, or even students of shamans. For those who also have shamanic spirits, however, playing the role of assistant can be quite difficult, as they must stay grounded and in control, and not fall into trance while the performing shamans draw in their spirits.

Midwives

Traditionally, midwives have fulfilled a very important role both physically and spiritually. In Mongolia, these practitioners are known as *bariyachi* (see chapter 3). Mongolian midwives typically work with the deity Auli Burkhan, a mountain spirit who takes the form of a fox. While women are pregnant, midwives are expected to care for both their physical and spiritual well-being. They are able to fall into a light trance to commune with Auli Burkhan—for instance, to divine the gender of the baby.[8] When babies are born, midwives deliver them and wash them in a salt bath.

Mongol midwives typically dry and preserve the umbilical cord (sometimes with an animal's vein). It is extremely important to retain the umbilical cord, along with hair from the baby's first haircut, which typically occurs when the child is around three or four years old. Both represent the child's karmic bonds to its past life, and they are often used in magic to protect and bless the child, even into adulthood.[9]

Among Manchus, midwives give children their first "spiritual" bath for blessing and protection on the third day after birth. For this, they fill a copper basin with hot water and steep mugwort leaves and small branches from the Japanese pagoda tree (*Styphnolobium japonicum*) in it. Family members and guests place coins, nuts, seeds, and even eggs in the basin as blessings for the child. Midwives perform prayers while tapping the child's head with a leek stalk to endow it with strength. Among Manchus, the role of midwife can be performed only by an elderly woman with at least one living adult son and one living adult daughter.

Bonesetters

Bonesetters can be described as spiritual chiropractors. In Mongol black shamanism, bones are considered to be one component of the tripartite soul, so bonesetters are extremely important, as they fulfill the role of soul healers (see chapter 2). When bones are damaged, the consciousness soul is damaged as well, and it is important for bonesetters to heal both the physical and spiritual damage. In Mongolic yellow shamanism, damaged bones disrupt the circulation of the ami and suns souls around the body, so bonesetters remain important in these traditions.

The positive mental and emotional effects of a soul being healed by a bonesetter can be felt immediately through the balancing of mood swings, improvements in focus and clarity, and in a general strengthening of mental capacities. Strong bonesetters are able to detect broken bones immediately upon sight and/or touch. Chinggis Khan's clan reportedly had some of the best bonesetters in Mongolia, and it is said that their descendants live in Inner Mongolia, primarily among the Khorchin. Researcher Marguerite Garner visited the office of Dr. Bao Renqinzungnai, one of the most famous bonesetters in Hohhot, Inner Mongolia. Bao, who can perform some shamanic practices—like making cleansing spirit water—is said to have descended from bonesetters who treated Chinggis Khan himself.[10]

Herbal Healers

All shamans, by nature of their training, have a basic knowledge of herbal healing, as one of the main divination questions is whether a particular sickness should be healed through medicine, ceremony, or both. However, the northern cultures recognize a clearly defined role for shamanic herbal healers. Among Buryats, they were known as *otoshi* (from the word *otochi* for "doctor," and the word *okin* for "girl"). Otoshi were exclusively women who were chosen by spirits—typically land spirits associated with wind and trees. These healers were guided both by their physical knowledge of ailments and herbs, and by information received from their spirits.

The otoshi also specialized in fertility and children's ailments and therefore sometimes assisted midwives. When connecting with their spirits, Buryat otoshis wore animal-hide skirts and colored hats, used colorful fans hung with silk strips, and sometimes used prayer beads. According to Sarangerel, they were heavily persecuted by Buddhists because of their feminist roles and power. Buddhist monks and doctors co-opted their role as herbal healers.[11]

The Daur are said to be the only Mongolic people who still use otoshis today. However, Daur otoshis are firmly rooted in goddess cults, which are typically referred to as *Niang-Niang* cults (from the

Chinese word for "mistress"). They refer to their spirits as *Tenger Niang-Niang*, including *Ome Niang-Niang barkan* (Umay). In Daur society, the otoshi's role often rivaled that of the shaman (*yadgan*), as they could be quite similar. In regions like Hailar in Inner Mongolia, both shamans and otoshis can be either male or female. The only differences between them are that they work with different types of spirits in nature, and shamans inherit their spirits from bloodlines, while otoshis can be selected by spirits regardless of bloodline. Otoshis also wear different regalia and do not use drums.[12]

Blacksmiths

Blacksmiths are extremely important for both the practical necessities of North Asian life, as well as for spiritual shamanic practice. For shamans to practice safely, especially for more difficult workings or when entering the spirit worlds, they must carry adequate protection, which is often provided by objects carefully made by blacksmiths. These include implements like copper mirrors, iron jingle cones, the frames of Khorchin iron drums, and the iron or copper antlers of Buryat and Tungus shamans, as well as bells and other tools (see chapter 8).[13]

Traditionally, most blacksmiths had some level of spiritual ability. They could go into light trance while working and bless items as they were being forged, imbuing them with blessings, protective power, and sometimes even spirits. Today, not many blacksmiths are spiritually trained, but shamans (elders and assistants) may participate in the forging process to make sure that the necessary items are made in the proper way. In northern Mongolia, there is even a type of shaman known as a blacksmith-shaman (*darkhan zairan*) who has enough knowledge of smithing to at least make more iron jingle cones when necessary.

Iron is the material most used for shamanic tools and regalia, as it is considered the hardest metal and most protective against spirits. Copper has protective abilities as well, but it is also considered pleasing for spirits because it represents wealth and pleasant objects—which is why copper is used to make shamanic mirrors.[14] Yakut creation legend indicates that the first blacksmith was the older brother of the first shaman. Because blacksmiths' abilities were so central to the success of shamans, they are the only non-shamans capable of overpowering shamans.

Shamanists

Shamanists are lay folk who believe in shamanism, the spirit worlds, and the power of shamans and other spiritual workers. They live conventional lives, but consult with shamans on spiritual needs or matters that need answers or insights, following the spiritual guidance they receive and respecting the taboos that regulate their cultures. They regularly give offerings to their ancestors and land spirits, and often maintain sacred spaces or altars in their homes to honor their ancestors and other spirits who look after their families.

The family members of shamans past and present tend to hold on to sacred items and spirit houses of past shamans and honor them, sometimes even drawing energy and magical power from them. Although they don't have shamanic spirits, they often have guardian spirits who watch over them and they can develop their own abilities to perform strong magic. It is said that, because the Turkic Dukha people are so powerful, even their non-shamans have strong magical powers they can use to influence and compel others.

CHAPTER 5

Turkic Shamanism

Now that we've explored the roots of shamanism and its spiritual components, let's take a look at some of the shamanic traditions that have flourished in North Asia.

Most people in the West tend to think of the country today known as Turkey when they hear the term "Turkic." But the people of Turkey make up only part of a broad group of people who are often referred to as Turkics—sometimes also called the Turuk, the Tureg, or the Turan—who originated in modern-day northern Mongolia and spread as far west as Anatolia and the Caucasus, and eastward toward the Pacific. In fact, the Turkic peoples are possibly the most widely spread family of peoples today.

While Turkics originally practiced shamanism through the religion of Tengerism (see chapter 2), most have since converted to Islam, with a minority converting to Buddhism and only a few tribes still practicing shamanism. While some Islamized Turkic peoples retain some shamanic elements in their spirituality, most retain very little if any of the original shamanistic practices or Tengerist cosmology. A nationalist movement gaining power in modern-day Turkey seeks to co-opt much of Mongolian history and culture. But it is important to note that the Turks in modern-day Turkey have become largely separate from both the Mongols and the Turkic peoples in Siberia. While modern-day Turks do have some ancestry that traces back to Central Asia and Siberia, their cultural and genetic identity has been so heavily influenced by Arab and Persian cultures that they retain very little of their original heritage beyond certain specific linguistic ties.

Early Turkic History

The first recorded accounts of shamanism come from Chinese records that describe their Hunnu/Xiongnu neighbors to the north roughly 2,000 years ago. Although the Hunnu may not have been the first nomadic civilization in North Asia, they certainly became the first dominant power across the Eurasian steppes. The Hunnu were a tribal confederation of nomadic peoples that was founded by the legendary Modu Chanyu around 209 BCE. According to the ancient historian Sima Qian, Modu's father plotted his death by sending him to a nearby kingdom as a hostage and then attacking that kingdom, hoping they would kill Modu in revenge. Modu was able to escape, however, and gather a group of loyal warriors whom he tested by ordering them to shoot his horse and wife, and then to shoot his father. After becoming the leader of his tribe, Modu proclaimed himself *Chanyu* (chief) and aggressively expanded his territory to neighboring kingdoms.

While there is some debate over whether the Hunnu confederation was a multiethnic empire consisting of Turkic, Iranian, Mongolic, Uralic, or even Tibeto-Burmese groups, some Western researchers believe that they were a Turkic civilization that practiced Tengerism. However, there is also evidence that suggests they may have been Mongolic, and this is what is taught in modern Mongolia today. Other researchers believe that they were Yeniseian, an ancient paleo-Siberian population that survives only in the modern Ket people.

Chinese anthropologists claim that today's Mongols descended from the ancient Donghu, another confederation of nomadic tribes to the east (eastern Mongolia and western Manchuria) that everyone agrees to be Mongolic. The Donghu were initially a rival confederation that was absorbed by the Hunnu. We know that the heart of Hunnu power was centered in modern-day Mongolia, but spanned eastward and southward into Inner Mongolia, northward into Siberia, and westward into Central Asia (Kazakhstan and Kyrgyzstan).

The Chinese empires that existed at the same time as the Hunnu confederation (primarily the Han Dynasty) left behind numerous records about it, as the two civilizations were arguably the largest players in ancient Asian politics and had deep interactions both peaceful and warring. What is important to us here is that the Hunnu established what is widely considered to be the first shamanist empire in history. Chinese chronicles note that, during shamanic ceremonies, the Hunnu made offerings to Tenger in the sky (see chapter 2).[1]

The Concurrent Han Chinese Dynasty

The Han Dynasty, led by Han Gaozu, was initially a vassal state of the Hunnu, then ruled by Modu Chanyu following the Chinese defeat at the Battle of Baideng in 200 BCE, at which time they were forced to pay tribute to the nomadic empire. About sixty years later, the new Han emperor, Han Wudi, adopted an offensive strategy against the Hunnu, reacting to years of raids by nomadic tribesmen against Chinese villages. This launched the Han-Xiongnu war (*Xiongnu* being the Chinese spelling of "Hunnu"), a fifty-six-year struggle that proved to be one of the largest conflicts Asia had ever seen.

The Chinese Han Dynasty emerged victorious, reversing the vassal relationship between the Hunnu and the Han. Over time, the Hunnu confederation crumbled from within, eventually splitting into the Northern and Southern Hunnu states. The Southern Hunnu, plagued by famine and natural disasters, submitted and were incorporated into the Chinese Han Empire. The Northern Hunnu continued their resistance and were eventually driven westward by Chinese forces. There is some indication that the Northern Hunnu may have been the ancestors of the Huns who later invaded Europe. Regardless, as the Chinese kingdom had no desire to rule over the grasslands and steppes that were inhospitable to their agrarian culture, North Asia now experienced a power vacuum that would soon be filled by the rise of the Xianbei.

The Xianbei

The Xianbei were a neighboring nomadic tribe of Donghu origin, from what is now modern-day eastern Mongolia, Inner Mongolia, and Manchuria. Although they were subjugated by the Hunnu and made a vassal kingdom, the deterioration and departure of the Hunnu (including the assassination of a Northern Hunnu king) allowed the Xianbei to rise as the dominant power in North Asia. There is much evidence to suggest that the Xianbei spoke a proto-Mongolic language, a distant ancestor of modern Mongolian.

As far as we know, the Xianbei were the first empire to refer to their kings as *khan* and *khagan*. They reportedly practiced shamanism as part of their Tengerist faith. The Xianbei state did not last long, however, falling quickly to the Rouran Khaganate (also of Donghu origin). Many splinter groups of the Xianbei settled in North China and adopted Chinese culture, language, and lifestyles. The most prominent of these was the Tuoba clan (*Tabghach* in Mongolian), who founded the Northern Wei Dynasty and became the primary opponent of the Rouran Khaganate.

The story of Mulan, now largely associated with China, is, in fact, from the Northern Wei Dynasty. Although this character's family adopted Chinese culture and lifestyle, she is of Tuoba Xianbei heritage and maintains some of her nomadic culture in her female equestrianism, which allowed her to develop great warrior skills that were uncommon for Han Chinese women. In the story, Mulan fights on behalf of the Northern Wei Dynasty against the Rouran Khaganate.

The Gokturks

The Rouran Khaganate lasted for about 200 years before falling during a rebellion by the Gokturks, a Turkic group that was founded by the Ashina clan and originated in the Altai Mountains of central Asia. They were vassals of the Rouran, as well as of several prior nomadic empires including the Hunnu, and were said to have been part of the Northern Hunnu Empire. *Gokturk* means "Blue Turks" or "Celestial Turks," reflecting the association of the color blue with heaven. According to legend, the ancestor of the Ashina clan was born from a gray she-wolf in the vicinity of the Altai, and the banner of the Gokturk Empire featured a wolf's head on a field of blue.

In 551 CE, Bumin Khagan (rendered *Qaghan* in academic circles), chieftain of the Ashina Gokturks, declared secession and independence from the Rouran Khaganate and allied himself with other kingdoms like the Western Wei, a Xianbei kingdom that came under Han Chinese influence following the disintegration of the Northern Wei. Within four years, he had conquered the Rouran. The kingdom he founded was known as the Gokturk Khaganate, sometimes also called the Old Turkic Khaganate.

The Gokturk Khaganate is considered to be the largest Turkic empire in history, as well as the last Turkic empire in which Tengerism and shamanism were considered the national religion. At its height, this empire stretched from Manchuria to the east, to the northern Caucasus to the west, near the borders of the Byzantine Empire. Although they came close, the Gokturks never reached the Pacific Ocean to the east or the Black Sea to the west. Eventually, thanks to civil war and infighting among Turkic nobles, the empire fractured into the Eastern Gokturk Empire and the Western Gokturk Empire.

Just as the rivalry between the Hunnu and the Han dominated earlier Asian power politics, the rivalry between the Gokturks and the Chinese Tang Dynasty dominated the Asian political scene in the 6th, 7th, and 8th centuries. Their relationship was volatile, alternating between periods of war and peace. During peaceful times, Chinese Buddhist missionaries often traveled to the Gokturk Empire, creating small Buddhist communities. Despite these missionary activities, however, the Gokturks remained staunchly Tengerist and maintained their shamanic traditions. A large portion of the conflicts that arose were tied to trade routes, specifically the Silk Road, which was already one of the largest sources of wealth in the region. The Gokturk and Tang Empires vied for control and influence over this and surrounding trade routes, and these clashes ultimately lead to the Tang-Gokturk wars.

Chinese-Gokturk relations soured quickly following the Tang's reunification of China and the increase of Gokturk raids into northern Chinese villages. The Tang emperors saw the Gokturks as the primary military threat to their regime and mounted several campaigns against them to secure their borders. They saw the Eastern Gokturk Empire as the primary threat and, in 630 CE, engaged them in battle all across southern Mongolia. After several battles, the Eastern Gokturk army was decimated and the Tang captured the Khan, as well as over 120,000 Gokturks. This signaled the end of the Eastern Gokturk Empire.

Twelve years later, the Tang took advantage of civil unrest in the Western Gokturk Empire to expand its influence into Central Asia, launching invasions that slowly drove the Gokturks back. By 657 CE, the Western Gokturk Empire fell apart completely. Twenty-five years later, the Eastern Gokturk Empire was restored as the Second Gokturk Empire, but, after several decades, it became a tributary and vassal state to the Tang. This situation lasted until around 740 CE, when it fell to the rising Uyghur Khaganate.

Although the Gokturks would not be the last Turkics to establish an empire in North Asia, they were certainly the last to practice shamanism and Tengerism as their national faith. The Uyghur Khaganate had already abandoned shamanism and converted to Manichaeism, a now-defunct, but once major, Persian religion that rivaled Christianity before the spread of Islam. Several centuries later, the Uyghurs abandoned Manichaeism and converted almost completely to Islam. The Uyghur Khaganate would be the last Turkic empire to rule North Asia, passing that torch to the Mongols (see chapter 6).

Although few people today know of the Gokturks, they left behind a legacy that had a great impact on Asian history, as well as on the history of shamanism. Although the Turkics would never again gain dominance in North Asia, their cultural legacy helped shape the future nomadic empires of the Mongols. Although only a few Turkic tribes continued to practice shamanism into the 20th century, Tengerism continued to thrive and was revived among the Mongols, while variations of it spread to the Tungus tribes to the east and to the Finno-Ugric peoples to the west.

The Turkic Peoples Today

Today, the Turkic peoples can be categorized into six branches based on the distribution of the Turkic languages: southwestern (*Oghuz*), southeastern (*Karluk*), northwestern (*Kipchak*), northeastern (Siberian), *Arghu*, and *Oghur*.

Oghuz is by far the most common Turkic language, spoken by Anatolian Turks, Azerbaijanis, and Turkmens, among others. Karluk refers to the languages of the medieval Karakhanid and Chagatai Empires, and is today primarily spoken by Uzbeks and Uyghurs. The Kipchak languages dominate in Central Asia and are spoken primarily by Kazakhs, Kyrgyz, and Tatars, including the Crimean Tatars. Arghu refers to the Persianized Turkic language spoken in parts of Iran. Oghur is the name of the language of the Turkic Chuvash people in southwest Russia, but may also have been spoken by the ancient Bulgars and Khazars.

The Siberian Turkic languages are the second least spoken after Arghu—all of them are considered linguistically vulnerable or severely endangered. The largest groups speaking these languages today are the Yakut and Tuvan, with considerably fewer speaking the Altai, Khakass, Yugur, Shor, Dolgan, and Tofa languages.

The Turkics have largely converted to Islam, with several scattered groups practicing Orthodox Christianity and Tibetan Buddhism. Although Turkic Tengerism and shamanism can still be found, it is currently practiced almost exclusively by the Siberian Turkic peoples, sometimes alongside Tibetan Buddhism or Orthodox Christianity. The most notable of these include the Tuvan, the Dukha, and the Yakut, whose traditions have remained largely intact, while Tengerist revival movements have emerged in the Altai regions. The Siberian and Central Asian Turkics are broadly referred to as *Uriankhai* in Mongolia.

Turkic Tengerism

As we learned in chapter 2, shamanism across most of North Asia was practiced through a sky-based spirituality known as Tengerism (sometimes spelled Tengrism). It is possible that these beliefs may first have been adopted by the Turkic peoples before spreading to other peoples. Here, we'll look at Tengerism in the context of ancient Turkic mythology and beliefs, which, although similar to the Tengerism practiced by other ethnic groups (like the Mongols), contain significant differences that will be covered more in the next two chapters.

Tengerism is grounded in a belief that the highest power in the universe is Tenger or Tengri, the chief sky god, who is considered to be the supreme being and creator of everything. Under Tenger, Turkics worshipped *Etugen*, the Earth Mother goddess who was considered to be second only to the sky god himself (see chapter 3). In keeping with the animistic roots of Tengerism, they also venerated the spirits of natural forces and elements—the sun, moon, stars, and clouds; water, fire, air, thunder, and lightning—as well as land and water spirits, and the spirits of elevated ancestors. These spirits were extremely diverse, some inclined to help, some inclined to harm, and some inclined to stay out of human affairs entirely. Generally, Tengerism divided these spirits into the gentle and heroic "white" spirits, and the wrathful "black" spirits, a distinction that refers to their temperament, not to whether they are "good" or "evil."

Tengerism began as a belief system centered on prayer rituals. Over time, shamanic practices developed out of these beliefs as a means by which spiritual elders could connect individuals to the spirits and deliver their actions to the physical world to serve the spiritual needs of the community. In both ancient and modern Turkic traditions, shamans acted as spirit-chosen bridges between humans and the spirit realms. But these practices developed differently across different nomadic groups. Here, we'll examine the shamanic traditions of three of these groups—the Tuva, the Dukha, and the Yakut.

Figure 5. The word "tenge" as written in the old Turkic script, a runic alphabet discovered in the Orkhon Valley in Mongolia.

Tuvan Shamanism

The Tuvans are a Turkic-speaking Siberian people who live mostly in the Tuva Republic of southern Siberia in Russia, with scattered populations also living in Mongolia and China. Tuva today is known for its throat-singers as well as for its shamanic traditions. It is interesting to note that, according to research by Ilya Zakharov of Moscow's Vavilov Institute of General Genetics, the Tuvans are the closest genetic relatives to the indigenous peoples of the Americas.[2]

Of all the Turkic peoples, the Tuvans perhaps maintain the most original form of nomadic lifestyle, and their shamanic practices date back to the Gokturk Empire. That being said, Tuvan culture has also been significantly influenced by Mongolic cultures. In fact, after the fall of the Uyghur Khaganate, Tuva was briefly ruled by the Turkic Yenisei Kyrgyz Khaganate, which peacefully submitted its territories to Chinggis Khan and his rising Mongol Empire in the 13th century. For the next approximately 600 years, the Tuvans were directly ruled by Mongol kingdoms. That is why Tuvan shamanism and original Mongolian shamanism (practiced primarily by the Darkhad Mongols in the Darkhad Valley, which borders Tuva) are said to be similar and to share many foundational roots.

In the mid-18th century, Tuva was conquered and ruled by the Tungus-Manchu Qing Dynasty (see chapter 6). This continued until its fall in 1911. While the independent Republic of Tannu-Tyva was established in 1921, Tuva was formally annexed by the Soviet Union in 1944. After 1944, the Soviets heavily persecuted both shamans and Buddhists, with many rounded up, arrested, incarcerated, and even executed.

After the dissolution of the Soviet Union, Tuva became a Russian protectorate as an autonomous republic in 1992 under the Russian Federation. The Republic of Tuva declared shamanism, Buddhism, and Russian Orthodox Christianity as their official religions. Today, Tuvans practice Tibetan Buddhism for the most part, but shamanism and Tengerism have seen a steady and healthy resurgence over the past thirty years.

Tuvan male shamans are known as *kam* (*kham*), while female shamans are known as *udgan*. In modern Tuvan shamanism, shamans are divided into black shamans (*kara-kham*) and white shamans (*ak-kham*), the main difference being that black shamans generally work with more wrathful spirits, while white shamans generally work with spirits who are more gentle and divine (see chapter 4). As we have seen already, black shamanism does not indicate evil in any form of North Asian shamanism. In fact, in some cases, shamans may refer to themselves as white shamans if they choose not to engage in harmful or wrathful work, even if they have black spirits in their lineage. Some claim that Tuvan shamans did not originally subscribe to black/white classifications, and that this is a modern distinction used to describe these practices.[3]

In modern Russia, shamanic ceremonies are known as *kamlanie*, a word derived from the Turkic-Tuvan word for shaman. This word is now even used by other Russian-speaking Siberian peoples when talking about shamanic ceremonies. Traditionally, a kamlanie starts with a purification followed by a prayer ritual. Shamans then invoke their spirits and enter trance to perform either spirit possession or spirit flight, as well as larger ceremonies (see chapter 1).

Tuvan kamlanies generally consist of two types: worship and healing. Worship ceremonies are performed chiefly by giving offerings of milk, meat, and/or bread to ancestral shamanic spirits, patron clan spirits, fire spirits, and spirits of the land and sacred trees. These ceremonies serve to strengthen the relationship and connection between the community, the shamans, and the spirits they work with, providing blessings and a solid foundation for shamans who must conduct healing ceremonies.

These worship ceremonies may take place at the household altar, or out in nature at land shrines known as *ovaa* (*ovoo* in Mongolia, *oboo* in Siberian Buryatia). These shrines often consist of a stone cairn with poles or branches sticking out of the middle tied with streamers and prayer flags. Ovaas are considered sacred sites that serve as meeting places for the local land spirits.

Healing kamlanies often involve purification, the removal of harmful spiritual pollutions, or, in some cases, the removal of curses and spirit attachments. If not removed, these pollutions and spirit curses can cause misfortune, physical illness, and even death. In one of the most intense forms of healing, shamans must beg and convince the spirits to release a person from impending death in exchange for a ransom or sacrifice, most commonly an animal like a sheep, ram, cow, deer, or horse. This "soul ransom" form of healing, referred to in Tuvan as a *tailyan,* is found all over North Asia.[4]

In modern times, a more radical form of healing known as "counter-cursing" has become popular. In these ceremonies, shamans perform curses to heal historical trauma. According to research by social anthropologist Konstantinos Zorbas:

> This ritual strand originates in [Tuvan] ancestor's rebellion against the colonial power. [These] retaliatory practices stem from a historical trauma—the disruption of ancestors' partnership with the spirits, as was the case elsewhere in Siberia [during Soviet rule].[5]

Zorbas notes one narrative in which a local Tuvan communist official visited the house of one of his informants' relatives, a shaman, after losing a government stamp bearing the official's signature. Through a kamlanie, the shaman was able to dispatch her soul over the land to search for the stamp. At dawn, the shaman's soul returned to her body and disclosed the whereabouts of the stamp, which the official found the next day. Because this story spread as an example of a victory of traditional customs over a Soviet official, the shaman's house was burned down in the middle of the night not long after. Stories like this became quite common and have shaped both post-modern Tuvan culture, as well as the re-emergence of Tuvan shamanism in the late 20th century.[6]

In modern-day Tuva, shaman clinics have been set up all over the republic, particularly in the capital of Kyzyl. In a distant Russian republic where ingrained cultural anger against former Soviet repression is rife—along with inadequate healthcare, overwhelmed police systems, and rampant alcoholism—people have flocked to these clinics for counter-curse ceremonies, revenge work (for instance, curses via spirit attachments and "black tongue," which can include curses, resentment, and harmful gossip), or even psychopomp work to aid the passing of recently departed relatives. This has prompted a rising interest in Tuvan indigenous culture, as shamans are, in many ways, representatives of ancient traditions.

Although Tuvans today speak Russian for the most part and adopt a modern Russian identity, many young Tuvans are becoming increasingly proud of their ancient heritage. Unfortunately, while this has allowed traditional Tuvan shamanism to re-emerge, it has also encouraged the rise of nontraditional, non-lineage forms of New Age shamanism that loosely resemble Western or core shamanic practices. While this sometimes reflects innocent enthusiasm, performing New Age spirituality for clients in the presence of traditional spirits can be very dangerous, potentially causing greater damage for clients who earnestly seek healing. Unfortunately, those who are unfamiliar with traditional shamanism may not be able to differentiate between traditional lineage shamans and New Age "shamans," as they may all wear traditional armor or clothes that resemble traditional armor. Nonetheless, these factors have ultimately contributed to the rapid re-emergence of Tuvan shamanism.

Dukha Shamanism

The Dukha of northern Mongolia deserve their own section here, even though they are actually a subgroup of the greater Tuvan people. They are sometimes known as *Dukhan* or *Duhular* and are often referred to as *Tsaatan* (Reindeer People) by Mongolians, although the Dukha consider this name offensive. The Duhka are, in fact, a branch of the Tozhu Tuvans who now live in Mongolia. The Tozhu Tuvan are themselves a subgroup of Tuvans from the Todzhinsky District of northern Tuva primarily known for herding reindeer.

After both Mongolia and the Republic of Tannu-Tyva declared independence in 1921, the borders between the two regions were open and reindeer herders crossed them freely. After Tuva was annexed by the Soviet Union in 1944, the borders closed. During Soviet rule, a number of Tozhu Tuvans fled into Mongolia, pressured by both food shortages and the requisition of herd animals to further Soviet policies of collectivization. As many Tuvan herders had established good trade relations with Mongolian herders, they were able to settle across the border. While the Mongolian government initially deported many of them back to Tuva, they finally granted these refugees citizenship in 1956. Most of these refugees, now known as the Dukha, settled in the taiga regions of Khovsgol Province, near Tsagaan Nur Lake, which has a climate suitable for reindeer herding.

The Dukha way of life revolves around reindeer herding, primarily for their milk, cheese, and yogurt, but also for their pelts and antlers, which are used to make clothing, medicine, tools, and art to sell to visitors. They also use reindeer for hunting and collecting firewood, and (along with horses) for transportation to visit, shop, trade, and collect provisions outside the Taiga. The Dukha are generally bilingual, able to speak both Tozhu Tuvan as well as standard Mongolian. They do not live in typical Mongolian *ger* yurts, but rather in *urts*, which are yurts that resemble Native American teepees.

Today, as their traditional lifestyle keeps them from modern economic development, the Dukha have become increasingly reliant on tourism from both Mongolian and foreign visitors who seek to experience reindeer-herder customs. For similar reasons, some younger Dukha are leaving the taiga to pursue a more ambitious lifestyle, leaving their traditional way of life. As I write, there are fewer than forty families that still maintain the traditional reindeer-herding lifestyle.

The reason the Dukha are important to us here is because of their shamanism. Dukha shamans and magic are among the most powerful in the region, and possibly in the world. In fact, both the Dukha and Darkhad Mongols are considered to have the most powerful shamans in Mongolia. These tribes are so magically potent that even non-shamans who do not engage primarily in spiritual vocations are known to have powerful magic.

Although they are powerful healers, the Dukha also have a reputation for specializing in curse work and hypnosis. There are numerous stories from the past fifty years alone that tell of people visiting the taiga and refusing to leave or return home, desperately choosing rather to stay in the taiga without electricity, plumbing, or cellular connectivity. Some say that the ancestral and shamanic spirits of the Dukha are so strong that the Dukha can easily compel others simply by using their eyes. There are many stories that tell of young Dukha women who may see someone as a desired suitor and use their eyes to compel that person to stay and marry them. In one story, a young Dukha shamaness forced two young strangers to marry her and stay with her for many years. It was only upon her death that these men awoke from their enchantment and fled the taiga.

Despite the decline of their reindeer-based lifestyle, the Dukha have gained greater international awareness in recent years. In 2009, a documentary film named *The Horse Boy*, directed by Michel O. Scott, followed an American family visiting Mongolian and Dukha shamans to help treat their son's autism. In 2016, photographer Hamid Sardar visited the Dukha and published his work showing them in their natural landscape. These efforts have helped spread awareness of the Dukha and their culture around the world, and have brought much-needed tourist revenue to these economically challenged people.

But this publicity (particularly *The Horse Boy* documentary) has also brought negative consequences as well. The increase in tourism has convinced some families to bring their reindeer outside of the taiga to resorts near Khovsgol Lake even in the summer, which is not an appropriate climate for reindeer. Moreover, some entitled Westerners have visited Dukha shamans and demanded that they be allowed to study with them or be initiated, often becoming angry or offering large sums of money when the shamans refuse. This has led to some bitterness and resentment among the Dukha and their shamans, some of whom now charge extremely high fees or even refuse to meet with tourists at all. It was not strange that we were unable to meet with any Dukha shamans.

Yakut Shamanism

The Yakut are a seminomadic people who make up almost half of the total population of the Sakha Republic (Yakutia). They are the northernmost group of Turkics, living for the most part in the Siberian taiga of northeast Russia, although some are scattered throughout neighboring Amur, Magadan, and Sakhalin oblast regions, as well as Taymyr and Evenkia autonomous districts. In the northern parts of the region, they are primarily hunters, fishermen, and reindeer herders, while in the south they are primarily cattle and horse ranchers. The Yakut refer to themselves as *Sakha* or *Urangai Sakha*, although they are officially known as Yakuts by the Russian government. The Russian word *yakut* is actually from the Evenk word *yako* or *yoko*, which means "stranger."

Before the Yakuts arrived in northeastern Siberia, they lived in the region around Olkhon and Lake Baikal. They are possibly descended from the Kurykan Turkics who migrated eastward to the Baikal region from the Yenisey River area during the 7th century, although this has not been confirmed. In the 13th century, they moved north along the Lena and Aldan Rivers under increasing pressure from the burgeoning Mongol Empire. As their Buryat Mongol neighbors in the Baikal region consolidated under the forces of Chinggis Khan, they began to flee north to escape the expanding influence of the rising empire.

In the 1620s, the Tsardom of Muscovy and Russian Cossacks expanded their influence into the Sakha region, eventually annexing the territory. Despite rebellions, both Russian oppression and Russian-brought diseases (notably smallpox) ravaged the native Yakut population. By the 1800s, although Russian government pressure began to ease, the discovery of gold along with the expansion of the Trans-Siberian Railway brought large numbers of ethnic Russians to settle in the region. As a result of Russian missionary activity, the Yakuts began to convert to Orthodox Christianity and to move away from shamanism. By the 1820s, all Yakuts claimed to have converted to Christianity, although they still retained shamanic practices and beliefs.

Despite Russification, the Yakut population and culture thrived throughout most of the 1800s and early 1900s, until the region found itself embroiled in the Russian Civil War and was fully annexed by the Soviet Union. The Soviet Union heavily persecuted the ethnic Yakuts, particularly during Stalin's reign. During this time, religion in general and shamanism were strongly repressed. Although the dissolution of the Soviet Union allowed the Yakuts to practice their culture and shamanism more openly, Yakut shamanism did not experience a rapid or strong revival. In the 1980s, shamans in the Sakha Republic were rare, and were more likely to be Evenk rather than Yakut shamans.[7]

The spiritual and religious beliefs of the Yakut are very similar to those of Turkic Tengerism and were quite possibly derived from the same roots (see chapter 2). There are many differences, however, due to both Mongol and Tungus influences. In fact, it is debatable whether the belief system can even still be considered Tengerist. Many across Yakutia and beyond argue that the Yakut faith, frequently known as the *Aiyy* faith among Yakut revivalist movements, is simply a branch of Tengerism that uses a different name. Like Tengerists, the Yakut believe in a chief sky deity known as *Urung Aiyy Toyon* or *Toyon Aga*, the White Lord Creator, who is master of all other spirits. He is sometimes known as *Aiyy-Tangra*, which demonstrates a clearer connection to Tenger (see chapter 3).

Aiyy Toyon rules the sky, which is believed to have nine levels. He sends souls to newborn children (via other spirits) and assures fertility in both plants and cattle. He does not, however, generally interfere in human affairs as other spirits do. Sometimes he is described as husband to the Earth Mother, but this is not very significant for the Yakuts. Below Aiyy Toyon are the *aiyy*, or white spirits of the heavens, the Upper World, and the direction of east. The Yakut sometimes refer to themselves as *Aiyy Jhono* (People of Aiyy).

The black spirits of the Lower World in the western direction are known to the Yakuts as *abaasy*. These spirits are not innately evil, although they are sometimes known to be dark and to bear diseases. Nonetheless, they can also bless black shamans, empower fires, and give humans a soul component. Note that the way the Yakut equate the east/west directions to white and black spirits is opposite to the way the Mongols interpret them.

For Yakuts, the Middle World is home to the *jhono* (humans), as well as to the *ichchi* spirits, a term best translated as "host spirit" that refers to all spirits of the physical world and all spirits who are associated with objects in the physical world. This includes land and nature spirits—like those of rivers, lakes, mountains, and rocks—but also, in true animist fashion, to those connected to natural forces, houses, hearths, and man-made objects.[8]

The Yakut word for a male shaman is *oyun*, while the word for a female shaman is *udagan*, which is quite similar to the words that refer to female shamans in other North Asian cultures. According to a Yakut proverb, the first blacksmith, the first shaman, and the first potter were brothers. Since the blacksmith was the eldest brother and the shaman the middle brother, blacksmiths were considered to have sacred power over shamans, and much of their regalia and armor, as well as many of their tools, were forged by sacred or spiritual smiths to ensure that they resisted rust and contained an ichchi spirit.[9] It is said that only a blacksmith descended from nine generations of blacksmiths can make some of the most important Yakut shamanic tools, like iron ornaments, copper breastplates (*amyagat*), and mirrors.[10] However, as there are now extremely few hereditary blacksmiths among the Yakut, it is practically impossible for new shaman coats to be made in the traditional way.[11]

Because of the importance of blacksmiths to Yakut shamanism, the patron spirit of blacksmiths, Kudaai Bakhsi (sometimes rendered as *K'daai Maqsin*) is one of the most important deities for both blacksmiths and shamans (see chapter 3). Similarly, fire spirits are also considered to be extremely important for both. Fire spirits (known as *aiyy uota* or *uota ichchi*, derived from the Altay/Old Turkic word *od iyesi*, meaning "fire spirit") serve many functions, including cleansing, protecting households and bloodlines, and attracting health, fortune, and happiness. They can also enhance the magical abilities of shamans and blacksmiths. As we have seen, there is an element of fire worship in that fire spirits are considered just as important as other shamanic spirits in all forms of North Asian shamanism.

Like Tuvan and other North Asian shamans, Yakut shamans are generally divided into categories of "black" and "white" (see chapter 4). White shamans work only with the *aiyy* spirits and perform ceremonies of spirit possession and spirit flight. They also perform healing ceremonies through *alghys,* a term that can refer to more complicated ceremonies, but typically indicates prayers. Alghys can also refer to sorcerous spells performed by both shamans and non-shamans, as well as to folk magic. In fact, most families know at least some kind of alghys prayers or narrations to bring about blessings and luck.[12]

Yakut black shamans tend to work with the *abaasy* spirits and can perform beneficial as well as vengeful or harmful work. Black shamans also have a particularly close relationship with *Kudaai Bakhsi,* who is known as one of the preeminent powers of the Lower World (see chapter 3).[13] While both white and black Yakut shamans work with drums, black shamans are known for wearing heavy, complex gowns with an apron on top, both of which are covered with metallic implements. This protective armor is particularly necessary when dealing with the more wrathful abaasy spirits. White shamans usually only need to wear an armored apron without an armored gown underneath.

Yakut shamans have become so rare that traditional shamans in the Sakha Republic tend to be Evenki rather than Yakut. Although the Sakha Republic is one of the more remote regions of Russian Siberia, the area has been experiencing both modernization and a general decline of traditional lifestyle as more of the population seeks to develop their economy or even move elsewhere for more ambitious careers. Although Yakut shamanism continues to decline, the Yakuts largely still maintain their belief in their spirits alongside newer Christian beliefs, often equating them with figures and saints in Orthodox Christianity. It is no surprise, then, that the mighty Aiyy Toyon is often equated with Jesus Christ.

There are some encouraging signs, however, that the youth of the Sakha Republic are beginning to take pride in their indigenous culture and to promote it as musicians and performers, like Yuliyana and Olena Uutai, who have brought Yakut cultural performances to the West.

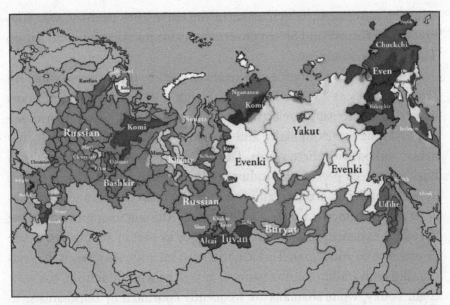

Figure 6. Geographic distribution of the many ethnic indigenous tribes of Russian Siberia. Note the Yakut, Evenki, Buryat, Tuvan, and Udihe (Amur) peoples who are explored in this book.

Turkic Shamanism Today

Turkic shamanism and Tengerism survive almost exclusively among the Siberian branches of the Turkic peoples. There is evidence of Tengerist revival among other Turkic groups, however. Just as many Caucasians, African Americans, and Latinx folks have been exploring their ancient ancestral faiths and practices, the youths of many Turkic populations have been exploring the pre-Islamic beliefs of their ancestors. Several of my friends and acquaintances of Anatolian Turkish descent have begun researching the Tengerist beliefs of their Siberian cousins and have become acutely aware that Tengerism was the original belief system of their own ancestors, despite centuries of Islamization and influences from Persian, Arab, and Greek cultures.

The Burkhanism (*Ak Jang*) movement is a new religious movement inspired by ancient Tengerism that arose in the Altai Republic. Although the Altai people have also converted to Islam, they retain some cultural practices (including a nomadic lifestyle) that have Tengerist roots. This religious movement, which arose in the early 20th century, was suppressed by Czarist and Soviet governments for fear that it would stir up Turkic-Siberian unrest.

The word *burkhan* generally refers to gods or great spirits, while *Ak Jang* translates as "White Faith." Although Burkhanism has deep roots in Turkic Tengerism, it rejects worship of traditional Lower World deities and was even originally anti-shamanic because many Turkic shamans worked with these spirits. Despite this, however, many aspects of Burkhanist folk practice are culturally shamanic in origin—for instance, juniper smudging, erecting and worshipping *ovaa* cairns, and tying ribbons and streamers to trees and headgear. Although suppressed by the Soviets, it experienced a revival in the 1990s as part of attempts to create or preserve an Altaic/pan-Turkic nationalist identity. As a result, its relationship with traditional shamanism, as well as with Buddhism, has softened. Today, white shamans are frequently consulted by Burkhanists.

There is also evidence of both Tengerist and shamanic survivals and revivals across Turkey, Kazakhstan, Turkic Siberia, and even parts of Turkic Central Asia. In Kazakhstan, remnant shamanism is still practiced by individuals who go into trance with the *kobyz kazakh* fiddle rather than with a drum, and traditional healers in Kyrgyzstan still perform pre-Islamic folk magic practices that can be traced back to Tengerist beliefs. In fact, in both these places, they still use ancestral trance possession and employ the shamanic practice of stone divination (see chapter 1). In the Republic of Khakassia, shamanism has re-emerged as individuals from pre-Soviet shamanic families (notably Tatyana Kobezhikova, who is leading the Khakass shamanic revival) received the calling and traveled to initiate and study with shamans in Tuva and Mongolia.[14]

Overall, Tengerism and shamanism are still very much at risk among those who, while credited as the forbearers of these traditions, have largely turned away from them in favor of Manichaeism, Zoroastrianism, Islam, and, to some extent, Buddhism and Christianity. However, Tengerism and shamanism continue to flourish and thrive across North Asia, as these ancient practices were carried by the Mongols, who rose to global prominence after the decline of the Golden Age of the Turkic khaganates.

CHAPTER 6

Mongolic Shamanism

Mongols are perhaps the best-known of all North Asian peoples, due in no small part to the Great Mongol Empire created by Chinggis Khan, which remains the largest contiguous land empire in history. Most people think of the Mongols as those who inhabit the country of Mongolia. But the modern nation of Mongolia encompasses only about half of all indigenous Mongol land. Much of the other half falls within the borders of the People's Republic of China (PRC) as the large province of Inner Mongolia (known by activists who seek independence from China and reunification with Mongolia as South Mongolia). Smaller portions fall in Russian Siberia as the Republic of Buryatia, located directly above Mongolia beside Lake Baikal, as well as the Republic of Kalmykia near the Caspian Sea.

For the most part, ethnic Mongols still retain strong beliefs and practices that are both shamanic and Buddhist. Although heavily persecuted by both the Qing Dynasty and the Communist regime, shamanism has experienced tremendous growth in the 1990s and into the 21st century, so much so that Mongolia now shines as a beacon of indigenous shamanic practice in North Asia.

Early Mongolic History

With the exception of the earlier Donghu confederation, the Mongolic Xianbei established the first confirmed non-Turkic empire in North Asia, one which later fell to the Turkic Gokturks and subsequently to the Uyghur Empire. After the fall of the Uyghurs, the Mongolic Khitan people rose to power across the grasslands.

The Khitans are widely believed to be a subgroup descended from the Kumo Xi tribe of the Xianbei. Although Mongolic, they may have originated in Manchuria. Prior to their rise, the Khitans were largely vassals of the Chinese Tang Dynasty. As the Tang Dynasty began to crumble and was replaced by the Song Dynasty in the Chinese heartland, the Khitan warlord Abaoji wrested control of the other Khitan clans and established their superiority over other Mongolic tribes, as well as over some Turkic peoples (notably the Shatuo).

The Liao Empire

In 916 CE, Abaoji declared himself the khagan of the Liao Empire, a new northern nomadic empire that competed with the Chinese for dominance in Asia. At its greatest extent, the Liao Empire occupied all of Mongolia, Manchuria, as well as parts of northern China, the Russian Far East, and Siberia, and North Korea. Because it was very much a multiethnic empire that promoted all races to high-ranking offices, it was open to heavy external cultural influences, notably in the southern region where Chinese traditions held sway. In fact, the Khitans had such a large influence in Central Asia and medieval Europe that the word *khitai* came to mean "China" and is still so used in many Turkic and Slavic languages today. The word "Cathay," still used most notably by the Hong Kong airline Cathay Pacific, is derived from *khitai*.

The Liao Empire was officially Buddhist, but the Khitans themselves relied heavily on shamans and worshipped the Tengerist sky god, even employing shamans in an official capacity within the Imperial court. The descendants of Abaoji, known as the Yelü clan, ruled the Liao Empire for just over 200 years. In 1125 CE, the Tungus

Jurchens rebelled against the Khitans and destroyed their empire (see chapter 7). The majority of Khitans fled westward and established the kingdom of Qara Khitai, which was soon conquered and absorbed by the Great Mongol Empire. A smaller group, which fled north and settled near Lake Baikal, eventually moved farther east, closer to their original homeland in Manchuria, and are known today as the Daur, or Daguur. Because they were never formally incorporated into the Mongol Empire, the Daur are one of the few Mongolic groups that do not revere Chinggis Khan. Today, they still practice a form of shamanism that is similar in many ways to that of the Buryats from the Baikal region as well as to the traditions of the Tungus in northern Manchuria (see chapter 7).

The Tungus Jurchen Jin Dynasty emerged in 1115, overthrew the Khitan Liao in 1125, and occupied Manchuria, northern China, and parts of Russian Siberia until 1234. Although they pushed the Khitans out of the Mongol heartland, the Jurchen Jin largely abandoned the Mongol regions and focused their efforts southward to expand into China, allowing the Mongols to establish what can be considered as the first incarnation of a pan-Mongol nation (rather than one dominated by one tribe). This loose confederation of Mongolic tribes, known as the Khamag Mongol, spread across the Mongolian plateau and grasslands and is considered by some to be a predecessor of the Great Mongol Empire.

When unrest emerged among several Mongol tribes in the northern regions of the Liao Empire, the Khamag Mongol confederation quickly stepped in to fill the power vacuum, and its first leader, Khabul Khan, successfully repelled the Jurchen Jin invasion, discouraging further incursions into Mongol territory. After the death of the fourth Khamag Mongol leader, Yesugei (who was never formally enthroned as khan), Mongolia erupted into political anarchy as the confederation began to disintegrate. Yesugei's son, Temujin, became the Khan of the Khamag Mongols in 1189 and waged war against other Mongol tribes and confederations. In 1206, he was given the title Chinggis Khan (Great Khan), who, in the same year, declared the formation of the Great Mongol Empire.

The Great Mongol Empire

Chinggis Khan's empire stretched eastward to Manchuria and Korea (destroying the Jurchen Jin Empire in 1234), westward to Hungary, Poland, the Middle East, and Anatolia, northward into Siberia, and southward through all of China and to the borders of southeastern Asia. The Khan was a devoted follower of Tengerism and shamanism; some stories even say he was a shaman himself. Even before he became Khan, he traveled to the sacred mountain Burkhan Khaldun to pray to Tenger.

After he established his empire, Chinggis Khan always kept two shamans by his side to perform ceremonies for his own personal well-being, as well as for the success of his military campaigns. Some traditions say that one was a black shaman known as Teb-Tengri (Kokochu) and the other a white shaman known as Usun, although this is likely a modern reinterpretation, as 13th-century Mongols did not use colors to distinguish between shamans as they do today. The darker shaman was especially powerful, although he was ultimately executed for attempting to consolidate political power and instigate rivalry between the Khan's brothers.

In Mongolic traditions, black shamans performed intense and highly ritualized ceremonies before battles to petition the aid of ancestral war spirits, often using the bones or remains of great warriors. They also often employed weather magic, calling down thunder and lightning to strike against enemy armies and cities. The work of these shamans is said to have determined the outcome of many battles— some in which barely 100,000 Mongol soldiers are reported to have defeated enemy forces of over a million. Mongolian shamans today advise against using human remains and even objects belonging to those who have passed away, as these objects can carry very dangerous death energy. Only the most powerful shamans with proper empowerments and trainings have the strength and ability to work with these objects, and, even then, they do it with utmost caution.

Many associate the Great Mongol Empire with cruelty and bloody acts, largely thanks to ancient Chinese and Russian propaganda describing them as such. And this is partially true. Mongol armies showed no mercy to any city or kingdom that actively resisted them, sometimes razing entire cities, executing all adult males, and carrying off women and children to be adopted or sold as slaves to Mongols and allied kingdoms that surrendered. But they were also known to embrace the kingdoms, cities, and cultures of those who submitted themselves to Mongol rule.

In fact, the Mongol Empire was unprecedented in its cultural and religious tolerance. In addition to Tengerism and shamanism, it actively sponsored Buddhist, Christian, Muslim, and Jewish institutions. Many of its high-ranking officials were Muslim or Buddhist, and Kublai Khan's own mother was Christian. Chinggis Khan himself even organized gatherings in which leaders from different religions were invited to debate on spiritual topics. To facilitate communication across their vast empire, the Mongols also created the first continental postal system and expanded trade routes to promote wealth and a flourishing economy.

Unfortunately, this great empire was plagued by political infighting among Chinggis Khan's descendants, notably his grandchildren in the House of Tolui and the House of Ogedei (two of the Khan's sons, along with Jochi and Chagatai). One of the key issues within the empire was whether it would become an established cosmopolitan culture or remain true to the Mongolian nomadic steppe-based lifestyle. Continued power struggles ultimately led to the empire fracturing during the reign of Kublai Khan, who, although called the fifth khan of the Great Mongol Empire, realistically controlled only the Yuan Dynasty, which occupied Mongolia, China, Manchuria, Tibet, Korea, and parts of Russian Siberia. Other fragments of the great empire, including the Chagatai Khanate in Central Asia and the Ilkhanate in Persia and the Caucasus, eventually became Islamized and Turkic in identity, as did the Golden Horde in Russia, Ukraine, and Kazakhstan, which would further fracture into smaller Turkic kingdoms.

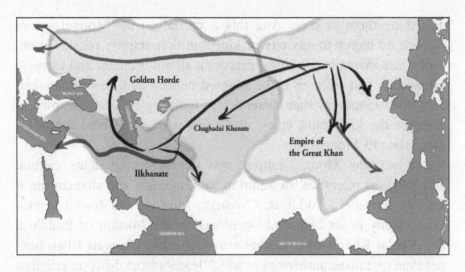

Figure 7. The four successor kingdoms of the Great Mongol Empire after it had fractured during the reign of Kublai Khan.

The Yuan Dynasty

Kublai Khan declared the advent of the Yuan Dynasty in 1271 as a "Mandate of Heaven," a Chinese tradition that acknowledges the passing of legitimate power through the surrender of Imperial seals and titles or the obliteration of the previous dynastic family. The Mongols of the other three remnant kingdoms, having not yet been Islamized, saw the Yuan Dynasty as "too Chinese." Eventually, after periods of famine, anarchy and unrest, and large-scale uprisings, the Mongols were pushed back north into the Mongolian heartland and the Chinese reclaimed their territory, establishing the Ming Dynasty in 1368.

In the same year, the Mongols established the Northern Yuan Dynasty under the rule of the descendants of Chinggis Khan, who were unable to control the various Mongol tribes effectively. In 1479, after almost ninety years of unrest, the warrior queen Mandukhai Khatun reunited many of the Mongol tribes with the help of her husband, Dayan Khan, into the Khalkha clan. Although the Khalkha identity still exists, the political union under Dayan would not last, however, as the tribes soon fell apart again after Dayan's death.

In the following century, the empire briefly reunited as several smaller khans banded together, and this period proved to be a pivotal point in Mongolian spiritual history. Although the Mongol and Yuan Empires had adopted Buddhism, with many emperors and kings becoming Buddhist themselves, most Mongols remained steadfast in their shamanic belief in Tengerism. But in 1575, Jasaghtu Khan declared Buddhism to be the state religion of Mongolia. Two years later, Altan Khan declared Sonam Gyatso, the leader of the Gelugpa (Yellow Hat) school of Tibetan Buddhism, to be the third Dalai Lama, after which Mongolia experienced its first large-scale conversion to Tibetan Buddhist beliefs as numerous Tibetan lamas entered Mongolia to proselytize. They were so successful that Buddhists gained political power that rivaled that of those who still retained their belief in shamanism.

By the 1600s, the Northern Yuan Dynasty was no longer a functioning unified entity. Around this time, the Jurchens arose again as a major power in North Asia under the leadership of Nurhaci, whose ambitions to conquer the Chinese Ming Dynasty led him to seek allies among the Mongols (see chapter 7). Between 1612 and 1624, the Khorchin Mongols made formal alliances with the Jurchen, followed by alliances with the Jarut and the southern Khalkha Mongols. In 1625, Ligdan Khan, who was then technically the great khan of the Northern Yuan Dynasty (although he had control only over the Chahar and Khorchin tribes prior to their defection), waged war on the Jurchens and their Mongol allies and was defeated in 1634. In the following year, his son, Ejei Khan, surrendered the Imperial Seal (*tamgha*) of the Mongols to the now-Manchu (formerly Jurchen) emperor Hong Taiji, formally ending the Northern Yuan Dynasty. Hong Taiji immediately declared the creation of the Great Qing Dynasty as the successor to the Yuan Dynasty, and all Mongols technically became subjects of the Qing.

The Great Qing Dynasty

Under the Qing regime, the Mongol territories under direct Manchu rule were governed as their own region. This marked the beginning of the separation of "Inner" and "Outer" Mongolia, although most people today (both Mongol and Chinese) believe this distinction began in the 20th century under Communist rule. In fact, however, Inner Mongolia was the Mongol area that was under Manchu rule prior to the establishment of the Qing Dynasty, and Outer Mongolia was the remaining Mongol territory that would later submit to Manchu rule. These two areas were ruled as separate regional entities with separate governors, thereby creating a sociopolitical division that still lasts today.

The conquest of Mongolia was completed when the Qing Dynasty, along with its Khalkha-Mongol and Uyghur allies, launched the Qing-Dzungar war in 1688 against the Oirat Dzungar Khanate. This conflict ended in 1757 with the Dzungar genocide, in which the Manchu Qianlong emperor ordered the mass extermination of the Dzungar people because of the rebellion of their leader, Amursana. This genocidal action by the Manchus is perhaps the greatest crime ever committed against the Mongol people, extinguishing the last great nomadic empire in Asia. Historians estimate that about 80 percent of the Dzungar population (between 500,000 and 800,000 people) were killed by either warfare or disease, and Dzungar women and children were given as slaves to Manchus and Khalkha Mongols. A large band of refugees escaped to their Oirat cousins on the northwest banks of the Caspian Sea.

As an ethnic Manchu, I acknowledge this tragedy and crime perpetrated by my Manchu and Inner Mongol ancestors and apologize to any descendants of Dzungar survivors who may be reading this. I offer my apology on behalf of my ancestors and want to help heal the scars that can still be felt in Mongolia today. Although Outer Mongolia submitted to the rule of the Manchus, the people there faced persecution and economic stagnation under them, especially compared to those in Inner Mongolia, who received much more favorable treatment by comparison.

Although the Manchus were originally shamanists themselves, they had officially converted to Tibetan Buddhism. In fact, they maintained control over Mongols by aggressively spreading Buddhism and driving people away from shamanism in the hopes that the peaceful philosophies of Buddhism would prevent any potential uprisings or resistance. As a result, Mongolia went through a second round of often-violent mass conversions. The Khalkha Mongols were so aggressively converted that many of their original shamanic traditions were severely damaged or extinguished. Buryat shamanism in the northeast (and Siberia) survived, but was heavily influenced by Buddhism. Even the Khorchin shamanism practiced in eastern Inner Mongolia was influenced by Buddhism, despite the favors they received for their early loyalty to the Manchus.

Only the Darkhad, Huular, and Tuvan shamanic traditions in the north and northwest (modern Darkhad Valley, Khovsgol Province) avoided heavy Buddhist influences and remained as a center of resistance against both aggressive Buddhist encroachment and Manchu rule. Among the Khalkha and Oirat tribes, many shamans were forced to convert to Buddhism and become Buddhist monks lest they face ostracism and even execution. By the end of the Qing Dynasty, it is estimated that about half of all adult Mongol men were Buddhist monks or lamas.

The Manchu Qing Dynasty officially ended in 1911. In the same year, the eighth Jetsundamba Khutuktu, the leader of Tibetan Buddhism in Mongolia, was declared the Bogd Khan of Mongolia. He declared Mongolia's independence, claiming that both Mongolia and China had been ruled by the Manchus during the Qing era, and that the fall of the Qing released Mongols from further submission. Although Inner Mongolian nobles largely supported Mongolian independence initially, they were unable to agree with their Outer Mongolian counterparts on questions of political structure. Outer Mongols wanted to create an independent theocratic nation with the Bogd Khan as both political and spiritual leader. Inner Mongols, on the other hand, wanted to create a restored (Qing-like) empire of Mongolia and Manchuria, and considered the Bogd Khan's theocratic rule to be an obstacle to modernization. As a result, Inner Mongolia became part of the newly established Republic of China (which claimed all former Qing territories, including Tibet and Xinjiang/East Turkestan, and attempted to claim Outer Mongolia), while Outer Mongolia declared independence and became the Bogd Khanate of Mongolia.

In 1921, the communist Mongolian People's Party took control of the Bogd Khanate, although allowing him to remain as figurehead. On his death in 1924, Outer Mongolia was transformed into the Mongolian People's Republic as a communist state. Inner Mongolia fought with the Republic of China against Japan during World War II. In 1949, however, the Republic of China was overthrown by the Chinese Communist Party and Inner Mongolia was incorporated into the communist People's Republic of China. Communist China sought to incorporate Outer Mongolia as well, but the Soviet Union wanted to maintain it as a satellite state that could serve as a buffer against China. Inner Mongolia thus remained a territory of China, while Outer Mongolia became the communist Mongolian People's Republic.

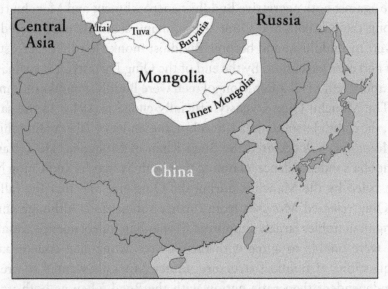

Figure 8. Territories of "Greater Mongolia," including the country of Mongolia, as well as Inner Mongolia in China and the Republic of Buryatia in Russian Siberia. Tuva and Altai are Turkic regions in Russian Siberia that share cultural influences with Mongolia.

Mongolians from Communism to Today

Communist rule in both Mongol regions had severe impacts on Mongolian spirituality. In both areas, the communists dictated that all forms of spirituality were harmful and feudalist in nature and must be rooted out. Both shamanism and Buddhism were strongly suppressed, with massive rounds of arrests and even executions for shamans as well as lamas/monks. Many shamans and monks went underground and either practiced their spirituality in secret or, in some cases, gave it up entirely. Metropolitan areas experienced the heaviest purges, and many temples were demolished or transformed into museums.

In Inner Mongolia, shamans all but disappeared—some giving up their practices completely, others practicing secretly at night. The Chinese Cultural Revolution (1966–1976) saw a violent crackdown in which many shamans and other religious figures were arrested and never seen again. In the northern areas of the Mongolian nation (Outer Mongolia), the Darkhads had to be discreet as well, but, given the remoteness of the Darkhad Valley, many shamans were able to practice more discreetly, using tools like the jaw harp, which is much smaller and easier to hide than a drum. The Buryats in Mongolia almost lost their traditional practices, but the Buryats in Russian Siberia were able to preserve their practices because they were far from major Russian metropolitan areas.

In 1990, Mongolia experienced a peaceful democratic revolution, in which the communist Mongolian People's Republic was transformed into the democratic nation of Mongolia. Since then, shamanism has experienced an explosive revival. The idealistic explanation for the revival is that hordes of ancestral spirits who had not been honored for generations resurfaced when shamanism became legal again, choosing many young Mongolians to be initiated as shamans for the next generation. The more cynical—and unfortunately perhaps more realistic—explanation is that many perceived shamanism as an easy way to make money and take advantage of others.

The sudden democratization of Mongolia and the collapse of the Soviet Union also saw the collapse of the Mongolian economy. Most Mongolians lost their livelihoods and most collectivized property never found its way back to individual families. As a result, the Mongolian social fabric crumbled as hunger, alcoholism, and violence grew. Since there were not many institutions that were equipped to handle these issues, many families sought the help of shamans, making it easier for fake shamans to exploit those who desperately needed help.

Shamanic researcher Amalia Rubin divides modern Mongolian shamans into four groups: A1, A2, B1, and B2. A1 consists of shamans
who descend from legitimate lineages and are very powerful, many being
the elders of their traditions. A2 consists of shamans who descend from
legitimate lineages, but are perhaps younger, less experienced, and less
powerful. B1 consists of those who mean well and have good intentions,
but do not have the proper lineage or training and are often trained only
in modern New Age styles, making them less effective in true healing
and spirit work. Despite their good intentions, their "healing" work may
even cause more damage to their clients. B2 "shamans" are simply frauds
and scam artists, pretending to be shamans to exploit others.[1] Currently,
Mongolia is full of "shamans" who fit into these last two categories, and
great care must be taken when seeking out a shaman in Mongolia.

In Inner Mongolia, shamanism is currently tolerated and no longer
persecuted, provided individual shamans don't become too famous or
express anti-government opinions. Several of my acquaintances from
Inner Mongolia have told me that famous shamans, lamas, and healers are often arrested on charges of "harmful superstition" and taken
away simply because they became too famous for their healing abilities, even though they didn't express any political opinions. Because of
this small but inherent danger, these B-class shamans are less common
than they are in Mongolia, but they still outnumber the A-class shamans. The Khorchin and Daur shamans of eastern Inner Mongolia are
among the very few groups in Inner Mongolia who still maintain an
original traditional shamanic lineage.

Modern Mongolic Peoples

Although Mongols today are considered to have a unified cultural
and genetic identity, they can still be classified into many different
ethnic subgroups, of which there are at least twenty in the country
of Mongolia alone (excluding Inner Mongolia). The largest of these
subgroups by far is the Khalkha Mongols, who make up roughly 80
percent of the total Mongol population. The Khalkha, which means
"shield," are an amalgamation of many different subgroups that were

united or created by Dayan Khan (Mandukhai's husband) to protect Mongolia. Technically, there is no such thing as "Khalkha shamanism," because the Khalkha consists of many different subgroups who each have their own shamanic traditions. Moreover, because of the Qing Dynasty's violent mass conversions, many shamanic traditions among the Khalkha were severely damaged or even extinguished completely.

That said, it is possible that there are still remnants of original shamanic practice among specific areas of Khalkha that descend from their original subgroup traditions. In major metropolitan areas like Ulaanbaatar, some Khalkha individuals who have shamanic spirits have also trained under Darkhad and Buryat teachers, and there are also many who have initiated under reconstructed Mongolian New Age traditions.

Western Mongolia contains the next largest, and perhaps most diverse, Mongol population, including the Turkic Kazakhs (not ethnically Mongol, but considered to be part of the Mongol nation), as well as Oirats, the Kalmyk subgroup of Oirats, the Turkic Altai Uriankhai, and other smaller groups like the Bayad, Zakhchin, Choros, Myangad, and Khoshut, most of which are also Oirat subgroups. The Oirat Mongols are said to originate from Tuva and Khovsgol Province, having moved southwest during the 14th century. They originally practiced shamanism, but were largely converted to Tibetan Buddhism in the 1600s, even participating in the conflict between the Gelug and the Karma Kagyu schools. The dominance of Buddhism, along with the Dzungar genocide, pushed Oirat shamanism to near extinction. According to Amalia Rubin, there is still evidence of shamanic practices (such as trance possession) among the Kalmyks, likely a holdover from ancient shamanic practices, but they no longer wear any form of shamanic armor.[2]

The northern Mongols still retain the strongest traditional forms of Mongolic shamanism. Chief among these are the Darkhad and Buryat. Generally, the Darkhad have preserved the most original form of Mongolic shamanism with the least Buddhist and other outside influences. The Buryats practice a form of Mongolic shamanism that contains local Baikal-area features, as well as heavy Buddhist and some Tungus influences. Other northern Mongol groups include the Huular, the Barga, the Turkic Dukha, the Tungusic Hamnigan, and the Daur or

Daguur in northeastern Inner Mongolia and northern Manchuria. We will explore some of these shamanic traditions in greater detail below.

The eastern Mongols are based primarily in Inner Mongolia and include the Khorchin, Dorbet, Kharchin, Uzemchin, Gorlos, Jaruud, Jalaid, and Aohan, among others. Among these, only the Khorchin have maintained a distinct traditional shamanic lineage, which includes unique tools, armor, and even possession and dancing methods that are uncommon among other Mongol groups due to historically heavy cross-cultural influences under the Manchus, the Tibetan Buddhists, and, to some extent, the Chinese. It is unknown if the other eastern Mongols still maintain distinct shamanic lineages, or if their traditions are more aligned with Khorchin, Darkhad, or even New Age practices. Unfortunately, Inner Mongolia has been experiencing heavy influence from the Chinese, and the local Mongols are being pressured to assimilate to mainstream Chinese culture and lifestyle for socioeconomic benefits. Nonetheless, there are those who still hold to traditional nomadic lifestyles and spiritual beliefs and honor the Mongolian shamanic worldview.

The southern Mongols, also based primarily in Inner Mongolia, include the southern Khalkha, as well as the Tumed, the Chahar, the Ordos, and the Abaga, among others. While there are shamans who still practice among these groups, it is unclear if they represent a distinct tradition, a subgroup of one of the larger traditions, or a New Age reconstructionist practice that combines Chinese and/or Manchu folk practices.

Due to the rapid industrialization and commercialization of some major metropolitan areas, the southern Mongols are experiencing a far greater level of Chinese influence than their eastern counterparts. Although the entire region has experienced some of the fastest GDP growth in China, modernization coupled with the migration of ethnic Han Chinese into the area has been so radical that many young Mongols are far more fluent in Chinese than they are in Mongolian, and identify far more with Chinese culture. Recently, local governments of Inner Mongolia (the southern areas particularly) have been pushing to reduce the teaching of the Mongol language in schools, and agricultural expansion and collectivist overgrazing have caused many areas that were once grasslands to be turned into deserts. This area is thus perhaps at greatest risk of losing its cultural and spiritual identity.

Mongolic Tengerism

Although Tengerism was originally the faith of the Turkic peoples, it was largely inherited by the Mongols, who dominated much of North Asia after the decline of Turkic influence. As a result, Tengerism shaped not only the shamanism practiced among different Mongol tribes, but also many Asian cultures, belief systems, and even history for centuries. In fact, because the adoption of Tengerism coincided with the creation and rise of a distinct identity for Mongols (who were formerly a collection of proto-Mongolic tribes scattered across the steppes), it is fair to say that Tengerism is as indigenous to the Mongols as it was to the Turkic peoples. Since the Tengerism of the Mongols is similar to Turkic Tengerism, this section will focus on aspects of it that are central and unique to the Mongolic traditions.

The foundations of Mongolic and Turkic Tengerist mythology are very similar. They begin with creation stories that describe how the physical world separated violently from the Upper and Lower spirit worlds (see chapter 2). The spirit worlds were ruled by a heavenly male father figure known as Tenger, sometimes called *Tenger Etseg* or *Munkh Kokh/Huh Tenger* (Eternal Blue Sky). The physical world, ruled by an earthly female figure known as *Etugen*, is home to physical beings as well as to land and nature spirits. Those most commonly encountered by humans are the *lus*, water-oriented spirits who inhabit bodies of water and areas of low earth like swamps and valleys, and the *savdag*, earth lords who inhabit areas of high earth like mountains and hills (see chapter 3).

In the Mongolian language, the word *tenger* means "sky." In fact, Mongolia is sometimes poetically known as *Munkh Khukh Tengeriin Oron*, or "Land of the Eternal Blue Sky." In many resources, the term *tenger* refers to both heaven and to the main sky father deity, as well as to the 99 realms into which the heavens are divided. Many Mongolians also refer to their ancestral spirits as tengers. The word is also used more generally to mean "higher power," which can be a spirit or group of spirits, or simply the spirit realms. Shamanic spirits are known as *ongod tenger*, and many Mongolian shamans refer to their own spirits as their tengers.

As we have seen in previous chapters, shamanism, and by default Tengerism, are very much regional practices, and this is clearly reflected in the traditions of Mongolian shamanism, which are extremely diverse across Mongolic tribes. In Mongolia, this regional variation is perhaps more pronounced than in Turkic traditions, and the regional variations between different shamanic practices can be separated into truly unique and separate traditions. Here, we will look at four of these traditions—the Darkhad, the Buryat, the Daur, and the Khorchin.

Darkhad Shamanism

The Darkhads retain perhaps the "purest" form of Mongolic shamanism, as it has been subject to the fewest external influences since the time of Chinggis Khan. Originally, the Darkhads were not an ethnic subgroup like other Mongols; rather they were families chosen by Chinggis Khan to protect sacred objects and places. The word *darkhad* translates to "untouchables," but its true meaning is "protected ones," meaning that it is taboo to harm them.

The Darkhad are generally divided into three groups.[3] Black Darkhads are based in the Darkhad Valley in northwestern Khovsgol Province, between the red taiga and the Khoridol Saridag mountain range. They were charged with protecting the black war flag of Chinggis Khan, in which his soul was enshrined. This flag was lost or vanished during Mongolia's communist period, so the black Darkhads are now technically unable to fulfill their duty. Some speculate that a family may have hidden the flag away for protection. Legend claims that, if the black flag of Chinggis Khan were ever to reemerge, Mongols would be called to war.

The second group are the yellow Darkhads, based in the Ordos area in Inner Mongolia. They were charged with protecting the personal items of Chinggis Khan, which became sacred relics. Despite their efforts, most of these relics have been lost or stolen. In the mid-1950s, the Chinese government constructed the Mausoleum of Chinggis Khan where the yellow Darkhads continue to conduct worship ceremonies honoring the Khan.

The third, and much smaller, group of Darkhads is based near the sacred mountain of Burkhan Khaldun in Mongolia. Chinggis Khan often worshipped there during his lifetime and is rumored to be buried somewhere nearby.

The black Darkhads were able to preserve their traditional shamanic lineages because of the isolation of the Darkhad Valley. The region is so remote that it takes two days to drive from the capital of Ulaanbaatar to the valley itself. There are no paved roads into the valley and the terrain is too rough for most modern vehicles. When I visited the valley, we had to switch from a sedan, to a Soviet-era van, and then a Land Rover. During the communist era, when Mongolian shamanism had almost completely disappeared elsewhere, the Darkhads were able to adapt, becoming less dependent on drum and full armor and relying more on the small jaw harp to induce trance.

Today, Darkhad shamans still reserve the use of drum and ull armor for heavier shamanic ceremonies performed at night (see Figure 9 on page 113), but largely prefer the jaw harp (which is easier to carry) for daytime ceremonies, which are performed wearing traditional Mongolian *deel* robes. As a result, shamanizing with the jaw harp is known as "walking shamanism," which can be performed anywhere at any time. In fact, some even say that now there are ceremonies that can only be performed with a jaw harp.[4] Unlike the black Darkhads, the yellow Darkhads lost their shamanic lineages for the most part and now perform only worship ceremonies.

Darkhad shamanism felt the fewest effects of external influences, although some Turkic influences were felt, particularly from its Tuvan and Dukha neighbors (see chapter 5). As a result, aside from a few key differences, the shamanic traditions of these two groups are very similar. The Darkhads retain many of the original Tengerist beliefs regarding the three worlds, the tenger spirits, and the *lus savdag* land spirits. They work exclusively with their shamanic spirits, known as *ongod tenger*, who are largely ancestral spirits of past shamans, but who can also include some lus savdag spirits, particularly the black lus, or *nagas* (see chapter 3).

The black lus spirits are especially dangerous because they are quite dark and wrathful and don't understand human lifestyles, limitations, and boundaries. Many of them are particularly known for heavy curses that last for generations. Many Darkhad families who survived shamanic battles and curses retain these black-lus curse spirits as their shamanic spirit allies. Once invoked, these dark spirits are nearly impossible to remove. In fact, often the only way to "remove" one of these curses is to persuade or bribe the spirits to curse on the family's behalf, rather than cursing the family itself. In this way, these shamans become naga shamans (fortified by the lus) and become much more powerful than shamans with only ancestral spirits (see chapter 3).[5]

In fact, many of the ancestral Darkhad spirits are quite dark. Many of them were warriors and act as war spirits capable of cursing and killing beyond the will of their shaman counterparts. These ancestral shaman spirits still reside in spirit houses all over the Darkhad Valley. The bodies of Darkhad shamans are given sky burials, in which they are placed in trees or often on the grass when there were no trees to be eaten by wild animals, as other Mongols likely did in ancient times. But shamans' sacred tools are interred in a second funeral grave within spirit houses at specially chosen locations that were significant to them during their lifetime. Living shamans with that ancestor then go to these places to conduct ceremonies.

Shamans' souls are enshrined in these spirit houses as well, and become guardian spirits of the mountain or forest where they are located. Because of the prevalence of ancient shamanic lineages in the Darkhad Valley, these spirit houses can be found everywhere, which in effect creates many "haunted" forest and mountain locations. Because many lineages battled each other at some point in time, it is considered extremely unwise for shamans and their relatives to spend significant amounts of time in unknown areas that are likely to contain spirit houses from other lineages, as the spirits housed there may be harmful to them. As a Manchu, I was once advised by my shaman friend not to visit a particular Darkhad spirit house because that spirit was reputed to have been a great warrior who fought against Manchu. Similarly, while we were driving in the valley, another visitor asked if we could do offerings in the forest we were passing through, as he felt called by spirits there. My friend immediately refused and told the driver to drive faster. She explained that we don't know what spirits or ghosts were in these forests, which were known to be extremely haunted. Those spirits might have been luring us; who knows what the spirits there wanted to do.

Black Darkhad shamans of northern Mongolia are generally regarded to be the strongest Mongolic shamans. In fact, many non-Darkhad shamans, especially those who follow New Age traditions, generally fear them and avoid angering them. There are many stories that tell of people being injured or even dying prematurely after angering a Darkhad shaman. This may even happen unintentionally. Because Darkhad spirits are often dark and vengeful, they may be able to act on their own to "eat" a person without their shaman counterparts intending to do so.

Figure 9. Darkhad shaman Surenjav in armor, entering a trance state while playing her drum in 2017. Photo courtesy of David Shi.

In Mongolia, the word "eat" is often used to indicate causing someone's death or absorbing others' cultural identity. For example, Mongols often say that the Manchus were "eaten" by the Chinese. There are also tales of Darkhad shamans who had the ability to fly, and powerful shamans are sometimes known to levitate during ceremonies. Their shamanic tools have also been known to start flying above them and drums have been reported to play by themselves.[6]

Despite (or perhaps because of) the strong reputation of these Darkhad shamans, this northern tradition is considered to be the true bearer of the legacy of Mongolic shamanism in its purest form.[7] To learn more about the Darkhad tradition of Mongolian shamanism, see Purev's *Mongolian Shamanism* or the teachings of the Mother Tree Shamanism group.

Buryat Shamanism

The Buryats are a Mongolic people who live primarily in southern Siberia along the shores of Lake Baikal in the Russian Republic of Buryatia. They can also be found in parts of northern and northeastern Mongolia. It is generally believed that, prior to Chinggis Khan, the current Buryat region was largely occupied by a mix of Turkic, Mongolic, and Tungusic tribes who gradually merged to form a unique identity. The historical text *The Secret History of the Mongols* describes them as a forest people.

In the early 1200s, Mongol forces under Jochi, the eldest son of Chinggis Khan, marched north to subjugate the Buryats. Since then, the Buryat Mongols have absorbed several other southern Siberian tribes with both Turkic and Tungusic roots into their cultural identity. During the time of the Northern Yuan Empire, the Buryats sided with the Oirats in opposition to the Northern Yuan under the Khalkha (see above). In the late 1600s and early 1700s, the Buryat region was formally annexed by Russia and remains so to this day.

Because of its mixed roots and diverse areas, Buryat culture and shamanism are Mongol in foundation, but retain many unique features that resemble those of the Turkic and Tungus peoples. The Buryats also underwent mass conversions to Buddhism in the early 18th century under heavy pressure from missionary efforts by Khalkha Mongolia and Tibet. As in many other places, these mass conversions were often violent, and Buryats today recount stories of battles that took place between Buddhists and shamanists. Unlike the Khalkha, however, which saw their shamanic lineages broken entirely, Buryat shamanic traditions survived, although they were deeply influenced by Buddhist beliefs and practices. By the 19th and 20th centuries, Buryat shamanism had transformed to such an extent that many other Mongols (notably the Darkhads) started referring to it as "yellow shamanism" (see chapter 4).

Of course, the Buryats contest this, as, in their belief, "yellow" shamans were formerly Buryat white shamans who were forced to become lamas and monks, essentially acting as monks during the day and conducting shamanic ceremonies at night. This type of hybrid shaman-monk no longer exists among Buryats today, so many claim that yellow shamans no longer exist.[8] Regardless, Buryat shamanism is perhaps the Mongolic tradition most heavily influenced by Buddhism. It retains a strong distinction between black and white shamans, whereas this distinction is less clear among the Darkhads. Buryat black shamans resemble the traditional Darkhad shaman in practice, in that they tend to work with and are often possessed by darker ancestral shamanic spirits. They claim to work with the forty-four black tengers and are known to heal and curse equally (see chapter 2). Historically, they were known to be heavily involved in political matters between the tribes and were often employed in conflicts because they could call upon war spirits.

Buryat black shamans also employ specific tools and can be recognized by their regalia. In keeping with tradition, only black shamans work with drums and (often metallic) horse-head staffs (see Figure 10). Advanced black shamans also wear an iron antler crown.[9] These were the shamans most heavily persecuted during conflicts with the Buddhists because of their strong resistance to outside influences. As a result, while Buryat black shamanism still retains some level of Buddhist influence, this influence is far less than in Buryat white shamanism. For example, Buryat black shamans work with darker and heavier Tibetan spirits as well, such as the blacksmith spirit Damdin Dorlig, one of the Tibetan spirits imported into the Buryat region (see chapter 3).

Типы инородцевъ Забайкальн. № 30.
Бурятъ-Шаманъ.—Le chamant des Bouriates.

Figure 10. Buryat black shaman with drum, iron crown, and horse-staffs in 1904.

By contrast, Buryat white shamans today heavily employ practices of Buddhist origin or influence, likely because they acted as Buryat yellow shamans in the past. White shamans are still technically chosen by the spirits and employ trance possession, but they are known to work with lighter ancestral shamanic spirits, as well as with the white tengers. While black shamans are more involved in political affairs and battles, white shamans act more as healers and mediators, and tend to work within communities rather than between them. Unlike black shamans, Buryat white shamans traditionally did not use drums to induce trance, but rather used a Buddhist bell and a wooden dragon staff.[10] However, these days many Buryat white shamans influenced by New Age practices have opted to use drums as well. Advanced white shamans do not wear iron antler crowns, however; instead they wear a bright multicolored cape with vertical stripes.

In addition to typical shamanic trance work, Buryat white shamans frequently employ common Buddhist folk-magic techniques, like chanting mantras and sutras to bring about healing and influence. During the conflict with the Buddhists, many white shamans were spared because they were deemed to work only with "good" spirits, while black shamans were thought to work with "evil" spirits. Nonetheless, most white shamans were forced to become monks and work primarily with Buddhist spirits—most commonly *Sagaan Obgon* (Buryat spelling), a Buddhist spirit known as Old White Man who appears only in Mongolian Buddhism and is depicted with long white hair, eyebrows, and beard, and carrying a dragon staff (see chapter 3).

Buryat shamanism may be the only form of Mongolic shamanism that traditionally designates shamans as black or white, hence their attire and tools are quite distinct as well. Both types of shamans wear a shaman cap known as a *maykhabsha*, which includes five long streamers hanging down the back, each with five colors to symbolize the elements. This cap is unique to Buryat shamanism.

The Buryat worldview has been deeply influenced by Buddhism, as have many of its practices. Although Buryats still retain a Tengerist cosmology, they combine it with a Buddhist view of the universe. Like other Mongols, they believe in the concept of the three souls, but believe they come from each of the three worlds, as opposed to the Darkhads, who define the three souls as bone, flesh, and consciousness (see chapter 2). Two of these souls reincarnate in the Buddhist fashion. Buryat altars often feature Buddhist spirits and Buddhas as well.

In keeping with the Buddhist habit of mapping as much of the universe as possible, Buryat shamans assign names and characteristics to each of the ninety-nine tengers, as well as to the various types of lus savdag spirits and other heroes. Moreover, they have the most complicated of all shamanic initiation structures, known as *shanar*. These initiation ceremonies are quite large and complex, and require the participation of community representatives and children. They are comprised of nine stages, each of which grants new teachings and empowerments (see chapter 4).[11] The first initiation requires that new shamans run around a stand of birch trees with community representatives and children while in trance (and drumming), then climb up and down a very tall tree (symbolizing the World Tree) while in trance.

Although Buryat shamanism is a traditional and unique lineage of Mongolic shamanism, it has been severely impacted by Russian New Age movements in modern times. As the Buryat Republic is currently part of the Russian Federation, the region has seen a large influx of Russian immigrants, which has significantly affected the Buryat culture. For the most part, modern-day Buryats speak Russian much more fluently than their own language and, every year, Buryat shamans incorporate more Russian themes into their shamanic practices. In fact, the Buryats of the western Baikal region (specifically in Irkutsk) have largely adopted Russian culture and introduced New Age beliefs. By contrast, Buryats in the eastern Baikal region and Mongolia have been better able to preserve their Mongolic heritage.

Moreover, since the dissolution of the Soviet Union, the region has seen an increasing number of people receiving initiations, which may also indicate growing numbers of fraudulent practitioners. A Darkhad shaman friend of mine told me that, although she has seen many "Buryat" shamans in Mongolia, she knows of only two whom she considers to be of traditional lineages. For better or worse, Buryat shamanism has become the best-known form of Mongolic shamanism around the world, due in large part to ethnic Russians exporting its practices to western Russia and Europe, and to the publication of Sarangerel's two English-language books, *Riding Windhorses* and *Chosen by the Spirits,* which are marketed as Mongolian shamanism, but are specifically geared toward the Buryat traditions. One of my hopes in writing this book is to show Western audiences that there are many other forms of Mongolic (and North Asian) shamanism beyond the Buryat tradition.

Daur Shamanism

The Daur, also known as the Daguur, are descendants of the Mongolic Khitans who fled north to the Baikal region after the fall of the Liao Empire (see above). Although it is unclear what form original Khitan shamanism took, we do know that, while in the Baikal region, Daur shamans adopted practices and tools that are similar to those of the Buryats.

The Daurs eventually moved eastward across the Trans-Baikal region toward northern Manchuria, both areas of which were formerly known as Dauria. During the Qing Dynasty, they migrated again from the Amur River region toward the southwest to the Nonni/Nen River region to escape encroaching Russian influence. They were thus frequently conscripted into the Qing armies and also became involved in Manchu high society, with several later queens and concubines coming from Daur lineage. The last empress of the Qing Dynasty, Wanrong, was a Daur Mongol. Today, the Daur live primarily in northeastern areas of Inner Mongolia and the Meilisi district of Qiqihar in Manchuria. They refer to both their male and female shamans as *yadgan/yad'en* (derived from *udgan*), but retain other spiritual roles like healer-priests (*bagsi*), bonesetters (*barshi*), and herbal healers (*otoshi*).

In northern Manchuria, the Daur encountered the Tungusic Evenk and Oroqen peoples, and were subsequently influenced by them culturally, spiritually, and even linguistically (see chapter 5). As an example, Daur communities are organized by surname clans known as *xal* or *hal* and subclans known as *mokon*, similar to the way Tungus-Manchu society was divided into *hala* and *mukun*. During this time, Daur shamanism, most notably with respect to its tools and armor, came under heavy influence from its Tungus neighbors. As the Daur lived exclusively within the Chinese territories of Manchuria and Inner Mongolia, they began to use Chinese terminology in their spiritual beliefs. One clear example of this non-Mongol influence is that, although the Daur still follow Tengerism, they place a heavier importance on the female spirits and goddesses than other Mongol groups do—primarily due to the influence of Tungusic traditions, which were historically more matriarchal. As a result, the Daur place special emphasis on both the Earth Mother and the goddess Ome (from the Turkic Umai).

Under Chinese influence, the Daur started referring to their goddesses as *Niang-Niang* (Chinese for "Madame"), the term the Chinese traditionally use to refer to their goddesses. In fact, the Daur typically combine languages and refer to their goddesses as *Niang-Niang Barkan* and may refer to specific goddesses (like Ome) as either *Ome Barkan* or *Ome Niang-Niang*. These goddesses are especially important to bonesetters and those who heal children, while midwives (*bariyechin*) work primarily with mountain spirits (*aulei barkan*).[12]

Among the Daur, both shamans and healer-priests (and sometimes even bonesetters and midwives) are capable of using trance possession to heal. Unlike shamans, however, healer-priests cannot engage in spirit flight (known as the "*dolbur* road" among the Daur). Nor can they engage in some of the more complicated ceremonies. They don't wear shamanic armor and the only spiritual tool they can use is the horse-tail whisk.[13] Moreover, while any spirit worker can work with the barkans, which are static images of spirits depicted in portraits and idols (see chapter 3), only shamans can work with *ongods/ongors*, which are the changing and dynamic (typically ancestral) spirits who can possess shamans.[14]

Another aspect that makes Daur shamanism quite unique is that they differentiate clan (*mokon*) shamans, who inherit their spirits only from the patrilineal line, from ordinary shamans, who inherit their spirits outside the patrilineal line—for instance, from the matrilineal line, land spirits, or other sources.[15] It is unclear if their roles and practices are different, however, as no resource suggests the distinction is anything other than an indication of where the spirits originate. Nonetheless, this distinction is quite similar to the Manchu distinction between patrilineal "domestic shaman-priests" and non-patrilineal "wild shamans," who do have different roles and practices (see chapter 7). According to multiple accounts, the most common work that Daur shamans do is to make cleansing spirit water known as *arshaan* (*rashaan* in Mongolia) and use it to cleanse and heal patients.[16]

Today, the Daur tradition of shamanism is primarily preserved and popularized by the Daur shaman Siqingua, who is based in the Hulun Buir region of Inner Mongolia. She has been recognized by the local Chinese government as an intangible cultural heritage, and the Harner-based Foundation for Shamanic Studies has recognized her as a living treasure and conducted field studies observing her practice. Although she practices only Daur shamanism, she has students and apprentices who are ethnically Tungus-Evenk and Solon, as well as non-Daur Mongol. She has taken them as students in order to help them develop their own practices, as well as revitalize their shamanic traditions.[17]

Siqingua's shamanic armor shows very heavy Tungus influences, carrying fewer rope-streamers than the armor of other Mongol traditions (see chapter 8). She does use prayer scarves, however, and is covered with bronze jingle cones and small mirrors in a more Tungus design. As she induces trance, she changes from lighter to heavier armor, and, at different times, wears a bronze antler crown or even a spirit mask. While deep in trance, she has been seen using large horse-head staffs to stabilize herself, riding them as steeds in the spirit world.[18] These are practices that are similar to the Tungusics and the Baikal Buryats.

Daur shamanism today is by no means widespread and its practitioners are few. But thanks to the efforts of shamans like Siqingua who have curried favor with the local government, this tradition is being revitalized. To learn more about it, consult *Shamans and Elders* by Caroline Humphrey (Oxford University Press, 1996).

Khorchin Shamanism

The Khorchins were the first Mongol group to ally with the Manchus in the 1600s. Thus their culture and spiritual practices have been subject to strong cross-cultural influences. In fact, many of the early queens and empresses of the Manchu Qing Dynasty were Khorchin Mongols, said to be descended from Khasar, one of Chinggis Khan's brothers. These queens convinced the Manchus to treat Mongols better than they had the Han Chinese—for instance, forbidding Chinese emigration into Mongol lands and even discouraging intermarriage with the Chinese, whom both the Manchus and Mongols disdained during the Qing era. Khorchin Mongols live in the Hulun Buir, Hinngan League, Tongliao, and Chifeng regions of Inner Mongolia for the most part, and may number more than a million, making their dialect possibly the most widely spoken Mongolian dialect in Inner Mongolia, even though Chahar is the official dialect of the region.

Khorchin Mongols, like other Mongols, follow a mix of Tengerism and Tibetan Buddhism. However, Khorchin shamanism is perhaps most easily distinguished from other Mongol shamanic traditions by their shamanic vestments. Rather than wearing a single armored robe, Khorchin shamans wear ceremonial garments that consist of multiple parts. One key component is the shaman skirt (*alag deel*), which is made up of multicolored streamers that hang from the waist. According to Khorchin legend, this skirt was originally all one piece, but, in a spiritual battle with a Buddhist monk, the shaman's skirt was ripped into many long strips. Khorchin shamans preserve the legend in the skirt's streamers today.[19] Each streamer is outlined in a thin band of either black or white, indicating whether the wearer is a black or white shaman.[20]

While most other Mongols wear either feathered headdresses or iron antler crowns, Khorchin shamans wear a bronze crown with miniature birds on top over a cloth cap, similar to the bronze crown worn by Manchu shamans. Numerous prayer scarves and colorful fabrics hang from the crowns and down their backs. They also use bronze shamanic mirrors that hang off the back and sides of a belt. These mirrors serve primarily to protect shamans (notably from behind) while in trance.

But perhaps the most distinctive feature of Khorchin shamans' regalia is their iron-framed drum. While most other Mongol drums are made with a thick wooden frame, Khorchin drums use a thin iron frame with a handle on the side. These drums produce a surprisingly power-ful resonance when the drumhead is struck with a thin flat drumstick.[21]

Figure 11. Left: Wang Serenchin performing, 1994. Right: Khorchin shamans possession ceremony performed by Bulin Bayaer, Altan Chichige, and assistant. Photos courtesy of Marguerite Garner.

Khorchins are also known to have some of the most powerful bonesetters among all Mongols, said to descend from the bonesetters who personally treated Chinggis Khan. When shamanic researcher Marguerite Garner visited and lived among Khorchin Mongols in the late 1980s and early 1990s, she visited the clinic of bonesetter Dr. Bao Renqinzungnai, who successfully treated her sciatica. She notes that, while these practitioners largely adhere to Mongol techniques, they have also started to incorporate Chinese Taoist concepts and tools, especially in areas of overlap that include acupuncture and moxibustion.

One notable aspect of Garner's treatment was that Dr. Bao prepared the spirit water (*arshaan*) he used in the Mongol way, but used Chinese-style *baijiu* liquor as opposed to the vodka used in Mongolia. He kept it in a blessed Chinese bottle gourd (*hulu*)—typically a sacred tool used by Taoists and featured in many Chinese folk legends. According to Dr. Bao, the shape of the gourd represents the unity between the upper and lower spirit worlds, while its neck represents the middle physical world.[22]

I have heard both Mongolians and Inner Mongolians accuse each of being overly influenced by either Chinese or Soviet Russian culture, each arguing that their side did a better job of preserving Mongol traditions. The truth is that, in Inner Mongolia, Chinese culture has indeed influenced Mongol customs, but Inner Mongolians have made many successful efforts to preserve the unique characteristics of their heritage. It is also true, however, that there are clear Russian influences such as vodka use and Cyrillic writing, but Mongols have been able to strongly preserve their culture by virtue of being an independent nation not subject to Russian immigration. As we have seen, parts of Mongolia (like the Darkhad Valley) are still quite remote and therefore have little contact with the outside world.

Both Garner and the Foundation for Shamanic Studies have separately videographed Khorchin shamanic ceremonies in the Tongliao region—most notably those of the famous late shaman Wang Serenchin, as well as the blind shaman Altan Chichige, who performs with her two trainees (see Figure 20). You can find Garner's footage on YouTube. As in other shamanic traditions, Khorchin shamans employ blue-flaming vodka in their ceremonies for cleansing, for opening opportunities, and for blessings, but they also appear to employ circular step-dancing more than other Mongol groups.

Like the Buryats, Khorchins engage in very arduous initiation rituals that often entail being stabbed with knives and needles without exhibiting physical pain or damage. According to several shamanic researchers, Khorchin shamanism appears to be growing in secret in Tongliao and Inner Mongolia, making it harder to find shamans, who keep an increasingly low profile away from government eyes.

Garner reports that, too often, government officials seek out Khorchin shamans and confiscate their tools, which later surface in regional museums or even at antique auction markets. Because many of these tools were made according to specific customs, Khorchin shamans have an increasingly difficult time replacing them. As a result, they often resort to using Tibetan Buddhist tools that are much easier to acquire.[23] Videos taken by shamanic researcher Mátyás Balogh of Khorchin shamans in the late 2000s show them still wearing streamer skirts and caps, but no longer wearing mirror belts or crowns. Some have even started to use Tibetan Buddhist cymbals to induce trance.[24]

Khorchin Mongols have been able to preserve their Mongol heritage better than most others in Inner Mongolia, and even to maintain non-shamanic spiritual practices, like the unique *andai* dance, which the Chinese government has designated to be the "national dance of the Mongols" in Inner Mongolia (see Figure 12). According to ancient legend, a Khorchin man was carrying his sick daughter on a wagon to find a shaman to heal her when the wagon broke down. He was able to reach the local village, and the villagers decided they would try to extend the girl's life energy. So they circled around her and started dancing, singing, and praying, stomping their feet and jumping while waving red scarves in one or both hands. Miraculously, the girl's condition stabilized enough that she could continue her journey on foot to the shaman for treatment. Khorchins have used this dance for healing, fertility, and celebration, and it has become a cornerstone of Khorchin spirituality and culture.

Figure 12. Korchin andai dance. Photo courtesy of Marguerite Garner.

Mongolic Shamanism Today

Mongol shamanic traditions went through long and dark periods of struggle, yet have endured as some of the strongest forms of indigenous shamanism that survive today. The formation of the democratic country of Mongolia continues to be a huge factor in maintaining the strength and integrity of these traditions. The traditions of the Khorchin and the Daur are no longer threatened by national communist initiatives, although they are still threatened by local government meddling.

Buryat shamanism is no longer threatened by Soviet crackdowns, but is now threatened by rising Russian New Age movements. While some may consider these movements to be simply an evolution of shamanic practices, the reality is that they are diluting the integrity of these traditions by introducing ideas that stand in direct contradiction to the original philosophies and taboos of Buryat shamanism.

In Mongolia today, one of the greatest socioeconomic problems is the rampant rise of alcoholism. Researcher Amalia Rubin notes that, in her opinion, alcoholism is perhaps the greatest threat to the Northern shamanic traditions. Even among Darkhad elders, it has become so great a problem that it has already impeded elders' ability to transmit knowledge, empowerments, and teachings to the next generation.[25]

The Northern traditions have played an important role in reinvigorating shamanic practice among the Mongols. The loss of many original forms of shamanism has led many in the Khalkha (especially those who still have shamanic spirits from an older lineage) to try mending their shamanic lineage practices. While some have been able to study under Darkhad and even Buryat elders, there is a growing trend toward reconstructionist New Age practices that are gaining popularity in large cities. Although these practices may have been birthed from Buryat teachings, they have now "evolved" to the point where they no longer resemble Buryat shamanism. As the capital Ulaanbaatar contains over half of Mongolia's population, attempts to rebuild shamanic traditions have resulted in a mixing of customs and practices from all over the country.

Because shamanism is a regional practice, many traditions may have conflicting practices or local beliefs that have been combined in modern reconstructions. This phenomenon, known as "city shamanism" or "the Central tradition," is creating a new generation of shamans who fall into the B1 category discussed above who may have genuinely good intentions and may want to help people. Many of them may even have legitimate shamanic lineage spirits and command some power. These new traditions, however, are based purely on the direct words of spirits and not on the rules, guidelines, and rituals from which the Northern tradition was honed over generations of unbroken practice. Naturally, the Northern traditions consider these Central traditions to be illegitimate and without true power, while those in the Central tradition consider those in the Northern tradition to be so rigid, orthodox, and rule-bound that their true connection with the spirits is diminished.

Thanks to the perceived and actual strength of Mongolic shamanism around the world, numerous cultures that formerly had shamanic lineages have been looking to the Mongols to try to revive and honor their ancestral roots. For the past several decades, pan-Turkic nationalists as well as young spiritual people in Turkey have been researching and even romanticizing Mongolic shamanism, using it as a basis to try to create a Turkish Neopagan movement. Writer Judika Illes, who is of Hungarian descent, has noted that a similar movement has emerged in Hungary, where people have been looking to Mongolic shamanism to rediscover their pre-Christian Central Asian roots.

Even many Manchus like myself have recognized the history and culture they share with the Mongols and have sought to study Mongolic shamanism in order to better understand their own heritage. Thus, although this book is not specifically dedicated to Mongolic shamanism, it is no surprise that it makes up a significant part of the material covered here, both because of its ancient cross-cultural influences with neighboring traditions, and because of the impact it is currently having on global shamanism.

CHAPTER 7

Tungusic Shamanism

The Tungus are one of the least-known groups even in Asia itself, although they occupy a large expanse of land that includes much of eastern Siberia, Manchuria, and even parts of northeastern Mongolia. They are one of the few peoples in North Asia who do not have their own country. As a result, they are at the greatest risk of cultural and spiritual erosion.

The Manchus, the largest group of the Tungus, have mostly been assimilated into Han Chinese culture, both voluntarily and involuntarily, while other ethnicities within China, like the Oroqen, the Nanai, and the Evenk have been pressured to leave behind their traditional lifestyles, and hence their spiritual practices. In 20th-century Russia, the Tungus regions experienced the least benefit from economic development, and large numbers of young people have been moving into more metropolitan areas and abandoning their cultural practices. As a result, many elders from the Evenk and Amur tribes have found it increasingly difficult to pass on their teachings. The most important legacies the Tungusics have left to the world are the word "shaman" (the only Tungusic loanword that is known throughout the West) and the impact of the Manchu Qing Dynasty on Asian history.

Early Tungusic History

The Tungusic people are thought to have originated around the Amur River, which is currently the border between Russia and China. They expanded outward into Siberia as far as the Yenisei River, as well as through Manchuria and parts of modern-day Inner Mongolia. However, folklorist Kira van Deusen believes that the original Tungusic tribes originated from Lake Baikal and Mongolia, and were pushed east and north by the Turkic and Mongol peoples.[1] The expansion of Tungusics into Siberia displaced the Paleo-Siberian tribes, who now occupy only the northeast edges of Siberia (the Chukchi and the Koryak).

There is not much documentary evidence to help us understand ancient Tungusic history. Based on Chinese records, the Tungusics may have been related to the ancient Sushen (c. 1100 BCE), the Yilou (c. 200 CE), the Wuji (c. 500 CE), and the Mohe (c. 700 CE), who were all recorded to be living in northern Manchuria.[2] The Evenks may have descended from a mixture of the early Tungus and Mongolic Shiwei peoples in northern Manchuria sometime between the 5th and 9th centuries. They are thought to have first spread between the Amur River and Lake Baikal, and then subsequently farther north, deeper into Siberia. By the 1600s, the Evenks had spread between northern Manchuria and northeastern Mongolia—to the Sakha Republic (Yakutia) to the north, to Kamchatka to the northeast, and to the Yenisei River to the west. Despite mixing with local Mongolic and Turkic populations, the Evenk language remains a distinctly Tungusic tongue.

The Mohe were the first Tungusics to appear in the records of multiple kingdoms. Chinese reports indicate that there were eight Mohe tribes, the strongest of which were the Heishui Mohe based around the Amur River, and the Sumo Mohe based around the Songhua/Sungari River.[3] The Mohe formed a large portion of the Korean-ruled kingdom of Balhae from the 7th to the 10th centuries. After the fall of Balhae, records of the Mohe are scarce. However, most tentatively agree that the Heishui Mohe were the direct ancestors of the Tungusic Jurchens. The Mohe are generally considered to have been seminomadic, with some tribes more nomadic and reliant on reindeer herding and others more settled and agrarian and reliant on pig farming. Before they were incorporated into the Khitan Liao Empire (see chapter 6), they were recorded to have ridden reindeer, as horses were rare before Khitan domination.[4]

The Jurchens

It is unclear when and how the term "Jurchen" first came into use, although some speculate that it was used by the Khitans to refer to the Liao Empire's Tungusic subjects (possibly originally *Luzhen* or *Julisen* in the Khitan language). After the fall of the Liao, the Jurchens started to use their own pronunciation of the word—*Jucen/Jusen*—to refer to themselves. In 1115, the chieftain Wanyan Aguda of the Wanyan clan unified the Jurchen tribes, declaring himself emperor of the Jurchen-led Jin Empire (*Aisin Gurun*, in Jurchen, "Golden Kingdom") and launching a ten-year rebellion against the Khitan Liao. The primary driver for this rebellion was that, although the Jurchens were granted aristocratic titles and were part of Liao governance, Khitans had very little respect for them and often demanded that Jurchen nobles prostitute their wives to Khitan nobles or face harsh punishment.

In 1125, the Jurchen Jin successfully overthrew the Liao and captured the Khitan emperor. After a failed invasion into the Mongol heartland, Jurchen armies marched south and took the northern half of the Chinese Song Empire. At the height of their power, the Jurchens controlled Manchuria (including Russian Manchuria in Siberia, modern-day Khabarovsk, and Primorsky), as well as northern China and parts of modern-day North Korea.

The Jin Empire, the first Tungusic empire, lasted for 119 years before it fell to the Mongols in 1234 CE (see chapter 6). By that time, the Jurchen population in northern China had become so culturally Chinese that the Mongol invaders didn't even consider them to be Jurchen. In the racial hierarchy of the Mongol Yuan Dynasty, the Mongols were considered superior, followed by non-Asian foreigners from the West (*semu ren*, "those with colored eyes"), the northern

Chinese, and the southern Chinese. The Jurchens in northern China were classified as northern Chinese in this hierarchy, while the Jurchens who remained in Manchuria were classified as Mongol, and therefore occupied a higher place in the hierarchy.

During the Mongol Empire, the Jurchens in China abandoned any remaining Jurchen identity, while those in Manchuria became more Mongolized by their rulers. The Manchurian Jurchens, treated favorably by Mongol princes, incorporated Mongol influences into their own culture, to the extent that they became more nomadic. They incorporated Mongol words and grammar into their language, and even adopted Mongol names and customs. By the end of the Yuan Dynasty, the Jurchens were often bilingual in Jurchen and Mongolian and had abandoned the old Jurchen script (based on the Khitan script), using the Mongolian alphabet instead to write Jurchen words.

In 1368, when the Mongol Yuan Dynasty fell, it was followed by the Ming, a Han Chinese dynasty that then ruled China proper. However, Manchuria and other Tungus lands remained under the rule of the Northern Yuan Dynasty. The Uriankhai general Naghachu succeeded in consolidating the Mongol and Jurchen armies in Manchuria into a force large enough to launch an invasion against the Chinese Ming. In anticipation, the Ming launched a military campaign against Naghachu in 1387 that concluded with his surrender. After this surrender, different Jurchen tribes pledged allegiance to either the Chinese Ming or the Korean Joseon kingdom, with many tribes maintaining cordial relations with individual Mongol tribes. As evidence of their earlier Mongolization, in 1444, when the Ming Dynasty sent communications to the Jurchens using the old Jurchen script, they replied that nobody could read it anymore, and that all future letters should be written in Mongolian.[5]

During this period, the Jurchens were broadly classified into three groups: the Jianzhou, the Haixi, and the Wild Jurchens. The Jianzhou Jurchens were comprised of what had originally been the Odoli, Tuowen, and Huligai clans, which later became the five clans—the Suksuhu, the Hunehe, the Wanggiya, the Donggo, and the Jecen. They lived primarily along the Changbai Mountains, the Liaodong peninsula, and east of the Mudan River. They were heavily influenced by Chinese and Korean cultures and therefore were fully settled and agrarian. Although they practiced Confucian values and Chinese methods of agriculture and textile manufacture, they still retained Jurchen aesthetics, hunting traditions, and even shamanic spirituality. The Holjaon were originally a major Jianzhou clan that was conquered and culturally absorbed into the Korean Joseon kingdom.

The Haixi Jurchens, also known as the Four Huluns and the Nara Confederation, included primarily the Yehe, Hada, Hoifa, and Ula clans and were based around and to the west of the Songhua/Sunggari River. They were more strongly influenced by Mongols than their Jianzhou counterparts. Those who settled to the west were largely nomadic pastoralists, while those who settled to the east became more agrarian. The Haixi became so Mongolized that, prior to Jurchen unification, the Jianzhou referred to them as *monggo nyalma*, or "Mongolian people." Their speech differed from that of the Jianzhou in that they used numerous Mongol words. Even today, the Manchu language often has two ways for expressing the same meaning— one based on Jianzhou and one based on Mongolized Haixi usage. Examples include "hello" (Jianzhou, *si sainyvn;* Haixi, *si sain uu;* Mongolian, *sain baina uu*), and "I love you" (Jianzhou, *bi simbe buyembi;* Haixi, *bi simbe khairambi;* Mongolian, *bi chamd khairtai*).

The term "Wild Jurchens" refers to the northern neighbors of the Jianzhou and the Haixi, including the Tungusic tribes of the Amur River Valley (Nanai, Ulchi, Udeghe), as well as the Evenki and the Oroqen. The term was sometimes even applied to the Mongolic Daur and Solon (see chapter 6). This suggests that, although we now consider the Evenki, Oroqen, Nanai, Ulchi, and Manchu to be different peoples, in the past, they were all classified as different branches of Jurchens by the Chinese, the Mongols, and even the Jurchens themselves. The Evenki and Oroqen were nomadic, while the Amur River peoples were settled hunters and fishermen.

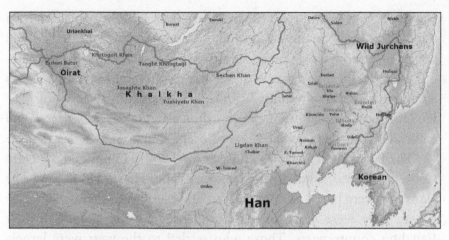

Figure 13. Jurchen and Mongol clans and rulers prior to Jurchen unification. Ruler names written in bold above the clan names.

During the Ming and Northern Yuan Dynasties, the Jurchens were a major source of contention between the Chinese Ming and the Korean Joseon, as both wanted to establish spheres of influence in Manchuria. Initially, the Joseon granted titles to the Odoli and the Huligai tribes and even expanded trade with them and organized marriages with Korean women. These tribes were even briefly considered to be Joseon subjects, and their elites served in the Korean royal bodyguard. Despite Korean attempts to acculturate and integrate the Jurchens into Korean culture, however, border tensions continued between them. In 1403, Huligai chieftain Ahacu and Odoli chieftain Dudu Mengtemu (Mongolian name: Möngke Temür) paid tribute to the Chinese Ming Empire and refused to pay tribute to the Joseon, thereby becoming subjects of the Ming and ending any further relationship with Korea. The Ming wanted to use the Jurchens primarily as a buffer against potential Mongol incursions. However, although the Ming maintained military bases across Jianzhou territories, the Jurchen tribes operated autonomously, even sometimes plundering Ming territory.

Jurchen Unification

In 1583, a young leader named Nurhaci succeeded his father as chieftain of the Jianzhou Suksuhu clan and launched a rebellion against the

Ming in retaliation for the murder of his father and grandfather by a Ming agent, Nikan Wailan. After the Ming executed the agent and ended the first rebellion, Nurhaci launched a series of Jurchen unification wars that lasted until 1619, successfully absorbing the other Jianzhou clans and establishing control over a large swathe of territory in Manchuria. During these struggles, Nurhaci began to use the name *Manju* (Manchu) to refer to his subjects, and to refer to his territories as *Manju Gurun*, or Manchu state. Initially the term applied only to the Jianzhou Jurchens.

In 1591, a coalition of nine tribes (the four Huluns, other Haixi and Wild Jurchen tribes, and the Khorchin Mongols) launched a combined assault against the rising power of Nurhaci, but they were defeated in 1593. Following this attack, Nurhaci's new Manju Gurun defeated the Haixi and absorbed their tribes—notably the Hada in 1601, the Hoifa in 1607, the Amur Wild Jurchens in 1611, the Ula in 1613, and finally the Yehe in 1619. The Koreans, sensing a rising threat in the north, launched an expedition in 1605 that destroyed the Jurchen Holjaon tribe (already allied with Nurhaci), but this did little to quell the Jurchen-Manchu threat.

With the successful unification of the Jurchens, the Haixi were formally incorporated into the Manchu identity. In 1616, prior to the collapse of the Yehe, Nurhaci declared that his territories be named *Amaga Aisin Gurun*, or "Later Jin Khanate," declaring his empire to be the successor to the earlier Jin Empire and granting himself the title of *Genggiyen Khan* ("Bright/Brilliant Khan"). In 1603, his Mongol allies had already granted him the title *Sure Kundulen Khan* ("Wise and Respected Khan"). Around this time, Nurhaci renamed his ancestral clan the *Aisin-Gioro* ("Golden Clan"), which is still known today to be the ruling clan of the Manchus.

Before his death, Yehe chieftain Gintaisi famously declared this curse: "Even if there is only one daughter left in my clan, we will overthrow the Manchus!" His curse, which indicates that the Manchu initially encompassed only the Jianzhou Jurchens and did not include the Haixi until after Jurchen unification, was arguably fulfilled by two of Gintaisi's descendants—the Empress Dowager Cixi of the Yehe Nara clan, who usurped power from the house of Aisin-Gioro at the end of the Qing Dynasty, and the last Empress Dowager Longyu (also of the Yehe Nara clan), who officially signed the abdication that ended the Manchu Qing Dynasty. In 1618, Nurhaci officially drafted the seven grievances that accused the Ming and Haixi of conspiring against him and performed a shamanic ceremony (the ritual burning of these grievances) that appealed to heaven to support his conquests.

In 1624, the Khorchin Mongols pledged their support to Nurhaci and the Later Jin Empire, the first Mongol group to do so, and this launched a centuries-long practice of arranged marriages between Manchus and Mongols. This momentous alliance was solemnized with a shamanic ceremony to heaven (Manchu, *Abka Enduri*; Mongol, *Tenger*) that stated:

In order to form one alliance, we two ulus [nations], the Manchu and Khorchin, offer a white horse to Heaven and a black ox to Earth. Wearing an oath of loyalty together, we offer one bowl of araki (alcohol), one bowl of meat, one bowl of blood, and one bowl of dried remains.[6]

In the years that followed, other Mongol clans pledged their loyalty to Nurhaci, including the Kharchin, Bayut, Jalaid, Dorbed, Gorlos, Aohan, Naiman, Bagarin, and Tumed clans. Ligdan Khan of the Chahars, who still held the official jade seal of the Northern Yuan Dynasty, attempted to unite the Mongols into a rival empire, but could not retain united Mongol support and was defeated by Hong Taiji in 1624.

Ligdan's son, Ejei Khan, transferred the Imperial seal to the Later Jin (Qing), thus ending the Northern Yuan Dynasty and establishing the Later Jin Dynasty (later known as the Qing Dynasty) as its true successor. After he pledged Chahar support to the Manchu empire, the alliance between the Manchus and the Mongols was cemented by royal marriages and all future Manchu emperors were declared to be legitimate descendants of Chinggis Khan. These alliances were all sealed with shamanic ceremonies employing both Manchu and Mongol shamans, largely to recognize that Nurhaci and his son, Hong Taiji, were legitimate khans as mandated by heaven.

The Manchus and the Qing

In 1636, Hong Taiji, who had been elected Sechen Khan of the Later Jin by a grand council of princes and lords following Nurhaci's death ten years earlier, officially renamed the empire to *Daicing Gurun* (Qing Dynasty) and proclaimed himself as its first emperor. This was a clever pun on the Mongolian word *daichin* ("warrior"). Thus *Daicing Gurun* may have also meant "warrior kingdom." In Chinese, this became *Da Qing*, which translates to "pure" and is associated with water (as *Ming* was associated with fire).

In 1640, chieftain Bombogor of the Evenk-Daur confederation was defeated and, with their collapse, the last of the Wild Jurchens were incorporated into the Manchu army. These Jurchen-Manchu groups, along with the Khorchin Mongols, were reorganized into the Eight Banners, a color-coded banner system created by Nurhaci when he organized the Jurchen clans into a military confederation. The Eight Banners (originally there were only four—yellow, white, red, and blue) remain, to this day, the cornerstone of Manchu identity. As the Qing Dynasty spread, additional banners were added. Most Jianzhou clans were assigned to four plain banners, while most Haixi clans were assigned to four bordered banners. The Imperial family (*Aisin-Gioro*) carried a plain yellow banner. The Emperor personally managed the three upper banners—plain yellow, bordered yellow, and plain white, while the five lower banners were managed by other princes and lords. Eventually, two additional groups of eight banners were created to encompass the Mongols and Han Chinese who joined the Qing military. At the height of Qing conquest, there were twenty-four banners in total consisting of Manchu, Han, and Mongol banners. However, the Manchu banners often contained both Mongols and Han Chinese, notably those who joined the Manchus prior to the Qing declaration, as well as those who married into Manchu families. My own family descends from the bordered yellow banner and contains bloodline from the Fuca clan as well as from the Mongol Borji clan that joined the Manchu banners.

Between 1636 and 1644, the Qing Empire defeated the Ming, although scattered Ming forces temporarily resisted Qing authority in both Taiwan and the western regions around modern-day Gansu/ Xinjiang. Many today, notably in China, claim that the Manchu people became Chinese under the Qing—that they recognized the "superior- ity" of Han Chinese culture and assimilated from their Manchu tra- ditions. Although it is true that some assimilation did take place, it is incorrect to state that the Manchus abandoned their culture entirely in favor of Chinese culture. Manchu banner garrisons were established all over the empire, and the Manchus who moved to these areas adopted local customs. Manchus in China proper became more Chinese; those in Mongolia became more Mongol; those in Tibet became more Tibetan; those in Turkic regions became more Turkic. This policy was encouraged to allow local governors more stability.

The Manchus were especially close with the people of Inner Mongolia, and many Qing empresses were Mongols. These empresses influenced and managed the inner court decisions that were announced by the throne and dictated interethnic relations, most notably banning non-Manchus and non-Mongols from entering their territories and forbidding marriages between them and the Han Chinese. To secure Tibet's allegiance, the Manchus officially adopted the Gelug school of Tibetan Buddhism as the official religion of the Qing Dynasty, elevating religious leaders like the Dalai Lama to political power. This official adoption ultimately led to a general suppression of traditional shaman- ism among the Manchus and forced mass conversions on the Mongols.

Under the Qing, most political offices were held by two indi- viduals—one Manchu and one non-Manchu (predominantly Han Chinese). In this way, although Manchus were the dominant ruling power, Mongols enjoyed direct influence in the inner palace courts and military offices. Tibetans oversaw religious and spiritual affairs (excluding the Imperial family's shamanic ceremonies) and the Chinese managed the empire's administrative responsibilities. In a sense, the Qing Dynasty ruled over a multiethnic empire in which four or five different races shared political power. Therefore, the Manchus did not abandon Manchu culture entirely and assimilate to Chinese customs as is commonly believed. Rather they became part of a complex patchwork of customs, adopting aspects of nearly every dominant culture within their empire. At the same time, however, they adhered to their unique cultural practices to the extent that they could distinguish clearly between what was Manchu and what was foreign in origin.

The Evenks

In Siberia, the Evenki people underwent a tumultuous period following years of peaceful nomadic living. As the Russian empire expanded and encountered the Evenks in the 17th century, they forcibly pushed them farther east, while simultaneously imposing heavy taxes on fur, a main source of their livelihood, and sometimes taking hostages to ensure payment. Resistance was often met with cruel punishments that included slavery or extermination of entire villages. This forced the Evenks to migrate farther east and south, often into Qing territory, with the largest movements occurring in the 19th century. These Evenks, classified as Wild Jurchens, were welcomed by the Qing and immediately employed as bannermen border guards.

The Manchus also tried to influence Evenki culture and language, although this was not cruelly implemented given the inherent similarities between the two cultures. This did, however, cause a "soft" erosion in Evenki culture as Evenks adopted more Manchu customs and traditions. The Evenks who stayed in lands occupied by the Russian Empire, on the other hand, experienced forced language erosion and loss of traditional lifestyle. This continued during the Soviet regime as policies of collectivization, forced sedenterization, and Russification were implemented, right up until the dissolution of the Soviet Union.

The Tungus Today

The Qing Dynasty lasted for nearly 300 years before its leaders officially abdicated in 1912 following a series of internal and external events that greatly weakened the empire—like the opium wars, the Taiping and Boxer rebellions, and the Dungan Revolt that culminated in the Xinhai revolution (1911–1912). The newly established Republic of China claimed Qing territories, including Inner Manchuria (Outer Manchuria had been ceded to Russia following earlier military defeats), Inner and Outer Mongolia, Tibet, and Xinjiang/East Turkestan. Many of these regions also declared independence, claiming that their allegiance had been to the Manchus and that they held no ties to the Chinese Republic. Although the newly founded republic contested this, it was initially so weak that many regions and provinces came to be ruled by local warlords. The Manchus, many of whom no longer spoke Manchu, either retreated to their ancestral lands (which had been heavily colonized by Chinese settlers) or assimilated into the local populations in China, Mongolia, and Tibet.

Many Mongols, including the Khorchin, broke away from Manchu association, although Inner Mongolian nobles still attempted to establish a restored empire of Mongolia and Manchuria. The former Wild Jurchens had already broken away, many of them forced to do so after Outer Manchuria was ceded to Russia. Others simply separated from the Manchu identity into separate ethnicities (Nanai, Oroqen, Evenki, etc.) and were officially recognized by the Republic of China and subsequently by the communist People's Republic of China. Only those who are descended from the former Jianzhou and Haixi Jurchens still adhere to their Manchu identity.

During the late Qing Dynasty and the Republic of China, Manchus and other Tungus peoples were heavily persecuted by the Han Chinese, who described them as barbarians and savages. During World War II, the Manchus (led by Puyi, the last Qing emperor) attempted to form their own independent country of Manchukuo, but this became a Japanese puppet state that was usurped by the Japanese military during World War II and disintegrated after the Japanese surrender and the Soviet-Chinese invasion.

In 1949, the Republic of China was overthrown, its government driven to Taiwan, and the communist People's Republic of China took power. The initial years of Communist Chinese and Soviet power were perhaps the most dangerous for Tungusic peoples. The Manchus were so closely associated with feudalism and aristocracy that, during the Chinese Cultural Revolution (1966–1976), they had to hide their identity or risk being harassed and attacked. This is why most Manchus today carry a Chinese-sounding last name instead of their original clan name. Although not officially labeled as such, Manchu culture became de facto "illegal" in Communist China, and thus Manchu spirituality greatly diminished in practice and almost disappeared entirely. Non-Manchu Tungusics could still maintain their traditional lifestyles, albeit with forced collectivization of herd animals, but traditional spirituality and shamanism were forbidden, and many had to practice in secret without their tools, often because they had been destroyed or confiscated.

For the rest of the 20th century, economic pressure forced many young people in these communities to leave their traditional lifestyles behind and move to more populous Chinese cities. While Soviet Russia had forbidden spirituality in the past, Russian Evenks have been able to revive their spiritual practices somewhat, although they face largely the same economic pressures as the Tungus people in China. After the dissolution of the Soviet Union, Tungusic spirituality could be practiced openly, but the economic hardships in Siberia forced many younger people to leave their communities for more prosperous cities with greater opportunities and potential for economic success. Moreover, these economic hardships increased alcoholism in these communities, greatly affecting elders' ability to pass on their knowledge.

And now a new threat comes from the Russian New Age movement, which is appropriating Tungusic spirituality while also diluting Evenki traditions with Western New Age practices. In China, communist repression relaxed significantly after the 1970s, but Tungusic spirituality still has to be practiced cautiously, as fame or success can attract the attention of local government officials, who are still able to arrest practitioners on charges of "harmful superstition." Despite these obstacles, however, Tungusic spirituality in both countries is cautiously re-emerging.

Today, the Tungusic peoples are largely divided into two groups—the Northern and Southern Tungus. All fall within the same language family, but these two groups were separated long enough that their languages and cultures evolved in somewhat different directions. Although the vast majority of Tungusics today speak Russian or Chinese as their primary languages, the Northern Tungus languages are mutually intelligible and the Southern Tungus languages are mutually intelligible, but the two groups have difficulty understanding each other beyond key root words.

The Northern Tungus include the Evenks (and their subgroup, the Even) in Russian Siberia and northern Manchuria, as well as the Oroqen (and their subgroup, the Orok) based in northeastern Inner Mongolia and northwestern Manchuria. Although the Northern Tungus may have mixed with Mongolic peoples in early history, their culture remained distinct and was shaped by the Siberian taiga climate. They remain generally nomadic, living in teepee-like structures, and are known to be reindeer herders. Their shamanic traditions can be divided into Evenki shamanism and Oroqen shamanism.

The Southern Tungus are quite diverse and can be further divided into two subgroups: the Amur River tribes (Ulchi, Nanai, etc.) in southeastern Siberia, and northeastern Manchuria, and the Jurchen-Manchu peoples, which include the Manchu and the Sibe. The Manchus were more heavily Mongolized than the other Tungusic groups and utilize the Mongolian script as their official writing system. Even today, nearly all Manchus have some Mongol blood due to political and military marriages. The Amur exhibit some influences from Evenk, Manchu, and Mongol populations, but maintain a unique culture for the most part. While they perhaps best maintain the original Tungus traditions, they (like the Evenk) were strongly influenced by the local climate, particularly the dense riverways of the region, which shaped their culture (for instance, fish-skin clothes) and shamanic practices. The shamanic traditions of the Southern Tungus can be divided generally into Amur River shamanism and Manchu shamanism.

We'll look next at how the complex history of the Tungusic peoples influenced their shamanic traditions.

Tungusic Tengerism

Although the Tungusic peoples practice shamanism in the context of a sky-centered animistic belief system, there is much disagreement about whether these beliefs qualify as Tengerism. While their Turkic and Mongolic counterparts undoubtedly practice Tengerism, even referring to it by the same name, the Tungusics use many different words for heaven. While Tenger is almost always male in balance with the female earth mother, heaven is almost always gender-neutral (beyond gender) or even female among most Tungusic cultures. Only the Manchus refer to a male Sky Father, although this is likely due to Mongol influence, as the ancient pre-Manchu Jurchen deity was known as *Abkai Hehe* or Sky Woman (see chapter 3). These differences may suggest that there is little evidence that Tungusic spirituality is related to ancient forms of Tengerism. Nonetheless, we know that shamanism came to the Tungusic tribes through early contact with cultures that had shamans. If shamanism did originate in and around northern Mongolia and southern Siberia, as suggested in previous chapters, it could only have come to the Tungus through mixing with the ancient Tengerist peoples who already practiced shamanism.

As we have seen, shamanic lineages travel by bloodline, as the spirits who choose shamans are often ancestors who were also shamans. The Evenks likely inherited lineages through interactions with the ancient Mongolic Shiwei people. Amur tribes and Manchus may have inherited theirs from the Mongolic Donghu tribes that had a strong presence in Manchuria. And in fact, although they do not share quite the same pantheon, many of the foundational and cosmological concepts of Tungus spirituality are very similar to Turkic and Mongolic Tengerism. For these reasons, some argue that Tungus spirituality is an extension of Tengerism, while others argue that it is a non-Tengerist belief system that adopted shamanic lineages from Tengerist cultures.

Two unique features of Tungusic spirituality are its matriarchal structure and its strong emphasis on animal gods and spirits. Like Tengerists, Tungusics believe that heaven is responsible for the world's creation. Some believe that the highest deity of heaven is without gender, while others believe it to be a Sky Woman. Many of those who believe that the highest heaven is a genderless deity also believe that this deity created a subordinate female deity who is more involved with life on earth and who, in turn, created other minor deities and land/earth gods and spirits (see chapter 3). In pre-Manchu Jurchen belief, Abka Hehe, the supreme Sky Woman, created the goddesses Banamu Hehe (Earth Mother) and Ulden Hehe (Light Mother), and the three were often worshipped as a trinity.

Animal gods also figure significantly in Tungusic spirituality and, in some cultures, were responsible for shaping the physical world. As in Mongolic belief, the physical world was believed to consist originally only of water, but various animal gods pulled earth from within the water to create land. Many Tungusic cultures also believe that animal gods were sent by heaven to accomplish and be responsible for specific tasks. One of the most iconic of these is the Eagle Mother, who is often considered to be either the first shaman or the mother of the first shamans (see chapter 3).

In some ways, Tungusic shamans are quite similar to Turkic and Mongolic shamans in that they do not work directly with gods and deities, but rather with ancestral spirits of past shamans (often known as "grandfather" and "grandmother" gods) and animal gods, although it is unclear whether these are representations of land spirits, representations of ancestral spirits and guardians, or simply gods who rule over animal types. What is clear is that they are not simply spirits of deceased animals. Like Turkic and Mongolic shamans, Tungusic shamans employ trance possession by these spirits, but they tend to employ spirit flights and journeys to the Upper and Lower Worlds via these spirits far more frequently than their Turkic and Mongolic counterparts.

The Tale of the Nisan Shaman

No discussion of Tungusic spirituality would be complete without the story of Nisan Shaman, possibly the most important and comprehensive example of ancient Tungusic shamanism that survives today.

Versions of this story can be found across nearly all Tungusic cultures, and even among the Mongolic Daur, likely because of their proximity to the Evenk and the Oroqen. Although it was originally transmitted orally, Manchu rulers of the Qing Dynasty decreed that it be written down and stored in the Imperial records. It is because written versions of this tale remained in the Imperial library in Beijing that we have the complete story today. This Manchu version has become the "official" version, but other Tungusic versions are consistent with it, with differences only in the details. Because the story can help us to understand what the ancient shamanism of the Tungus may have looked like, I summarize it for you here.

The story tells of how the Nisan Shaman (sometimes called *Teteke*) performs a spirit flight and soul retrieval for an adolescent boy (Sergudai Fiyanggo) whose soul was kidnapped by the Lord of the Lower World (*Ilmun Khan* in Manchu). In another version, a small boy accidentally breaks a sacred spirit figure and collapses into a deathlike coma, his soul having been taken. In both versions, the boy's parents beg Nisan Shaman for help. Correctly determining that the boy's soul has been taken by Ilmun Khan, she knows that retrieving it will be an extremely dangerous task. Out of compassion, however, she agrees to help the family.

Nisan Shaman prepares offerings of seeds, packets of bean paste and paper, a rooster, and a dog (required to pass the Lower World gatekeepers). Then she gathers her assistants into a circle around the fire and starts them drumming. The main assistant continues the drumming so that Nisan Shaman's path may be propelled forward, and so that she can return. As they drum, she puts on her armored robe, which is adorned with bells, horse tails, and a large bronze mirror, as well as her antler cap, whose deerskin fringes cover her eyes. As she begins to drum, her soul descends into the Lower World. When she arrives, she sees the child's soul traveling to the other side of a river in a boat.

When the boat comes back empty, Nisan Shaman asks the boatman (*Monggoldai Nakcu*, Mongolian Uncle) why he has taken the boy's soul. The guardian of the river to the Lower World says he harbors no ill will against the boy or his family, and that he was simply following his lord's orders, which he dare not question. Nisan Shaman asks the boatman to carry her across the river. As she travels, she sees snakes, dragons, and giant fish swimming in the water. When she reaches the other side, she leaves bean paste for the boatman as payment. Some versions of the story describe three underworld rivers (one red, one yellow, one black). One-legged *Toxolo Age* (Lame Brother) manages the red river, while Monggoldai Nakcu manages the yellow one.

After crossing the river, Nisan Shaman crosses a vast, dark, and mountainous land, eventually arriving at a fortress that marks the entrance to the land of the dead. Leaving the rooster and the dog with the gate guardians, she charges her way through the fortress, fighting and bribing the spirit guards who confront her. Exhausted, she eventually encounters a powerful god (likely the demon Yeruri) who attacks her. Her "soul body" collapses and she awakens in a strange land.

Still weak from her encounter with the demon, Nisan Shaman tries moving forward, but collapses again. Fearing that her soul could be trapped in the Lower World land of the dead, she offers a quick prayer. The reindeer god, one of her closest shamanic spirits (symbolized by her antlered cap), appears and heals her, then carries her on its back to the inner keep of Ilmun Khan, where she finds the boy's soul.

Nisan Shaman sends an invocation song and drumbeat up the World Tree to the Middle World (see chapter 1). Her main assistant, still drumming next to her unconscious body, hears the cry and repeats it up the World Tree to the Upper World to summon a mighty bird of heaven that descends to the Lower World and penetrates the inner keep like a projectile. As the Nisan shaman distracts the attention of Ilmun Khan, the great bird snatches the boy's soul and brings it to her, who places it in her mirror. As Nisan Shaman races to escape, Ilmun Khan's servants pursue her, but are held back by her animal spirits, who cover her tracks to mislead them.

The rest of the story describes Nisan Shaman's journey back, which was equally fraught with difficulties. She stops by a soul registration building to ensure the boy has a long life. At one point, her long-dead ex-husband's soul confronts her and tries to force (or beg) her to take him back. She replies that she cannot, because his body has long rotted away. When he becomes violent, she must fight him to get away (it's noted that he was also cruel in life). Eventually, she wanders into a temple of Omosi Mama, the goddess of life, where she gives offerings to an old woman who is cleaning the temple. The old woman then lifts her disguise and reveals that she is the goddess herself. Omosi Mama claims that she has personally ordained that Nisan Shaman will be a great shaman, having sent one of her own disciples to be her teacher.

Because Nisan Shaman is now too exhausted to complete her trip back to the Middle World, her main assistant performs a drumming ceremony and Nisan Shaman rides the remainder of the way on the drumbeat. Upon returning to her body, she returns the boy's soul from her mirror into the boy and he wakes up instantly.

Different versions of this tale have different endings. In the Qing Imperial version, her late husband's family, furious that she did not bring him back, convinced the royal court (backed by Buddhist monks) to punish her and take away her tools, so she can never practice as a shaman again. In other versions, after Nisan Shaman rescues the boy's soul, a giant reindeer appears (implied to be the reindeer god), and she travels away with the reindeer, never to be seen again.

The story of the Nisan Shaman highlights the shared connection and shamanic roots between the different Tungusic peoples. Sarangerel believes the story to be of Mongol origin, given its importance among Daur Mongols. Given that this story is so widespread among all Tungus peoples, but not known among most other Mongol tribes, this theory seems highly unlikely. It is certainly interesting that the Lower World boatman is known as Mongolian Uncle, although it is unclear why he is referred to as such. The Russian anthropologist Shirokogoroff believes the word meant "senior of the mother's clan" in ancient times.

The story also highlights much of a shared Tungusic cosmology—the importance of various animals, the goddess Omosi Mama, the Lower World landmarks, ancient forms of soul retrieval, and even the shamanic vestments that were used in ancient times. In addition to the official Manchu version in Beijing, different versions of the story were recorded and stored in Russia and Korea, and these versions have been invaluable in preserving the folklore of these deeply shamanic cultures.

Evenki Shamanism

The Evenks are the primary group of Northern Tungusic peoples. In their sky-centered belief system, heaven is known as *buga,* which, like the word *tenger,* can have multiple meanings—among them "world," "universe," and "heaven." Among the Amur Evenks, Buga is the highest deity, sometimes depicted as a reindeer or an elk, but generally considered to be without form. In fact, Buga is so far beyond comprehension that it has no image or gender, and cannot be described in exact detail. Although Buga is omnipresent, it rarely interferes with human or physical-world affairs, but acts rather as the lord of *Uga Buga,* the Upper World.

Uga Buga has three layers—the realm of celestial bodies and deities such as spirits of the sun, moon, and stars; the realms of the dead, which exist simultaneously with the Lower World realm of the dead; and the realm of the Sky Woman, Enekan Buga (Heavenly Grandmother), master of the world, and Seveki, who oversees all taiga life. Whenever the Evenk offer sacrifices to the sky, they are generally made to Enekan Buga. Many shamanic spirits, known as grandfather and grandmother gods, also reside in this realm.

The Middle World is known as *Dulin Buga* and consists of the earthly world and all the humans, animals, plants, and spirits within. The Lower World is known as *Khergu Buga,* which also consists of three parts: *buni,* the realm of the dead (farthest from earth); the underworld river *Tunete,* which cannot be crossed by inhabitants of the other two realms but only by the strongest shamans; and *khargi,* the realm of demons and evil spirits (closest to earth).[7]

Evenki shamans (and other Tungus shamans) do not classify themselves as black or white. Instead, they are usually classified by their power or preferences, notably their ability and desire to go to the Upper or Lower Worlds (or both). Some shamans work only with Upper World spirits (from the second and third layers of heaven); some work only with Lower World spirits. Sometimes they are also classified based on their areas of specialization—for instance, healing or treatment, divination, psychopomp work, or specific rites like attracting successful hunts. Most Evenki shamans can safely travel to the Upper World, as their shamanic spirits reside there. But only the most powerful shamans can travel to the treacherous realms of the Lower World, either because their spirits reside there or, on very rare occasions, because their Upper World spirits have the ability to engage against Khargi's demons.

Researcher Sergey Shirokogoroff notes that different Evenk shamans wear distinctly different armor and attire based on the primary animal gods they work with—most notably "reindeer suits" and "bird suits."[8] On these suits, the metallic implements, fringes, and fabrics are arranged to represent the skeleton of the animal. The headdresses of bird suits consist of feathers, while those of reindeer suits display either real or iron antlers. All headdresses have fringes that cover the eyes and parts of the face. It is important to note, however, that different groups of Evenks have different rules and taboos regarding how shamans practice and what they wear, so these are broad generalizations.

In Evenki yurts, which are shaped like teepees, the sacred place of honor lies opposite the door. Known as *malu*, this space contains a little table that acts as an altar on which sacred objects and tools are kept. As for other North Asian peoples, these include idols and other spirit representations, as well as shamanic armor and drums, and objects that act as spirit containers (see chapter 8). The malu also contains the ritual rugs and carpets known as the *namu* and the *kumulan*, which are distinctly Evenki. The namu are made of buckskins that have been processed to soft suede. They are decorated with images of spirits and deities, celestial bodies, animals, people, and even stories and legends. They may include ribbons, fringes, and fur pieces. The namu act both as vessels for a family's spirits and as talismans that can protect and bless the family.

Namu are prepared and empowered during a ceremony called the *sevekan*, which is performed in the spring to bring about the magical revival of nature and life. During these ceremonies, shamans imbue the namu with *musun*, the sacred power of life. Musun relates to a shaman's power, large reserves of which exist in sacred mountains. Shamans empower their drums, beaters, armor, attire, and other tools with musun before they are used. Ordinary families keep namu as repositories for musun. In Evenki belief:

> ... namu promotes and awakens the forces of life weakened by the pernicious impact of winter ... In a ritual of prayerful appeal, the power musun becomes more active and radiates to the surrounding space by sprinkling namu with sacrificial blood, filling it with the energy of movement.[9]

During these ceremonies, when offerings are given to the spirits, sacrificial reindeer blood is sprinkled onto the namu to revive its musun and life energy.[10]

The Evenki lifestyle is dependent on both hunting and reindeer herding. In fact, the Evenki economic calendar is divided between the herding season (roughly April to October) and the hunting season (roughly October to April).[11] Shamans and their ceremonies are intimately tied to these annual cycles. The two main ceremonies of the Evenk include the *sevekan*, which is centered around the herding season, and the *sinkelaun*, which is performed at the start of the hunting season, with simpler versions performed before each hunting trip. When performing the sinkelaun, shamans create ritual images of game animals with their shamanic staffs or walking sticks, then enter trance to petition Enekan Buga to send animals and luck for the hunt. Hunters are then purified by passing between *chichipkan* (idols or spirit houses made of young larches) that also provide protection from malice and evil spirits. Shamanic staffs are dressed and used in a spiritual "hunt," which acts as a divination for how the hunt can be successful.[12]

Although shamanism is still widely practiced among the Evenks, shamans are becoming more rare in Evenk communities. Many potential shamans have failed their initiations due either to a desire for modernization or to conflicting Christian values. In many cases, candidates are too corrupted by Russian New Age movements, which at times conflict with traditional practices or have diluted them beyond what is approved by elders.

One of the last great Evenk shamans, Semyon (Savey) Vasilyev (1938–2013), was born in the Amur region, but lived most of his life in southern Yakutia. Coming from a family of shamans, he was suspected of shamanism by Soviet officials when he was twenty-five, although he would not be struck by shaman sickness and hear the spirits' call until a decade later and did not complete his initiation until five years after that.[13] Vasilyev received requests for training from Evenks of both the Amur region and Yakutia, as well as from Russians and Yakuts. Despite the endangered state of Evenki shamanism, however, he did not train any students. According to Zabiyako:

> [Savey] was not really anxious with the continuity problem, and he relied entirely upon the will of the spirits. He believed that the spirits would "choose" the new applicant sometime after he left for the other world, and they would also teach him or her.[14]

As the revival of national consciousness spreads among Evenks, many are even seeking help from shamans of neighboring cultures. In one peculiar example, the ethnic Evenk Svetlana Voronina was trained by a Buryat Mongol shaman and performs according to Buryat tradition.[15] In Inner Mongolia, Daur shaman Siqingua also trains Evenki students in the Daur tradition.[16] Although the future of Evenki shamanism is still unclear, interest in shamanism will likely continue to grow among the Evenks.

Oroqen Shamanism

The Oroqen are another notable group of Northern Tungus who live primarily in the Chinese territories of Heilongjiang (in Manchuria) and Inner Mongolia. Like the Evenk, they are hunters and reindeer herders based in the mountains, although the southern Oroqen are also known for breeding horses and trading furs. My grandmother remembers that, when she was a little girl in northwest Manchuria, the Oroqen sometimes came down from the mountains into her town to trade furs for supplies. She described them as looking like ancient wild men dressed all in furs. The Oroqen may have originated near the Outer Khingan Mountains (Stanovoy Range) as a mixture of the ancient Tungus and the Mongolic Shiwei. Also called the Khingan Tungus and Mergen Tungus, they eventually migrated south into the Ilkhur, and the Greater and Lesser Khingan mountain ranges.

Traditional Oroqen dwellings are similar to those of the Evenk in that they are shaped like teepees and are covered with deer furs in winter and birch bark in summer. In fact, although they are officially recognized as a separate ethnicity, many anthropologists believe there is fundamentally very little difference between the Oroqen and the Evenk. During the Qing Dynasty, the Oroqen were formally incorporated into the Manchu banners and were influenced by Manchu and southern Tungusic cultures. They are organized into clan villages (*mokun*) like the Manchus, which consist of individual family units (*urireng*) like the Evenks. Like the Evenks, the Oroqen believe in the three worlds: the Upper World (*Buwa*), the Middle World (*Berye*), and the Lower World (*Buni*).[17]

The history of Oroqen shamanism is as tragic as it is important to our understanding of North Asian shamanism. In 1952, Chinese Communist Party cadres forced the Oroqen to give up their "superstitions" and spiritual practices. In particular, the Oroqen villages of Baiyinna and Shibazhan were forced to conduct a three-night ceremony called Twilight of the Spirits in which they sent away their spirits (*bukan*) and begged them never to return.[18] At the time, Chuonnasuan and Zhao Li Ben were two of the most respected and powerful shamans among the Oroqen. However, Zhao Li Ben (who was half Oroqen, half Han Chinese) had been converted to communist ideology, and he was largely responsible for forcing fellow villagers to attend these ceremonies. Communist party officials invited both these respected shamans to travel to several of the largest, most prosperous cities in

China to convince people of the futility of their "superstitions."[19] After these ceremonies, large numbers of Oroqen shamans were rounded up and imprisoned (possibly executed), especially those who did not participate.

Eventually, Chuonnasuan became the last fully initiated shaman of the Oroqen. In 1994, clinical psychologist Richard Noll and anthropologist Kun Shi received permission to visit Manchuria to study the spirituality of the Tungus peoples. By luck, they were able to meet Chuonnasuan, who agreed to be interviewed, photographed, and recorded as he spoke about his life as a shaman. This is perhaps the most important and insightful resource we have for understanding Oroqen shamanism. Here is some of what they learned.

Chuonnasuan (Chinese name Meng Jin Fu) was born in 1927 into a lineage that included his grandfather and paternal uncle, both of whom were powerful shamans. He was struck with his first bout of spirit sickness at sixteen after losing a younger brother and sister, which caused him to wander around the forest, often alone and in trance state. Shaman Wuliyen identified him as having shamanic spirits and performed a three-day healing ceremony, during which she introduced fifty of her spirits who wanted to work with him, singing fifty songs, each specific to a spirit. He learned the songs and dances for each spirit while in trance.[20]

At nineteen, Chuonnasuan fell ill a second time after the death of his first wife. As he was walking near the Huma River, he heard a thunderous noise, saw a brilliant flash, and lost consciousness. New spirits had entered him—spirits that Wuliyen's spirits could not accept. The spirits fought within him. His uncle, a powerful shaman named Minchisuan, performed a healing ceremony with many offerings (antelope, moose, duck, deer, and similar local creatures) that put an end to the conflict and introduced ten new spirits who could coexist with Wuliyen's. Minchisuan was said to be so powerful that he successfully cured two cases of tuberculosis and could even use a spirit to slaughter a pig. The most powerful of these new spirits was a two-headed eagle spirit (*sheki*) who greatly increased his powers.[21]

Chuonnasuan fell ill for a third and final time when he turned twenty, following the death of his shaman uncle. Many of his uncle's spirits descended upon him, and he was finally cured by Zhao Li Ben.[22] One year prior to this, Zhao Li Ben had fallen ill to spirit sickness and it was Chuonnasuan who performed the healing ceremony that initiated Zhao as a shaman. Zhao became an extremely powerful shaman who cured Chuonnasuan's final sickness. At the height of his powers, Chuonnasuan mastered more than ninety spirits.[23] He performed countless healing ceremonies, although only once did he have to conduct spirit flight to the Lower World to save a person's life.[24]

The information gathered by Noll and Shi places a notable importance on the role of shamans' assistants, known as *jardalanin* (second spirits). This role is critical across most North Asian shamanic traditions, yet is often glossed over and underappreciated (see chapter 4). Among the Tungus in particular, shamans are of little worth without strong assistants—as seen in the tale of the Nisan Shaman. When shamans are in trance possession, they generally are not able to communicate what is happening, let alone report new information given by the spirits. But assistants can read both shamans and their spirits, and act as interpreters. Sometimes shamans are only able to mutter information, which assistants then convey to the audience. But good assistants also understand shamans' chants, as well as the movements of the dance and the sounding of drums and the bells, and they can use these to determine how successful a healing is.

After shamans invite a spirit, their assistants may be able to determine that the spirit cannot, in fact, help and may suggest to the shaman another spirit who can help. When assistants see the arrival of a different spirit, they can announce it to both the shaman and the audience. Moreover, assistants are necessary to address the needs of both shamans and spirits during ceremonies—for instance, determining what offerings are required, and even preventing shamans from getting hurt or falling.

Many young shamans-in-training may serve as assistants to elders. Often, however, they are just spiritually talented and intelligent individuals who are not destined to become shamans. These individuals can be especially effective assistants, as they are capable of reading the spirits, but are not susceptible to falling into trance themselves. Chuonnasuan himself served as an assistant several times after his first illness.[25]

After the summer of 1952, Oroqen shamanism was officially banned by local communist officials. While many Oroqen were unwilling to give up their spirits and maintain belief in them to this day, shamans

Figure 14. Chuonnasuan (1927–2000), the last shaman of the Oroqen people, photographed in July 1994 in Manchuria near the Amur River, border between the People's Republic of China and Russian Siberia. Photo courtesy of Richard Noll.

were encouraged and even coerced into renouncing their practices and destroying their sacred tools, although some kept their tools hidden and continued to practice in secret. Guan Kouni, who was then only a seventeen-year-old shaman-in-training and serving as an assistant to elders, recalls that about 200 people attended the Twilight of the Spirits ceremony in her village, in which everyone begged the spirits to leave and never return. Her husband snatched the birch-bark box that contained her sacred items and threw it into the ritual fire. Her grandfather took her shaman's gown and hid it in the mountains, but she never discovered where.[26] Many journalists write that she is the last Oroqen shaman, but she herself claims that she is not, as she never completed her training.

After 1952, no Oroqen shamans openly performed ceremonies, although Chuonnasuan occasionally performed songs and dances for visiting researchers and interviewers, and sometimes fell into a light trance. He passed away on October 9, 2000. Today, there are no more shamans among the Oroqen, and Oroqen shamanism is officially extinct.

Amur River Tribes

Areas along the Amur River and its tributaries are home to a collection of tribes that include the Ulchi, the Nanai, the Udeghe, the Orochi, and the Negidal. These tribes are interspersed throughout both northern Manchuria (Heilongjiang province) and Russian Siberia (Khabarovsk, Primorsky, Amur Oblast, Zabaykalsk, and Sakhalin). Although each of these tribes maintains a separate identity, they interact and live so close to each other that many of their cultural practices (including shamanism) are quite similar. In fact, several of these tribes identify themselves as Nani, which means People of the Earth. For this reason, I group them together here as the Amur River tribes to examine their shamanic practices. Bear in mind, however, that this may result in some generalizations regarding their cultural identity and spiritual practices.

As the ancient Tungus likely originated from areas around the Amur River, the Amur tribes are likely descendants of those who did not migrate away from the region, although there is evidence that people from other areas moved in and mixed with them. In fact, it is extremely likely that several Mongolic peoples have settled with the Amur throughout history.[27] Prior to the Qing Dynasty, these tribes were collectively known as Wild Jurchens by the Chinese (see above). Due to strong influences from their Manchu cousins during the Qing Dynasty, however, they were heavily impacted by both the Manchu and Chinese cultures, although, unlike the Manchus, they were not as strongly influenced by the Mongols.

During the Qing Dynasty, many of these tribes identified themselves as Manchu bannermen, but this identity quickly faded in the early 20th century with the Qing's collapse. Amur River cultures often incorporated both Manchu and Chinese motifs, which included dragon and bird symbolism, equestrianism, silk and cotton fabrics (in addition to pelts and fish skin), iron-working, and heated homes. For both the Amur tribes and the Manchu, New Year celebrations and astrological calculations are more closely aligned with Chinese astrology, whereas Turkic and Mongolic calculations were more aligned with Tibetan astrology (see chapter 2).

The Amur also followed a Tengerist sky-centered spirituality and viewed the universe as consisting of three worlds (see chapter 2). The heavens (Upper World) are the realm of the great sky dragons who preside over everything on heaven and earth. The chief deity of this world is worshipped as either a great dragon known as *Ba*, *Ba Adja* (an honorific indicating Master), or *Enduri*, or as a pair of dragons known as *Ama* (Father) and *Unya* (Mother) *Enduri* (see chapter 3).[28]

The term *ba* is perhaps as confusing as the term *tenger*. At the broadest level, it can indicate everything within the three worlds, or it can indicate the Upper World or heavens. It can also be used to refer to the chief sky spirit, or to a specific spirit or group of spirits, or to elemental forces. Like tenger, *ba* can also refer to higher powers and to the universal life force or energy. Van Ysslestyne, who spent much of her life studying and living with the Ulchi, equates the term to the Chinese concepts of *Tao* and *chi*.[29]

The Amur refer to the Middle World, which is divided into the realms of land and water, as *Duentey*. The land is co-ruled by the tiger and bear spirits; the water is ruled by *Temu*, the master of the water spirits (see chapter 3).[30] Other Middle World spirits include water spirits, fire spirits, earth spirits, and the *kuljamu* (yeti) of the forested mountains. Although they generally agree on this cosmology, the exact details of it vary and even conflict among different tribes and even among individual shamans, primarily due to the unique perspectives that shamans gain from their spirit flights.

The Amur Lower World is known as *Buni*, although not much is known about it as it's taboo to discuss this realm, and shamans avoid traveling there unless necessary. What we do know is that the Lower World partially overlaps with the water territories of the Middle World and that, in the Amur worldview, the Lower World does not have a lord or master spirit. As Amur shamans tend not to interact much with each other for several reasons, these differing perspectives on the details of the spirit worlds are not reconciled for the most part.[31]

Figure 15. Nanai (Goldi) shaman and assistant in 1895, with thin-framed soft-handled drum and shamanic mirrors worn around the neck. Photo courtesy of William Henry Jackson.

Children of the Amur River tribes are taught how to drum and they learn sacred songs and dances. Therefore, all Amur River adults have some spiritual ability and can perform basic ceremonies for their families. In Amur cultures, anyone can become a "small shaman," meaning that they can develop their abilities sufficiently to perform some shamanic work, but only enough for themselves and their families (see chapter 4). Therefore, every family has at least one drum that is used for its spiritual needs and these drums are passed down from generation to generation.

Amur "big shamans," on the other hand, are selected by the spirits to perform deeper and more complex and difficult work, and are responsible for performing rituals and healing for the entire village or community. These big shamans (henceforth referred to simply as "shamans" here) are often born into shamanic families, as their spirits tend to choose shamans from the same bloodline. They usually possess multiple drums, each for a different purpose. When shamans pass away, their drums are usually kept by the family, but can only be used by future shamans from the same family.[32]

Unlike many other North Asian traditions, Amur shamans do not wear a single armored robe with attached implements as their main shamanic outfit. Instead, they wear multiple garments for ceremonies. Traditionally, they wear a vest and skirt specifically dedicated for shamanic work. The vest includes feathers sewn on the shoulders to allow their souls to fly. Both include designs and images relating to shamans' spirits and the three worlds. Their headgear may be made of cotton, leather, or metal, with fringes to cover their eyes, but often it is made completely from wooden streamers. These streamers (usually willow, rowan, or bird cherry) are worn around the head, arms, and legs, and act like spiritual antennas that allow shamans (and sometimes non-shamans) to contact and connect with spirits (see chapter 8). In ceremony, the spirits of the wood fly into the streamers to provide strength and protection to the respective parts of shamans' bodies. These streamers can also be used to cleanse patients and sometimes act as a net to catch, trap, or repel harmful spirits.[33]

One unique feature of the southern Tungus (both Manchu and Amur tribes) is a metal spirit belt known as a *yampa*. This contains large metal cones and bells, and sometimes also miniature talismans and tools made of metal and wood. When in ceremony, shamans swing their hips so that the belts create loud clanking noises to protect from and drive away harmful spirits. Like other North Asian traditions, the Amur make extensive use of bronze shamanic mirrors, as well as drums. Although Amur drums are usually round or egg-shaped, they are unique in that they have a thin frame (Turkic and Mongol wooden drums are usually thick-framed) and are made with flexible strap handles that allow both sides of the drum to be struck—hit by a beater on the outside and tapped or lightly punched by the hand holding the drum from the inside (see Figure 14 on page 155).

Luckily, the Amur region in Russian Siberia is remote enough that communism never forced the tribes there to give up their traditions. In fact, the tribes that live north of the Russian-Chinese border have preserved their traditions better than those who live south of the border, like the Oroqen. Nonetheless, modern development and Westernization have already started to place a strain on these traditions in Russian Siberia, especially since the 1990s. Although young people are still trained in their tribes' traditions, few want to be shamans and would much rather pursue economic opportunities outside their villages. As a result, many Amur shamanic lineages have not been passed on within the families. Luckily, however, the teachings of these traditions remain intact and are available for study by anyone interested within the tribe.

To learn more about the Ulchi tradition of shamanism, consult Van Ysslestyne's Pathfinder Counseling website as well as her book *Spirits from the Edge of the World*. To learn more about the Nanai tradition, consult Tatiana Bulgakova's *Nanai Shamanic Culture in Indigenous Discourse*.

Manchu Shamanism

The Manchu are the largest group of Tungus, yet little is known today of the role of shamanism played in Manchu (Qing) culture, due in no small part to the fact that very few Manchus still have knowledge of Manchu spirituality, let alone maintain traditional shamanic lineages. Moreover, most Manchus are now so impacted by Chinese influence that they are no longer culturally distinct from the Han Chinese. However, ancient pre-Qing Manchu (Jurchen) shamanism strongly resembles that of the Amur tribes, with heavy influences from the Khorchin Mongols.

While acknowledging belief in the three worlds, Manchu spirituality involves working with three types of spirits: gods and high deities (*enduri*), household and ancestral spirits (*weceku*), and animal nature spirits (see chapter 3). The high deities are Upper World spirits who sometimes include ancient master-gods of nature. In ancient Jurchen belief, the chief sky spirit was *Abka Hehe* (Sky Woman), who created *Banamu Hehe* (Earth Women) and *Ulden Hehe* (Light Woman).[34] However, in the Later Jin period, the Manchus no longer acknowledged Abka Hehe, but instead venerated a male lord of heaven known as *Abka Enduri*, *Abka Khan*, or *Abka Mafa*. The weceku include clan protector spirits, ancestral spirits, and elevated heroes (*manni*). The animal nature spirits are spirits who originate or appear in animal form; some may be ancestral spirits, some may be heavenly animals come down to earth, and some may be land spirits or gods who rule over specific animals.

These three spirit groups were honored and invoked in different ways. The enduri and some of the weceku (clan guardian spirits, house spirits, collective ancestors, and specific orthodox gods) were honored with offering rituals that didn't require trance. However, some of the other weceku—like grandfather and grandmother spirits (specific ancestors who were past shamans), manni spirits, and animal nature gods—were invoked through shamanic trance. Over time, these practices came to be classified as "domestic" or "wild" (see chapter 4).

Domestic rituals reflect the liturgical religious side of Manchu spirituality, which used elaborate, complex ceremonies that included prayers and offerings. These grandiose ceremonies honored heaven and other gods together and were conducted by shamans or by clan leaders. In the Qing Dynasty, domestic ceremonies for the nation (like the Imperial *tangse* ceremony) were co-performed by the emperor, the empress, and court officials ("clan" leaders), while individual clans conducted their own household weceku ceremonies. Prior to Jurchen unification, every tribe had its own *tangse*, or clan temple, that symbolized the clan's spiritual autonomy to its gods. After Nurhaci defeated the other Jurchen clans, he desecrated these temples, and clan leaders were forced to pay homage to Nurhaci's clan temple, although the clans were still allowed to perform weceku ceremonies in their own households.[35]

Wild rituals reflect the shamanic side of Manchu spirituality. In these, because of the nature of trance possession, each individual spirit must be called separately to possess the shaman. Although domestic ceremonies were conducted to gain blessings and luck, wild shamans were sought out to combat sickness, conduct spiritual warfare, and perform general sorcerous and magical workings. Moreover, wild shamans could use these practices to communicate directly with spirits and spirituality intervene directly in actions conducted in the physical world.[36]

Almost all North Asian shamanic practices have both domestic and wild elements that often blend and overlap each other. However, due to the institutionalization of Manchu spirituality at the beginning of the Qing dynasty, they were given separate classifications, and many anthropologists and researchers refer to both domestic and wild ceremonies together as Manchu shamanism. Even during the Qing Dynasty, those who performed domestic ceremonies were called shamans, regardless of whether or not they were able to perform trance. While domestic practices can be used in shamanic ceremonies, however, they do not fundamentally represent true shamanism. They are simply a system of liturgical religious practice. According to the original definition and usage of the word, only "wild" shamans are true shamans.

When Nurhaci established his Later Jin Empire, he employed both domestic and wild rituals. He often performed ceremonies before battles in which he called on heaven to imbue his troops with divine favor. He also performed ceremonies formally establishing his empire and validating important alliances. The *Old Manchu Chronicles* state that, on multiple occasions, signs and manifestations like divine fiery light appeared to signify heaven's approval of his endeavors.[37] Because these ceremonies invoked heaven, they were considered domestic. At the beginning of his campaign, Nurhaci also employed wild ceremonies to receive the divine right to rule from his clan's grandfather spirits and animal spirits (the magpie spirit was particularly important for his clan).

Thus shamanism was not only a spiritual practice; it was extremely political as well. According to Manchu researcher Stephen Garrett, shamanic authority was one of the core components of the Manchu ruler's legitimacy. Even after Jurchen unification, there was frequent tension between the Manchu tribes and princes, as well as among different Mongol and Turkic tribes living farther inland. Through conquest and subsequent shamanic ceremonies of alliance with defeated leaders, Nurhaci and his son, Hong Taiji, demonstrated through shared shamanic beliefs that their rule was endorsed by heaven. Even when individual leaders and tribes rebelled against the khan, this recognition of shamanic legitimacy held the various tribes and armies together, without which the empire would have fallen apart.[38]

Because shamanism became so political for the Manchus, however, Hong Taiji quickly realized that rebellious clans with wild shamans could receive blessings from spirits and could thus act as heavenly conduits to challenge his legitimacy. To solidify his own position as the sole supreme voice of heaven on earth, Hong Taiji declared wild rituals to be heterodox and illegal, and purged all wild shamans from the empire.[39] Many Manchu tribes and banner garrisons who had retained wild practices (although this happened more among commoners) were forced to give them up entirely or be executed for treason. This proclamation extended beyond the Manchus themselves and joined its destructive force to the violent spread of Buddhism among Mongol and Turkic subjects.

In essence, the Manchu leaders, who had established a shamanic empire, proceeded to ban shamanic practices and forced all Manchus to adhere to a non-shamanic Manchu religion that consisted of domestic ceremonies, thereby monopolizing the emperor as the sole voice of shamanic authority. In 1747, the Imperial family published *The Imperially Commissioned Manchu Rites for Sacrifices to the Spirits and to Heaven*, which dictated a standardized protocol for domestic ceremonies on both the Imperial and clan level. As the authority of the Qing weakened in the late 19th and early 20th centuries, however, wild rituals began to reappear among Manchu clans.[40] After the Boxer Rebellion (1899–1901), the Imperial tangse in Beijing was destroyed by foreign powers, and the

Imperial family performed tangse ceremonies in the Kunninggong palace only as a formality. The majority of indigenous Manchu spirituality today (nominal to begin with) is very fragmented, with some villages only practicing wild rituals, and other only practicing domestic rituals.

One of the last remaining Manchu clans that still fully adheres to traditional Manchu shamanic practice is the Shikteri clan in the Jiutai area of Jilin province. Remarkably, the Shikteri incorporate a hybridized practice containing both domestic and wild components, which they frequently implement in three-part ceremonies that last multiple days. The first part consists of sacrifices to domestic spirits, including household spirits and gods like Fodo Mama, Aodu Mama, and Grandfather Chaohazhan-ye (see chapter 3). This is performed indoors at the clan's tangse hall and altar by the clan leader and multiple domestic "shaman-priests," who sing and dance specific songs while beating tambourine drums, shaking their spirit belts, and conducting prayers and presenting offerings to the spirits. The worship of Fodo Mama revolves around a spirit rope that is used for both the first and third parts of the ceremony. The rope, tied with knots, ribbons, and anklebones that record births within the clan, is usually kept in a golden sack at the tangse altar.

In the second part of the ceremony, performed only at night, the clan's wild shaman goes into trance possession, calling the grandfather and grandmother spirits, animal spirits, and sometimes even manni spirits individually. The shaman also plays the tambourine drum and spirit belt, but, unlike domestic shamans, wears at least one copper or bronze mirror as well as a fringed headdress with bells and bird motifs that has multicolored cloth strips or scarves hanging down the back. This part of the ceremony takes the longest time, given the number of spirits invited. The grandfather and grandmother spirits are those of past shamans, and the Shikteri clan's animal spirits take the form of the jackal, wolf, tiger, leopard, eagle, python, snake (non-python), hawk, and otter. These spirits are given offerings that include boiled black pig, millet and red-bean pastries, and clear liquor (typically *baijiu*), among other items.

In the third and last part of the ceremony, domestic shaman-priests return and perform a final sacrifice to heaven. This takes place outside, where an altar with incense and a pig's head is set up. The Fodo Mama spirit rope connects the altar with a nearby spirit tree (typically a willow) or *somo* pole (spirit pole), joining heaven and earth. The pig's innards are tied or placed at the top of the spirit pole. Domestic shaman-priests pray to heaven and the spirits for health and prosperity, notably for the clan's children. If magpies or crows peck at the innards on the spirit pole, it signifies that the offerings were accepted. If the offerings are not accepted, the ceremony must be performed again on a later day, and a new spirit pole must be constructed.[41]

Figure 16. Manchu shaman's outfit and tools at the Manchu museum at Xiuyan Autonomous Manchu County. The iron-frame drum and skirt are inspired by Khorchin Mongol design, given the significant cross-cultural relationship. Spirit belt at the bottom. Photo courtesy of David Shi.

Tungusic Shamanism Today

Compared to their Turkic and Mongolic counterparts, Tungusic shamanic traditions are at the highest risk of extinction. This is not to say that they experienced greater damage or were attacked more than these other two groups, but rather that their rebirth and recovery have been the slowest—if not stagnant within the past several decades. As with the Evenk, the few remaining shamanic lineages have not necessarily been passed down through direct teaching and guidance, as elders have confidence that the spirits will teach young shaman students when appropriate. While some younger shamans have been trained in Evenki ways, some of them are also seeking nearby Buryat Mongol teachers to initiate and train them.

Based on my own observations, Evenki shamanism is not necessarily declining, but it is not growing much either. Among the Amur tribes, existing lineages are similarly not being passed down through apprenticeships as far as I know, but, given how much shamanic knowledge is ingrained in the daily lives of these tribes, information for potential new shamans is widely available. However, as multiple elder shamans were traditionally required to sing road-opening songs for new shamans in their initiation process, it is unclear how initiations may look for future generations of Amur shamans.

Although Manchus are the largest population of Tungusics, an extremely small number of them still retain their Manchu cultural identity, let alone their shamanic practices. Even among Manchus, there is bitter disagreement as to how much they want to adhere to modern Chinese culture versus retaining the old Manchu ways. Although there is not yet rising interest in Manchu shamanism (beyond learning performance dances), there has been a growing interest in their general cultural heritage among Manchus across North China in recent decades. Nonetheless, Manchu shamanism remains a stagnant practice, still found in a handful of clan villages, but passed down only through village descendants and not expanding to other clans.

Ironically, Manchu shamanism can perhaps be seen as having been inherited by several Chinese villages in Manchuria. After the mass migration of the Han Chinese into Manchuria in the late 19th and early 20th centuries, they intermarried with many of the Manchus. As a result, shamanic spirit lineages have been passed down into families that are Han Chinese in identity. These Chinese families now perform a light version of wild ritual known as *TiaoDaShen* or *ChuMaXian*, which incorporates components of traditional Manchu wild practice. But these "shamans" rarely wear shamanic implements and often incorporate Chinese Taoist motifs. In these cases, assistants (who drum and call the spirit into the shaman) may incorporate yin-yang and trigram designs on their drums, although their drumsticks still have multicolored ribbons attached in the Manchu style. These Chinese shamans work almost exclusively with animal spirits whom they claim are ancestral spirits tied to the village land. They do not work with Manchu ancestral spirits, perhaps because these spirits are unwilling to work in a different or Chinese way.

Due to their lack of formal rituals, TiaoDaShen is like Mongolian city shamanism in that it relies only on direct communications from spirits (see chapter 6). Although this type of Chinese shamanism in Manchuria can be considered a remnant of Manchu shamanism, it is different enough that it cannot be considered true Manchu shamanism. In fact, it has syncretized to Taoism so much that the Chinese in Manchuria believe the animal gods of the Middle World help connect people to Upper World Taoist gods and underworld ancestral gods.

The overwhelming reality among these traditions is that young people do not necessarily want to study shamanism and would rather move to larger cities and pursue Western education and economic opportunities. This was especially the case in the 1980s and 1990s. In recent decades, as people have become more comfortable economically, there has been a growing awareness of and desire to learn about their ethnic heritage. In addition to increased conversations with grandparents and other elders, Manchu and Tungusic language classes are appearing in more schools and universities, which hopefully may help their critically endangered status.

It may take some time before this growing interest extends to shamanism, but hopefully it will be preserved long enough for these traditions to experience true revival. Despite their slow growth, it is at least true that these practices are not being actively persecuted anymore and, with time, may be passed on to future generations to be preserved and to thrive as ongoing living traditions.

CHAPTER 8

Shamanic Tools

Many believe that, in order to be powerful, shamans must be enlightened and spiritually detached from the material world, but this could not be further from the truth. Spiritual enlightenment has never been the purpose of shamanism, as it is in Buddhism or Western mysticism. The purpose of shamanism, in its original North Asian sense, is to act as a bridge and connection between the physical and spiritual worlds. In other words, shamans must maintain one foot in the spiritual and one foot in the material, and treat both spiritual and material needs. Moreover, shamans do not become shamans by choice or through study. They are chosen and forced by spirits to take on that role.

Because of this, shamans employ many sacred and ritual tools. While these vary across traditions, many are similar and are used in similar ways. Shamans employ so many tools, in fact, that even traditional shamans joke that shamanism is a materialist path that involves collecting implements, items, herbs, and ingredients. Tools are so integral to shamanic practice that some, like shamanic regalia and armor, are even required for shamans to practice safely.

Shamanic Regalia and Armor

Almost every shamanic tradition employs regalia or armor of some sort as a necessary means to ensure shamans' protection while in ceremony.

While these shamanic garments vary across tribes, many of them share common characteristics.

Most Turkic and Mongol shamanic regalia consists of three parts: a coat, a headdress, and boots. Underneath the coat, a traditional robe is typically worn. The Tungusic Evenk and Oroqen, and the Mongolic Daur also use a coat, a headdress, and boots, although they are very different in style. Buryat shamans don't necessarily wear coats, but don very elaborate caps with streamers, scarves, and snake bundles hanging down the back and sides, although some (typically advanced elders) have adopted a coat as well. In ancient times, Manchus and Khorchin Mongols wore shamans' coats, but in modern times this has been simplified to a skirt accompanied by a spirit belt, a cap or crown, and possibly a vest or apron. The Amur wear a coat, boots, and spirit belts, and use many different types of headwear, depending on the work being done (see chapters 5, 6, and 7).

Shaman Coats

Shamans' coats are their main source of protection. In most cases, their main implements consist of streamers (or "snakes"), jingle cones, and bells. Among the Darkhad and the Dukha (and most likely the ancient Mongols), they feature a set of horizontal backplates on the back that have large jingle cones and tether bells attached across them. According to Purev:

[these] consist of three types [of bells], the [flat] plate, the shooter [pointed jingle cone], and the bell [round jingle cone] . . . [I]t is evident that the main purpose of the tether-bell was to protect the shaman from external damage or danger.[1]

Given their location, these plates are likely meant to protect shamans' backs.

The coats of these northern traditions also feature bundles of streamers or "snakes" sewn along the middle or top of the coats that hang down to the ground. These serve the dual purpose of drawing in land spirits and providing protection via the land spirits. Jingle cones and smaller snake bundles are sometimes attached along the joints and all over the coats. Central Asian and Tuvan shaman coats use jingle cones and streamers as well, but they're typically more spread out over the coats rather than bundled together. The armpit seams of these coats are often left open (unsewn) so that shamanic spirits can easily pass through to the shamans. As Darkhad and Dukha shamans conduct their ceremonies, their clients tie prayer scarves onto their coats that carry prayers and blessings, and, as shamans become more advanced, their coats become heavier with them.

Southern Evenki, Oroqen, and Daur coats are distinguished by an attached vest that's covered with cowrie shells. Around the midsection of these coats hang many small or medium-size bronze mirrors, while the bottom is adorned with rows of large tiger bells (although Chuonnasuan's coat featured jingle cones). Covering almost the entire back of these coats are one or several very large bronze mirrors (rather than jingle cones or bell plates) that are also meant to protect the shamans' backs. These coats aren't covered with the snake bundles seen on other Mongol and Turkic coats, but they do feature wide embroidered fabric streamers or an additional skirt made of fabric streamers that are meant to draw in land spirits. These are often intricately decorated to indicate areas where the land spirits may reside.

While most shamanic coats are made from fabric, the Yakuts and northern Evenks wear coats that are made entirely of leather and animal skins and are heavily decorated with metal tools and implements to reflect their blacksmith heritage—not just jingle cones, but also metal items that represent human and/or animal bones. The backs of these coats, which can often weigh thirty-five to forty pounds, also feature a plate and more metal implements than on the front in order to protect the shamans' backs. Rather than bundles, and long streamers that are attached to the coats, the bottoms of the coats are made into long fringes that may start as high as the waist.[2]

Amur shaman coats don't use quite as many metallic implements, but do have small bronze mirrors sewn on both the front and the back to protect shamans. These coats are distinctive for the large feathers that are sewn on their shoulders (instead of on the headdress) that indicate the shamans' ability to fly. Although these coats are not adorned with as many other objects, they are heavily embroidered with representations of each of the shaman's spirits. Upper World spirit helpers are embroidered at the top; Middle World spirits decorate the middle; Lower World spirits are shown at the bottom. Sometimes a spirit may require that it be represented by a metal amulet instead, and these are made into metal plates and sewn onto the coat. These coats almost always feature depictions of the World Tree and dragons.[3]

Figure 17. The back side of a shaman coat, worn by the Ulchi shaman Grandma Nadia Duvan (1950–2016).

Shaman Boots

Most shamanic cultures include boots that are dedicated for shamanic practice as part of their regalia and armor. According to Purev:

Darhad shamans considered their boots to be the legs of a spirit. The reindeer herder shamans believed that their boots were the hind legs of a doe, which was depicted on their drum

> ... the figure depicted on the drum was a late shaman's spirit, while the boots symbolized its two legs. A pair of boots preserved in the Museum of History [in Ulaanbaatar] belonging to a Darhad shaman had thick and soft soles and the uppers were made from reindeer skin.[4]

Jingle cones and small snake bundles are attached for protection as well.

Buryats sometimes use skin or leather boots, but may also use traditional boots that are dedicated to shamanic purposes. Sarangerel notes that each boot may be made with different patterns to signify that shamans have feet in both the spiritual and material worlds.[5] Among the Tungus, these boots are made of elk, leather, or even sealskin (Amur tribes) and are decorated with spirit motifs. The spirits represented on the boots are meant to provide strength, protection, and endurance to shamans' legs while in ceremony. Today, with the rising New Age influence, shamans wear boots less frequently and may wear modern footwear like sneakers.

Shaman Headdresses and Caps

Headdresses and caps are found in almost all North Asian shamanic traditions. Since the head is the body part closest to the Upper World, it is very important that it be protected. In most Mongolic and Turkic traditions, these headdresses consist of a large strap that goes around the head, with feathers attached to the top, a face stitched into the front, and fringes that cover the eyes. They are left "open" at the top to allow the spirits to come in through the crown of the head. The feathers are meant to help shamans fly in the spirit world; sometimes these are tail feathers to help them steer. The face stitched into the front serves two purposes: to represent the faces of spirits when they possesses shamans, and to help protect shamans when they are in the spirit world. As shamans' faces are hidden by the fringes, both the headdress and the coat are meant to disguise them so they can appear as spirits or ghosts and avoid unwanted attention in the spirit world.[6]

By contrast, Buryat Mongols and almost all Tungusics wear caps that fully cover the top of the head, usually with a fringe that covers the face or only the eyes. Buryats call the cap *maykhabsha*. Although the maykhabsha does not display a stitched face, it has eyes stitched on that fulfill the same purpose. It also features five long streamers that hang down the back and sides, each containing the five elemental colors and each with tiger bells attached. Among modern Buryats, black shamans wear a cap that is black on top, while white shamans wear a cap that is blue on top. Evenk, Oroqen, and Manchu caps also have fringes that cover the face or the eyes, and may have additional cloth streamers down the back. These are primarily worn to cover and protect the head, and to provide support for shamans who also wear a crown. Khorchin Mongol caps don't have fringes, as these are typically attached to the crown. However, as crowns are becoming increasingly rare (due to government confiscation and difficulty in replacing them and making new ones), Khorchin shamans are increasingly wearing just caps without a fringe.

Figure 18. Buryat maykhabsha cap from Mongolia, refitted by Nicholas Breeze Wood. Photo courtesy of Nicholas Breeze Wood.

Shaman Crowns

Crowns are worn by Buryat, Khorchin, and Daur Mongols, as well as by Yakuts, Evenks, Oroqens, and Manchus. Most of these crowns depict either antlers (especially groups living in the Siberian taiga) or birds. The Evenk, Oroqen, and Buryats tend to use iron crowns, as iron is one of the most protective metals, although some crowns are also made with reindeer antlers. Among Buryats, only advanced shamans who have achieved the seventh degree of initiation can wear antler crowns, which are known as *orgay*.[7] Among all these peoples, antler crowns are tied with streamers, prayer scarves, and snake bundles (Buryats), which are usually accumulated through experience in successful ceremonies, like the prayer scarves tied to Darkhad shaman coats (see above). The Daur use antler crowns as well, but they can be made of iron, copper, or bronze.

Khorchin Mongols and Manchus use copper or bronze crowns decorated with bird motifs. Khorchin crowns resemble those of Buddhist monks, but are topped by three copper birds and copper branches (signifying the World Tree), as well as copper bells. Multi-colored prayer scarves hang off the backs of these crowns. Manchu crowns usually don't incorporate the Buddhist crown design, but instead consist of a copper crosspiece that is topped with three copper birds and bells. The base of these crowns is decorated with small bronze mirrors on the front and sides, as well as multicolored banners that hang from the top to symbolize clan designations.[8]

While almost all wear skullcaps underneath their crowns, Yakuts sometimes wear just a fabric-lined crown directly against the head. These crowns appear to incorporate both iron and copper, and use rather minimalist designs that don't include antlers or birds. The fabric lining sometimes has fringes attached.

Shaman Skirts

Shamanic skirts are mostly used within cultures that do not use coats. Modern Manchu shamanic regalia consists of only a skirt, a spirit

Figure 19. Iron orgay crown forged by Nicholas Breeze Wood, in the style and form of those worn by Daur Mongols. Photo courtesy of Nicholas Breeze Wood.

belt, a headdress cap with copper crown, and mirrors, although many believe that Manchus may have used coats prior to the Qing Dynasty. Manchu skirts are usually brightly colored with blue, red, yellow, or even pink, depending on the type of spirit involved.

Similarly, modern Khorchins no longer use coats, but instead wear a skirt, a spirit belt, mirrors, and a cap with a copper crown. Khorchin skirts are distinctive in that they consist of wide, layered, multicolored streamers—recall the folk legend that tells of an ancient battle between a shaman and a Buddhist monk in which the shaman's skirt was ripped to shreds.[9] As the streamers are used to draw in land spirits—a core Mongol belief has ancestral spirits riding land spirits to enter the shaman—this may be an allegory of Khorchin shamanism adopting Buddhist views of serpentine *nagas* as land-spirit representations. Although Daur shamans do use coats, they also incorporate a multicolored streamer skirt that is usually worn over the coat, covering the back and sides.

Shaman Vests and Aprons

In many cultures where shamans don't use coats, they may use aprons or vests. Among Mongols (notably Buryats), aprons, known as *dudig,* usually cover both the front and back. They almost always contain metal implements similar to those used on coats, which are meant to protect the wearer. Among Amur tribes, some shamans wear vests instead of coats, but these serve nearly the same purpose and differ only in the shape of the garments. They generally contain similar metallic implements and spirit designs.

Manchu shamans sometimes wear vests over traditional clothing, but today these are usually just decorative, although they resemble the cape-like vests that ancient Manchus (and Qing Dynasty officials) used to wear. They may also have been decorated with spirit symbols, as were Amur vests.

Figure 20. Yampa spirit belt of the Kusayli clan, who live in Bulava Ulchi village. The Kusayli clan traces its roots up through the Amur River to the Kurile Islands and Sakhalin.

Spirit Belts

Spirit belts are worn primarily by the southern Tungusic peoples (Manchu and Amur tribes) and Khorchin Mongols. They are worn for protection, particularly against attacks from behind. Manchu and Amur belts consist of very large iron jingle cones (around eight to ten inches on average), bells, and metallic tools that hang off the back and sides. Shamans shake their hips while drumming so that the belts create loud clanging noises.[10]

Khorchin spirit belts usually consist of a set of copper mirrors that also hang off the back and sides. While Khorchin shamans don't shake their hips as much as the Tungus, the mirrors still create loud sounds as they hit each other (see Figure 21).[11] These spirit belts likely perform a function similar to the backplate jingle cones found on Turkic and Darkhad Mongol shaman coats.

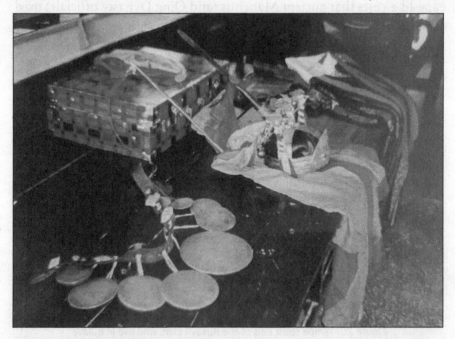

Figure 21. Korchin shaman Wang Serenchin's mirror spirit belt, bronze crown, and other tools. Photo courtesy of Marguerite Garner.

Shaman Capes

Although not many North Asian cultures use capes as part of their shamanic regalia, they are a notable feature of Buryat white shamans. While advanced Buryat black shamans receive antler crowns, the white shamans do not. Instead, advanced white shamans receive a cape that contains many multicolored brocade strips hung with bells that they wear along with their shaman caps. Like spirit belts and backplates, these capes also protect the shamans, while the strips draw in land spirits.[12]

Shamanic Tools

Shamanic tools and implements are remarkably consistent across all North Asian shamanic cultures, although there are some significant differences. The list I give here, although not complete, includes the most important of these tools.

Drums

Drums are used by almost every North Asian shamanic tradition, with the exception of several Central Asian reconstructed traditions. These specially crafted drums are considered to be enlivened objects that contain their own spirits. Drums are used primarily to induce trance while simultaneously calling shamans' spirits. Sometimes drums are used to store and transfer energy, and also to bless or cleanse attendants.

During soul retrievals, shamans can store souls in their drums, mirrors, or other objects.[13] When they conduct spirit flight, their drums often become mounts that they ride into the spirit world—usually in the form of the animal whose skin was used to make them. In many cultures that live in or near the Siberian taiga forest, these drums are made of reindeer or elk skin. Cultures that live away from the taiga (or don't have reindeer or elk) typically use goatskin. Traditionally, however, only the skins of specific animals are deemed appropriate for use in making shamanic drums.

Although almost all shamanic cultures use drums, each has very detailed specifications for how these drums should look and how they're supposed to be made. Because these drums are living objects endowed with spirits, some traditions require that they be pierced after a shaman dies to release the spirit(s) that reside in them and to prevent them from being used by other shamans, which could create problems of spirit incompatibility. In other traditions, these drums are sometimes kept within the family and passed down to the next generation of family shamans.

Drums are among the most important, powerful, and flexible of all shamanic tools. When shamans conduct spirit flight (or attract unwanted spirits during possession), their drums act as natural shields against attack. They can also act as weapons. In many Mongol cultures, the inside handle of the drum is designed in the shape of a bow and arrow that can be used to attack hostile entities. In Tuvan and Central Asian Turkic traditions, the drum's handle is a figure that represents the spirit that dwells in the drum. Khorchin Mongols use drums with a thin iron frame that enhances their protective abilities. Tungus tribes historically use thin drums with a flexible cross-handle that allows them to be tapped from the inside in addition to being struck by drumsticks on the outside. This enables greater variations of beat and melody that allow shamans to perform a wide variety of spiritual actions.[14] Today, only the Amur still use this type of drum.

Modern Manchu drums use a thinner skin (with a thin drum paddle) that allows for beats to be played very fast, highlighting the shaman's frenzied power. In almost all North Asian cultures, drums feature jingle cones, bells, and/or Chinese copper coins on the inside that jingle loudly when the drum is struck, essentially acting as a rattle.

Drumsticks

Among North Asian cultures, drumsticks (or drum paddles) are not simply components of shamanic drums; they are enlivened objects that contain a separate soul that works with the drum's soul to perform shamanic magical work.[15] In most North Asian cultures, the flat striking side of the drumsticks is lined with fur or soft leather. In Turkic and Mongolic traditions, the backs of the drumsticks feature metal rings that jingle against each other as the drum is struck, also serving as a rattle.[16]

Today, only Manchu drumsticks lack a fur lining, consisting instead of a thin flexible wood strip that bounces and raps against the drumhead, producing a bright, fast-paced sound. These drumsticks somewhat resemble the bamboo *yeolchae* sticks used on Korean *janggu* drums, which are used for both musical and spiritual purposes.

Shamanic drumsticks often have multicolored streamers or snake bundles attached to their handle end. In many cases, the sticks may be carved with scales or depictions of snakes or dragons, highlighting their connections with land spirits. When in trance, shamans sometimes use their drumsticks to cleanse, striking them on various parts of the body to drive away pollution or unfriendly spirits. Drumsticks are also used as divination tools, with shamans tossing them and observing how they land to determine the efficacy of their ceremonies.

Jaw Harps

Almost all North Asian cultures use the jaw harp as a musical instrument. Only Mongol groups frequently use it as a shamanic tool, although Dukha and Tuvan shamans have been known to use it as well. In Mongolia, use of the jaw harp evolved as a way for shamans to practice discreetly (see chapter 6). Although most anecdotes regard the jaw harp as a tool used during the communist period, this practice may have existed during Manchu rule as well.

Among Darkhad Mongols, jaw harps are used for "walking shamanism," shamanic practices performed during the day in traditional clothing (see chapter 6). Drums and armor are used for nighttime and/or more dangerous ceremonies. Jaw harps are now so ingrained in Darkhad shamanic practice that some ceremonies can only be performed using them.

Jaw harps, like drums, are considered to be enlivened objects with their own souls. They are used to induce trance states while calling spirits, and as vehicles for shamanic travel to the spirit world. Like drumsticks, they can also be used for divination by tossing them and observing how they land.[17]

Bundles

In most cases, jaw harps are attached to larger bundles of snakes, miniature tools, and spirit representations that contain everything shamans need for walking shamanism ceremonies. In Mongolia, these bundles are known as *manjig*. When a jaw harp is attached, they are known as *khuur* (harp) *manjig*. Bronze mirrors may be attached to these bundles as well, especially in the case of Darkhad Mongols, who don't wear mirrors around their necks as Buryats do, but attach them instead to their bundles.

Even when shamans are performing with drums in full armor and regalia, bundles are draped over their shoulders, with jaw harp and mirror in front and snakes falling down the back. Bundles can be used for both blessing and cleansing, and prayers spoken into the snakes as they are pressed against the forehead can yield a direct connection to land spirits.[18]

Mirrors

While drums are now common in global animistic traditions, mirrors remain the most unique feature of North Asian shamanic practice. These mirrors are almost always made of copper or bronze, but may contain other metals when forged for specific purposes. On occasion, a silver mirror may be used in addition.

Shamanic mirrors have a loop welded onto the back so that a string, ribbon, or thin scarf can pass through, allowing them to be worn or attached to other objects. One side of these mirrors is reflective, while the other side may be adorned with designs like the zodiac wheel, Chinese characters (typically "Four Happinesses"), or other images (see Figure 22 on page 184). The reflective side often becomes cloudy through oxidation, and patina, but, spiritually speaking, this cloudiness develops in ways specific to each shaman and can aid in visualization and scrying. Mirrors are referred to as *toli* in almost all North Asian cultures.

Sarangerel referred to the mirror as a shaman's Swiss army knife. At their most basic level, they protect against spiritual attacks by reflecting them back. They are also commonly used as divination tools and for scrying. Shamans may gaze into them looking for images or messages from spirits while in trance to identify issues, to read fortunes, or to receive any messages the spirits may wish to impart. They may look directly into them after stating a client's name and astrological information, or they may look at the client's reflection in the mirror.

Like their drums, shamans' mirrors are also enlivened objects endowed with spirit. They can serve as containers used to absorb and accumulate energy, acting as spiritual "batteries." Shamans can use them to transfer energy and blessings onto clients or tap into the energy for more complicated workings. They can also use them to draw spiritual pollution out of clients, or to store soul parts and return them to clients when conducting soul retrievals. When engaging with hostile spirits, they can lure and trap them in their mirrors. In cases in which mirrors have extracted pollution or hostile spirits, they must be cleansed, or the trapped entities can create problems for the shaman.[19] Once, after I cleansed a house that a friend of mine had just moved into, my Mongolian shaman friend noticed that one of my mirrors had developed a human-shaped smudge. The mirror had captured a ghost that was residing in the house. I was able to clear the ghost by cleaning the mirror every day for a week with cleansing spirit water and vodka.

According to many North Asian legends, the leaves of the World Tree are made of mirrors. According to the Amur Nanai, in ancient times, great spirits (like fish spirits) sometimes plucked these mirrors from the World Tree and gave them to great shamans.[20] In some stories, the most powerful ancient shamans were able to call to the World Tree, causing its leaves to fall and descend from heaven to become their mirrors. If this is true, the technique is long lost, although many unbroken shamanic lineages, like the Darkhads and the Amur, still retain ancient methods of crafting these mirrors—methods that, of course, require the skills of blacksmith-shamans or spiritual blacksmiths (like Yakuts) who know the techniques and materials needed to forge them properly.

North Asian tribes all differ in how they handle old or used mirrors. Some groups, like the Evenk, Oroqen, and Daur, like to keep old mirrors of past shamans and pass them down the family generations, believing that they have accumulated great power from their connection with ancestral spirits. Other groups, like the Darkhads and Tuvans, completely abstain from using old mirrors, believing that the spirits in them (even of shamans within the bloodline) may be incompatible with the spirits of new users and may create problems. They believe that old mirrors must be interred in the spirit houses of dead shamans, and that new mirrors must be made for new shamans. Both groups agree that it is a bad idea to use old mirrors from outside the bloodline, as there is a high probability that the spirits will be incompatible and may work against new users.

This was true of my earliest mirror—a beautiful bronze mirror from Inner Mongolia with the zodiac and Chinese trigrams on the back. It had been polished to a shiny gleam and sold as a new mirror. My Darkhad Mongol shaman friends immediately realized that the mirror had previously been used by another shaman. Unfortunately, it had been blocking me from my own ancestral spirits and delaying and obscuring my shamanic path. I wrapped that mirror in a black prayer scarf, hid it away, and have never touched it since.

Figure 22. Unused Mongol shamanic mirror, with engraved reverse side. Photo courtesy of David Shi.

Staffs

Staffs were once a common tool among most North Asian shamanic tribes, although today, they have largely been replaced by drums to induce trance and only a few tribes use them. In ancient times, staffs were at least as common as drums, with shamans inducing trance by repeatedly striking them on the ground. This action was used to both call the shamanic spirits and summon land spirits so that all would be present within the staff. Because staffs allowed for deeper connections to land spirits than drums, they were used only by shamans who were fortified by land spirits (see chapter 4). The heads of the staffs varied by tradition and lineage, but they generally all featured jingle cones, miniature tools, and ribbons or streamers attached along them. The bottom was usually flat, but occasionally took the shape of a foot or paw.

Buryat Mongols have retained the use of staffs, their black shamans typically holding a staff known as a *horbo* in each hand that is carved with a horse's head. They beat both staffs, which only come in pairs, on the ground and use them for spirit flight when they need to ride them into the spirit world.[21] Buryat white shamans use a single wooden dragon-head staff, which is an homage to the Buddhist deity *Tsagaan Obgon* (White Old Man) who carries a similar staff.

Daur Mongols in Inner Mongolia also use two horse-head staffs. Although no Darkhad staff shamans have been born since the early 1900s, local museums still retain the staffs of the last Darkhad staff shamans. Staffs were sometimes three-pronged or depicted the head of a snake at the top to represent the *lus* spirits. Staff shamans were noted to be more powerful than drum shamans. Some Amur shamans used staffs that carried the image of their spirit's head carved at the top. Khorchin Mongols and pre-Qing Manchus used bell staffs made from tamarisk, generally for healing.[22]

Jingle Cones and Bells

Jingle cones and bells are used in all North Asian shamanic traditions. While their jingling sound helps induce trance, they are primarily used for protection. Jingle cones can be small when attached to a drum, or large when hung from a spirit belt. They are primarily made of iron because of its strong protective nature, although copper cones are sometimes used as well.

Tiger bells are the most common form of bell. These are typically round and hollow with a small stone or metal piece that rings against the bell body when shaken. As the name implies, they are typically inscribed with a stylized tiger or frog face on both sides. Tiger bells are used like jingle cones as protection amulets that can be sewn onto objects or worn on the body (for instance, around the neck or ankles) or even on animals. Originally made of copper or bronze, most tiger bells today are mass-produced using brass.[23] Traditionally, jingle cones and bells were made by spiritual blacksmiths, although sometimes they were purchased and then empowered for use.

As far as I know, Buryat white shamans are the only shamans who primarily use bells to induce trance instead of drums or jaw harps. They use Buddhist-style cup-shaped bells, ringing them to induce trance and summon their spirits. Today, it is not uncommon to see a Buryat white shaman using a drum, but, traditionally, only Buryat black shamans used drums. White shamans typically used only a bell in one hand and a dragon staff in the other.

Wood Streamers

Wood streamers are used primarily by the Amur River tribes, who refer to them as either *gemsacha* or *sisakun*. They are commonly made of willow, rowan, or bird cherry, and are fashioned into caps and headdresses, arm and leg bands, and belts worn during ceremonies. When used by shamans, the spirits that reside in the wood or tree (land spirits) help them by providing strength, protection, and connection with other spirits. Van Ysslestyne refers to them as spiritual antennae, as they can be used by shamans and clients who wish to connect with ancestral spirits and great spirits or deities of the forest, water, heaven, etc.

These streamers can also act as nets to catch or repel harmful entities, who can get tangled up in them and confused. Shamans also use them to cleanse and heal clients, as they can trap and remove pollution and illness.[24] Very similar forms of streamers are used by the Nivikhs and the Oroks of Sakhalin (nearly identical practices to the Amur tribes, as the Nivikh live in both areas), as well as by the Ainu of Hokkaido, who refer to the streamers as *inau*. As Amur tribes frequently sailed between their rivers as well as Sakhalin and Hokkaido, this is likely a shared shamanic practice. The Shinto practice of using paper streamers (*shide* or *onusa*) is likely related to these Amur/Sakhalin wood streamers.

Figure 23. Ulchi shaman Grandmother Indkyeka Djaksul (1911–2007) wearing a headdress of wood streamers while performing for clients who traveled to her home. Photo courtesy of Pathfinder Counseling.

Swords, Knives, and Implements

Most North Asian shamanic traditions use only miniaturized weapons and other implements like blacksmith tools, ladders, boats, and others. These hang on the coat or on another tool and are used primarily when shamans are in the spirit world. These miniature weapons, which become larger in the spirit world, help shamans fight hostile spirits, while the other miniature tools help them overcome "physical" obstacles they encounter there.[25]

Very few traditions used actual full-size weapons. The Manchus perhaps used them the most. In addition to using weapons for protection and defeating hostile spirits, Manchus sometimes used them as divination tools. For example, sometimes a knife (*hama*) with loops was hung by shamans at night; if the loops jingled or made certain signs, it was seen as an omen.[26] The jingle patterns made by the loops could also be used to divine meaning while in trance. When in trance, shamans whose spirits were warrior spirits sometimes danced wielding full-size weapons to cleanse and purify the space, similar to those in both Korean shamanism (warrior-general spirits) and Himalayan shamanism (wrathful Buddhist spirits). Buryat shamanism sometimes employs full-size weapons as well, although this may be due to Tibetan/Himalayan tantric influence.

Whips

Turkic and Mongolic traditions use whips as shamanic tools. The "soft" whip is typically a bundle of streamers made of long thin rolls of sheep's wool wrapped in cloth (snakes) tied into a handle, or a bundle of horsetail hair tied together. The "hard" whip is known as a *bardag*, which resembles a Mongolian riding crop—the closest North Asian shamanism comes to using a wand. The bardag consists of three parts: a handle made of deer antler, a body made of red wood (usually tamarisk), and an end that consists of a metal arrowhead. Multiple clusters of metallic ornaments hang from the bardag body—including jingle cones, bells, and miniature tools and weapons.[27]

When shamans are possessed by their spirits, they use the whip to both bless and cleanse. When using a "soft" whip, the bundle of streamers invokes land spirits and can be used for both blessing and cleansing. White horsehair whips are used only for blessing; black horsehair whips are used only for cleansing.

"Hard" whips can be used for both functions and thus allow for more flexibility. They are used for different types of healing or for battling harmful spirits, depending on the different tools attached to them. Shamans typically use "hard" whips to tap clients' heads or strike their backs, but may occasionally use them on other areas of the body where pollution is present.

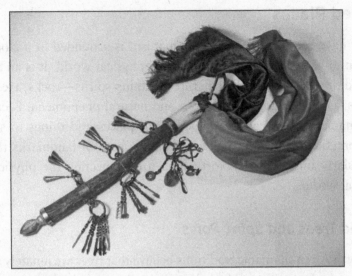

Figure 24. Mongolian bardag whip made for Nicholas Breeze Wood by a blacksmith shaman in Ulaanbaatar City and linked to a mountain spirit from one of the mountains outside the city. Photo courtesy of Nicholas Breeze Wood.

Offering Spoons

Offering spoons are not specifically shamanic tools, but are worth mentioning here because of their importance in North Asian spirituality. Throughout North Asia, offerings almost always consist of liquids—milk, or tea, or some clear liquor. While sometimes an entire bowl (either large or small) may be poured or thrown as an offering, often a special spoon is used to sprinkle or throw the liquid.

Mongolian offering spoons are distinct in that they are generally flat wooden spoons with nine small holes—nine (3 times 3) being a sacred number because of its reference to the three worlds (see chapter

2). Because of these nine small holes, each throw is akin to making an offering nine times. Other traditions use metallic spoons or even a wooden spoon with just a single large hole in it. Whichever type of spoon is used, however, it is almost always reserved only for offerings and spiritual use, as are the bowls that hold the offerings.

Sacred Places

As we have seen, North Asian shamanism is grounded in a close connection to both the spirit world and the physical world. It is an animistic tradition in which all of nature contains spirits—rocks, trees, and objects, as well as animals, people, and natural phenomena. Because of this, shamans often call on the spirits of places and things to support their practices. I give you a few examples here of landmarks that are particularly important in North Asia for connecting the physical and spiritual worlds.

Sacred Trees and Spirit Poles

All North Asian shamanic traditions believe that trees are innately sacred, as they are the property of land spirits and cannot be harmed without good reason. There are certain trees, however—sometimes known as "shaman trees" or "spirit trees"—that are especially sacred, as they either host a land spirit(s) or act as a strong connection point between people and spirits. Van Ysslestyne refers to these sacred trees as the "telephone" to the spirit worlds.[28] Mongols sometimes affectionately refer to them as "mother trees."

These sacred trees are not identified arbitrarily. They typically stand out in some way that makes them different from the other trees around them. They may have been struck by lightning yet still survive. They may tend to grow in very distinct and odd shapes. Many shaman trees in Mongolia grow in an umbrella or mushroom shape unlike any other trees around them. They may be remarkably tall or extremely strong. Some groups recognize only specific species of trees as shaman trees—typically pine, larch, or birch—and mark them by tying prayer scarves and cloth ribbons to them. Some marked trees belong to specific tribes or families and use them as sacred places in which to conduct ceremonies, pray, and leave offerings.[29]

The Tungusic peoples traditionally have designated spirit trees for each family or bloodline, often trees that grow a fair distance away from the family so they won't cause too much spiritual interference in their daily lives. When Russian settlers moved into Siberia, however, they indiscriminately chopped down these trees—even those marked as sacred—often leading to conflict between Russian settlers and native inhabitants, notably the Evenk and Amur tribes. As a result, many (notably the Amur) moved their households closer to their sacred trees, often fencing them within the household area.[30] Some Manchu families also moved their households nearer to their sacred trees so that Chinese settlers moving into Manchuria wouldn't chop them down.

During the Later Jin and Qing Dynasties, many Manchus stationed across the empire could no longer easily access their sacred trees for spiritual ceremonies. As a result, many (domestic) shamans erected spirit poles, known in Manchu as *somo/solon* poles, harvesting wood from their spirit tree and fashioning it into a sacred pole. These poles often have a little bowl attached to the top to hold meat offerings. If birds come to peck at the meat, it is a sign that the spirits have accepted the offering (see chapter 6). Today, many village households in Manchuria have both a spirit tree and a spirit pole, although these families usually replace the pole with a new one after each ceremony. The Evenk use similar spirit poles, but carve birds on top. These are not used to give offerings, but rather as a spirit house for various bird spirits.

Land Shrines

Land shrines (Mongol, *ovoo*; Buryat, *oboo*; Turkic, *ovaa*) are like sacred trees in that they mark a connection point to the spirits and often have spirits residing in them. They are typically found on mountains and at borders or gates to specific areas. Often, especially among Mongols and Turkics, they appear as a large pile of stones with branches or wooden poles emerging from the top (see Figure 25). Sometimes they consist of a conical or triangular group of large branches or poles that are tied together at the top and set into the ground. These branches are often tied with prayer scarves and fabrics. In the former case, offerings are given on the stones; in the latter, they are given inside the conical or triangular space. In Manchuria and Inner Mongolia, land shrines may also appear as a small stone cave in the ground or small shrine boxes or rooms built into the ground. The shrine box is likely the result of Chinese influence, as they resemble Chinese temples.

Visitors who pass land shrines while traveling leave offerings in hopes of general good fortune and blessings, and to help protect themselves and ensure safe and smooth travels. Today, many simply leave coins if they do not have food or drink to offer. It is also acceptable to add an additional stone to a stone land shrine, thereby strengthening it.[31] In areas like Mongolia, travelers may pass many of these shrines on a single journey. Rather than stopping to leave offerings at each one, they just leave them at important shrines (at gates or entrances) to ensure smooth and safe travels.

Figure 25. One of the ovoo land shrines on the road to the Darkhad Valley in northern Mongolia. Photo courtesy of David Shi.

Spirit Houses

Spirit houses are essentially grave shrines of past shamans. In parts of Mongolia and Siberia, they are found on mountainsides or hidden away in the forest. In Mongolia, they typically appear as fenced areas about the size of a yurt, with a fire pit, a raised platform for offerings, and two trees at the end with sheets and ribbons tied between them that act as spirit representations and cloth offerings. In other areas, they may appear as small sheds with altar structures inside.

Although they act as grave shrines for shamans, spirit houses do not contain the bodily remains of shamans, but rather their shamanic tools. After death, shamans' bodies are returned to nature, either through sky burials to be eaten by wild animals (Turco-Mongol peoples) or placed in open wooden coffins in trees out in the wild (Evenks). The Amur bury their dead shamans, but only with their wooden streamers. Among the Tungusic peoples, shamans' tools are kept within the family (generally in the attic or near the roof on wooden beams) or interred in a special location like a spirit house. Among Mongol and Turkic peoples, living and younger shamans who have deceased shamans as one of their shamanic spirits make regular journeys to their spirit houses to conduct honoring rituals and other ceremonies, as being there allows for a deeper connection and more powerful workings.[32]

Spirit Containers

In all shamanic traditions, it is not unusual for shamans to create, bless, and/or activate objects to act as amulets and talismans to bring people luck, protection, and prosperity. These function as temporary "spirit containers." Activated shamanic tools like mirrors, drums, and regalia already act as spirit containers because they have shamans' spirits residing in them.

In some traditions, additional objects like small amulets and talismans, masks, dolls, and figurines are also made into spirit containers. Turkic and some Mongolic peoples (Darkhads and Oirats) generally don't use additional items as spirit containers beyond shamans' regalia and direct tools. Even their household altars consist of only five colored prayer scarves (blue, white, red, green, and yellow), offering bowls, and ribbons or streamers hung on the wall or ceiling that represent spirits. Sometimes these ribbons or streamers may have small figures attached to them that represent ancestral spirits.

Tungusic traditions, as well as those of the Buryat, Daur, and Khorchin Mongols, make spirit containers of items in addition to regular tools and use them as spirit representations. Many are dolls or figurines, while others are more abstract. These are typically made of wood, leather, felt, fur, paper, rocks, feathers, straw, and/or metal.

According to Sarangerel, Buryat Mongols often maintain spirit containers (*ongons*) of various Mongolian deities, most commonly *Zol Zayaach*, *Avgaldai*, and *Umay*. Zol Zayaach's figure protects the household and typically appears as a male-female pair. Avgaldai is commonly represented by a copper mask that is used during honoring ceremonies.[33] Umay is not typically a figure, but is represented rather by drawings that are sometimes burned in a fire to dedicate the fire and associated magical works to her. Daur Mongols maintain many of the same spirit containers and figurines as the Buryats, suggesting some degree of shared roots.

Siberian Evenks refer to their spirit figures as *seven* or *barelak*. One story tells of a family whose yurt burned down. They lost nearly everything they owned, but found their main barelak doll on the ground several meters away. It is believed that the spirit in the barelak, although kept in a birch-bark box, sensed the danger and somehow escaped to safety.[34]

Among Amur tribes, these spirit containers are known as *saiven/seven*. These can be containers for specific purposes or simply effigies that are given offerings and prayers. The functional saivens often take the form of *ponga saivens*, which contain spirits employed for divination, or small healing saivens (keychain size) that are given to people who are sick. These must be treated with respect as living objects and regularly fed and prayed to. One of the more common saivens that is less functional and simply given offerings and prayers is the *kuljamu*, which is distinguished by its conical head (see chapter 3). Many families also keep saivens that depict specific ancestral spirits and deities. These are normally kept near the roof of the house and brought down and honored at the house's southern side. Shamans' main helping spirits are typically represented by silver saivens (only initiated "big" shamans can carry silver saivens), which are fed every day.[35]

Both Manchus and Khorchin Mongols still maintain spirit figures or containers, but these are used mainly as honored figures and not for functional purposes. On their altars, a family tree mural may be accompanied by multiple figurines, each representing a specific ancestor.

CHAPTER 9

Divination, Folk Magic, and Ceremonies

This last chapter explains some of the divination, folk magic, and ceremonies that are practiced across North Asia. Some are given with specific instructions for using them safely, while others are described in more general terms, as they should be used only by those who are ready for heavier spirit work.

Please bear in mind that performing these practices in no way makes you a North Asian shaman. Nonetheless, I hope that you can draw inspiration from them and credit aspects of them as part of a profound spiritual tradition derived from North Asian spiritualities.

Divination

Divination is a vital component of North Asian shamanic practice. Before consulting a shaman, or even proceeding to do their own magical work, people turn to both astrology and divination to ensure that the work will be safe and successful. Shamans also employ astrology and divination to make sure that certain ceremonies or magical works are appropriate (see chapter 2). Although here I highlight methods used in North Asia, I encourage you to use the method most comfortable for you. And remember that basic astrological information must be given before divination can begin.

North Asian divination can be classified into two broad types: reading signs that appear in nature and using tools to find answers to questions. The first type is passive and spontaneous, as diviners can read signs only when they appear and not on demand. More active divination methods include observing the movements of stars and celestial bodies (Eastern astrology), reading the movements of birds, domestic animals, and fish, and interpreting the condition of flowers, plants, trees, and even grasses. Because of their reverence for fire, shamans also gaze into it for signs and images, especially if the fire is used in ceremony or worship. Manchus held dream divination in especially high reverence and often planned to ask certain questions of the spirits before sleeping, then interpreted their dreams to find answers. Divination with tools is more active and detailed, and is therefore more commonly used.

Stone Divination

Most Mongol and Central Asian Turkic shamans prefer using stone divination, a method known as "forty-one stones" among Mongols and *kumalak* among Turkics. I won't go into detail on stone divination here, as it is extremely complicated and also because traditional shamans are very selective about whom they choose to learn this method. The basic idea of the practice is that shamans are guided by their spirits to separate stones into a square of nine piles, removing stones as guided by spirits. Eventually, each pile will contain between one and three stones, and shamans then read both the individuals stones and the piles into which they are divided. Because this method requires a small degree of trance (and therefore strong intuitive powers) as well as a deep understanding of Mongolic shamanic cosmology, it is generally only taught to and performed by shamans.[1]

Bone Divination

Non-shamans often divine using sheep knucklebones or anklebones (astragalus bone, known as *shagai* in Mongolian and *galaha/gacha* in Manchu), tossing them like dice and divining answers based on how they land. However, these knuckle bones are more effective if activated or blessed by a spiritual elder. In the past, shamans ceremoniously cut these bones out of specifically chosen sheep before they died to ensure that there was active life energy in them.[2] Goat, deer, or even pig knucklebones can also be used, as they have a similar shape. In these cultures, knucklebones are sometimes also kept for good luck.

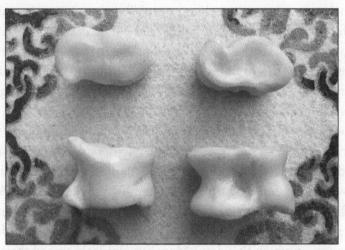

Figure 26. Shagai sheep knucklebones. From top left to bottom right, the horse, camel, sheep, and goat sides of bones used for divination. Photo courtesy of David Shi.

The four sides of these bones are known as horse, camel, sheep, and goat (see Figure 26). The sheep and goat sides are the "larger" sides; the sheep side (bottom left) has a rounded hump, while the goat side (bottom right) has a large inward indentation. The horse side (top left) and camel side (top right) are the smaller sides and both have an S-shape, but the camel side has an indented bowl, while the horse side is flat. In general, the horse is fast and delivers good news quickly. The camel is persistent and steady, but slower. The sheep is good, but aimless and directionless, and capable of being led in any direction. The goat is difficult to manage and mischievous, and tends to stray or invite the unexpected or unwanted. I encourage you to call on your intuition when considering these animal behaviors to guide your readings. A complete chart of the possible combinations and their meanings can be found online or in my book *North Asian Magic*.[3]

Other Divination Techniques

While stone and bone divination are the most common today, there are historically many other divination types that were used in North Asia. Different Manchu clans used several tools, including a ritual knife known as a *hama* (see chapter 8). While in trance, shamans held the knife horizontally in both hands and chanted and shook it while praying. The knife had distinctive loops on it that jingled, and shamans interpreted the rhythms of the knife loops to make predictions. Sometimes, when the knife was hung horizontally, its loops jingling on their own indicated an omen.

Another divination method found in Manchuria involved tossing small grains of pearls onto one or more mirrors and divining based on how and where they landed.[4] A common method used across all North Asia involved tossing long objects to see how they landed. Turkic and Mongol shamans asked questions and then tossed their drumsticks or jaw harps, reading answers based on the side on which they fell and the direction in which they lay.[5] Manchus similarly tossed their drumsticks, but also ritual knives (hama) and willow branches. Modern Korean shamans toss knives, Chinese coins, and rice grains; in ancient times, they tossed even rocks and sticks.[6]

Advanced Divination

Some less common divination practices require a higher level of skill or involve inherent dangers. For example, direct trance possession by spirits, the cornerstone of North Asian shamanism, can be used to gather insight directly from spirit voices. In North Asia, only initiated shamans can use this technique, as only they can rely on trusted spirits to take control of their bodies without potentially harming or abusing themselves, their clients, or anyone in attendance.

The most advanced and dangerous divination technique is "fire scapulae" divination. For those familiar with ancient Asian cultures, this resembles ancient Chinese oracle bones. The scapulae bone from a cow, a sheep, or a reindeer is removed and sometimes inscribed with words, spells, or pictures related to what is being divined. The bone is then tossed into a fire until scorch marks appear on it, which are then interpreted for meaning. Although used during the Shang Dynasty, it has long gone out of practice in China, but it survived in Mongolia, among the Evenk and Oroqen, and some of the Amur tribes. Mongolian elders have noted, however, that, while this practice is extremely powerful, it is also extremely dangerous, as it carries a high risk of karmic consequence or curse if not performed correctly. For this reason, many Mongolian elders today refuse to pass this practice on to most younger shamans.[7]

Folk Magic

The spiritual techniques below are drawn from folk traditions and can be incorporated into any practice. They include simple ceremonies open to non-shamans, as well as folk practices that have intended spiritual effects.

Smoke Cleansing

Before any spiritual or magical work, the person performing it must be cleansed. The easiest and quickest way to do this is to use smoke from a sacred herb. Mongolic and Turkic peoples most commonly use juniper for cleansing. Juniper is also preferred because it can calm energy and spirits, which is why juniper smoke can also be used as an offering. Amur tribes use marsh labrador (*Ledum palustre*), while Manchus prefer Asian thyme (*Thymus mongolicus*) for cleansing and Daurian rhododendron *(Rhododendron Dauricum)* for offerings. Please note that all of these herbs are used by all North Asian peoples, but some tribes prefer one over the others.

Smoke cleansing works in ways similar to what many know as "smudging." After the herbs are lit, the smoking herb is passed around the body clockwise three times, then passed over the crown of the head and under the armpits. Individual users may choose to cleanse other parts of the body as well. Smoke can also be used to cleanse spaces. When cleansing a room or a house, pay extra attention to the corners, as pollution tends to gather there. The armpits are seen as the "corners" of the body.

Although juniper, marsh labrador, and Asian thyme are preferred among North Asian peoples, elders encourage every person to use either the sacred cleansing herbs of their ancestors or herbs that are indigenous to where they live. By using the herbs of your ancestors, you connect with and invoke ancestral power. By using herbs that grow naturally where you live, you connect with and invoke the power of local land spirits.

Offering Prayer Ceremony

Prayer is an integral part of all spiritual traditions. In North Asia, practitioners frequently perform structured prayer ceremonies that are combined with offerings, giving gifts to the spirits and gods while simultaneously asking for blessings, protection, health, and prosperity from all of them at once. Below I give you an example of one such ceremony that has been adapted from shamanic prayer ceremonies.

As with every working, this ceremony should be preceded by a smoke cleansing. Then lay out the offerings in ceremonial cups or bowls and sprinkle a small pinch of a cleansing herb into each one to purify the offerings. It is typically appropriate to dress in spiritual regalia or traditional clothes to show respect to the spirits.

Although this ceremony does not require heavy protection, it never hurts to set up spiritual safeguards, either through protective amulets or in the Western style by casting a circle. In North Asia, practitioners typically wear mirrors and cover their crowns with simple hats. If performing the ceremony inside, uncover the altar holding your spirit representations (if you normally keep it covered) and begin by reciting a prayer to all the higher powers, starting with the most supreme and ending with the "lowest." Invite each god or spirit one by one and announce your offerings, then ask them to answer your prayers. Here are the words I typically use when performing a prayer ceremony like this:

I bow and give respect to the highest being, the Master of Heaven.
I invite you to come and accept my humble offerings.
We welcome you and your glory.

I call the great star spirits that shine to us our destinies!
The North Star, Big Dipper, Orion's Belt, and others.
I call the beloved ancestral spirits, my Grandfather
    and Grandmother spirits,
who watch over me unconditionally.
I invite the heavenly beings and gods, both wrathful and gentle,
and beg for your kindness and favor.

I bow and give respect to the Earth Mother
    whose breath gave me form.
I call to the land spirits!
The nagas and sprites who rule the shimmering kingdom of water.
The earth-lords who rule the strong rugged
    kingdom of mountains.
May your magnificence never diminish, may
    your wonders ever inspire.
From the smallest plants, to the rushing rivers, to the
    mighty forests, mountains, and caverns!
Please bless us with health and fortune.

I beg the presence of Omosi Mama, the Manchu goddess of life!
May your willows grow strong yet graceful,
    and may your fires never falter.

With your rope, tighten my bonds with family
and friends as you do with all life.
Strengthen my household fire, as you do with
the fires of the Middle World.
Watch over our children as they are born and grow,
and our elderly before they return to you.

To all the spirits called, please accept these offerings.
I offer you the purest untouched milk, the
white life essence of nature.
I offer the blue-green smoke of my herbs as
it rises to the highest heavens.
[List out any other offerings that are prepared.]
Please accept these offerings evenly and fairly, without ignoring any.

To all the spirits and gods I have called,
Please grant to us your protection and blessings.
Forgive the trespasses and mistakes I have
committed, for I am silly and stupid.
And in your kindness, grant us health and prosperity.
Protect me from calamities, both physical and spiritual,
and guide me when I am lost.
Allow true friends to share my table and
turn away my enemies' eyes.
Open the roads to opportunities so that I may
flourish and present offerings to you again.
May my wishes be granted. So shall it be.

Note that this prayer begins with an invocation to the Master of Heaven. I kept the wording gender-neutral, as the master of heaven can be male or female depending on the cultural tradition. Next, I invoke the star spirits. Although different cultures honor different stars, I name some of the notable ones here by their western names. Star prayer is a quite universal ancient practice, even in Western fairy tales—praying to the "first star I see tonight," for instance (typically the North Star). Then

I invoke ancestral spirits, which can include general ancestral spirits as well as shamanic spirits. Afterward, all other relevant helpful sky spirits and heavenly gods are invoked.

Next, I call upon the Earth Mother and invoke the land spirits using compliments and flattery. As we have seen, land spirits are vain and materialistic, so any work with them must contain words that describe their majesty and brilliance, and the wealth and beauty of the natural world. Finally, I follow this with a direct invocation to the Manchu goddess of life, Omosi Mama, who oversees all life in the world, including birth and death. She is associated with the willow tree and, although she is not specifically a fire goddess, she feeds spiritual fires and strengthens family/household bonds. Because Omosi Mama is a "domestic" and not a "wild" spirit, she is invoked only through prayers and never engaged through shamanic trance, despite being a patron of shamans in her mythology. Feel free here to invoke the spirits of your own tradition.

Next, I give offerings of milk and juniper, but you can add any other offerings you feel are appropriate. I sometimes also include barley, cookies, nuts, and unwrapped candies. You can also offer cooked dishes, but these are typically reserved for more complex ceremonies. Note that I clearly state that the offerings are for *all* the spirits called and ask them to share them equally. If you wish to invoke other spirits, you can add additional prayers after the fire section and before presenting offerings.

Once all your offerings have been presented, tell the spirits what you want. The prayer above asks for health, prosperity, protection, and blessing, and generally wishes for your aspirations to come true. If you have a specific request, add it here.

The shamans and elders of North Asia believe that prayers are best said spontaneously and strongly advise against memorizing them, as this can limit their effectiveness. Every time I perform this offering ceremony, I say the prayer slightly differently.[8] Among Mongols, all sections end with the word *shoog* (a sacred word used when calling shamanic spirits), repeated three times. After saying the prayer, I formally give the offerings, either tossing liquid offerings directly from the bowl or sprinkling them with an offering spoon or a sprig of juniper. Toss your offerings upward when offering to sky spirits, and forward when offering to other spirits. Make sure you throw your offerings in each of the four directions, otherwise spirits from the neglected directions may get jealous.

I used to throw offerings only toward the north for simplicity, even when outside, but immediately after returning home, I either collapsed in exhaustion or was struck with short-term sickness. Once I started giving offerings to all four directions, this no longer happened.

Food offerings like grains, cookies, or candies should be given in a similar manner. Present cooked dishes using both hands, then leave some out in nature near a tree or body of water, and take the rest home. You can also share them with attendees. If performing this ceremony by a body of water, never toss or pour your offerings directly into the water. Instead, place or pour them a small distance away. When your offerings have been given, pay your respects in an appropriate manner and leave.

Hurai Blessing

Like prayers, blessings are a part of every North Asian shamanic tradition, although they are performed in different ways by different groups. The easiest way to call down blessings is to use the sacred Mongolian word of power, *hurai* (*khurai*), which specifically calls blessings and attracts them to you. Simply hold your hands out, palms facing up, and rotate them in a clockwise motion while shouting the word (pronounced like "hooray," but in a guttural voice) three times.[9] There are no strict rules for how to do this. I like to rotate my hands three times, repeating the word three times with each rotation, for a total of nine times.

Because this blessing is so simple, many people perform it as a daily practice. It is also frequently employed at the end of larger ceremonies, including prayer ceremonies, and can be used informally to conclude ceremonies. The *hurai* chant can also be performed with a prayer scarf held in both hands and rotated in a similar fashion. Some also use their sacred instruments or drums, collecting the blessings into them, then pouring the blessings over their heads to transfer them to their bodies.

Prayer Scarves

Prayer scarves, called *khadag* in Mongolian and *khata* in Tibetan, come from Tibetan practice and are primarily used by cultures influenced by Tibetan Buddhism (Mongols, Turkic Tuvans, and Qing-era Manchus). Tibetan prayer scarves are white to symbolize purity and have the eight Buddhist treasures printed on them. In Mongolia, most scarves are blue to symbolize the eternal blue sky, although they retain the eight Buddhist symbols. These blue scarves can often be found both at land-spirit shrines and in Buddhist temples.[10] Mongol shamanic altars also typically have green, red, white, yellow, and blue scarves folded and stacked on top of each other. Although blue scarves are dominant, white scarves are also used in Buddhist ceremonies, as well as at formal events and to honor guests. Manchus commonly use gold-colored scarves, since gold is a sacred color in their tradition.

Prayer scarves are quite versatile and can be used in many ways. Typically, people press them against their mouths or foreheads, and whisper their prayers and wishes into them. Often, these prayers are concluded with the *hurai* chant (see above) and the scarves are then tied to sacred spiritual and/or energetic locations that can carry and activate the prayers held in them. These locations include land shrines, sacred trees, temple doors, or even outside homes, so that the wind can carry the prayers.

Among Darkhad Mongols, the intentions of every ceremony are whispered into prayer scarves (or other long cloths), which are then tied to shamans' coats. For this reason, ceremony attendees sometimes wear scarves around their necks throughout ceremonies and attach them to shamans' coats at the end of them. Whenever these shamans perform ceremonies wearing their ritual coats, the spirits come in and energize the scarves, thereby strengthening their prayers. As we have seen, the experience level of these shamans can be judged by how many scarves are attached to their coats, indicating how many ceremonies they have conducted (see chapter 6).[11]

Prayer scarves can pass blessings on to others as well. At many cultural events, attendees place scarves around each other's necks as a sign of respect. In spiritual work, prayers are often spoken into the scarves and then transferred to others, thereby passing blessings on to them.

Milk Blessings

Milk is an innately sacred liquid. It is the means by which mammalian mothers provide sustenance to newborns. Thus it is the pure essence of both life and motherly love. For this reason, many in Mongolia and Turkic Siberia sprinkle milk onto objects to bless them. Today, it's not uncommon for people to sprinkle milk onto new cars. If you buy souvenirs and/or spiritual tools in Mongolia, these items may smell slightly of sour milk because they have received milk blessings.

If you want to perform milk blessings yourself, be sure to obtain whole milk in the purest form possible. When I use milk for spiritual purposes, including in prayer ceremonies, I try to buy unhomogenized whole milk (even if I don't drink it). If this is not possible, regular homogenized whole milk also works.

Protection

Protection is key in every magical or spiritual tradition, thus it is not surprising that it also plays an important role in North Asian shamanism. Here are two methods shamans in these traditions use to protect themselves from negative energies and malign spirits.

Thread

The most common form of protection in North Asia is thread—most often red, but sometimes sky blue. This is not thin sewing thread, but rather a thicker thread more like Chinese knotting cord or embroidery floss. It is usually made of cotton, wool, or silk. It's not uncommon to see people wearing these colored threads tied around their necks, wrists, or ankles for protection.

To empower these threads, shamans cut a piece and place it in their palms, then bring it close to their faces and pray to the spirits to bless it and imbue it with protective power. They may go into shamanic trance as they do so. Then they blow on the thread three times to close the working and tie it around the person requiring protection. Responsible shamans will tell clients how long this protection lasts until they need to return to renew it.

Although this method is commonly used for protection, it can be used for healing as well.[12] I have received thread protection twice—first from a Tuvan American shaman who tied the thread around my wrist, and then from a Darkhad shaman in Mongolia who tied it around my ankle.

Sharp and Pointed Objects

Sharp and pointed objects can be used in effective ways to protect spaces, typically homes. They are usually hung by a home's entrance, but can also be hung by a window. As with all protection talismans, these objects must be prayed over to empower them. They can be pouches full of needles, or miniature weapons like a bow and arrow. Sarangerel notes that Buryats sometimes use bear claws or porcupine quills for protection.[13] Bear claws are empowered by prayers to the bear spirit; porcupine quills are empowered by prayers to *Zar Zargaach*. Herbs that are sharp and spiky can also be used in this way, as they protect against harmful energies. Different cultures use different herbs for this, but generally any herb or plant that is sharp or spiky will work.

Another variation on this is to place sharp objects (knives, nails, broken glass, needles, etc.) outside the home pointing away from it. Sometimes the figure of a warrior holding a weapon is placed outside the entrance of a home, which is somewhat similar to East Asian warrior-god statues or images that guard the doors of homes and temples.[14]

Spirit Water

Water is the oldest physical form of existence in North Asian cosmology and thus has a very close connection to the spirit worlds (see chapter 2). Almost all North Asian cultures have a practice for creating a special form of water that is spiritually charged, giving it strong cleansing, healing, and protective properties. In Mongolia, it is known as *arshaan* or *rashaan*. Some sacred springs that have a strong spiritual presence naturally produce sacred spirit water. When I traveled into the taiga to meet with families of Dukha reindeer herders, they brought me to springs that each had specific healing properties.

Spirit water is used primarily for personal cleansing, but it can be used to cleanse your sacred tools or sprinkled around a room to cleanse the space. If no spirit water is available, you can use salted water as a substitute to remove lighter forms of pollution. As with smoke cleansing, remember to pay special attention to corners. Spirit water can also be applied topically to cleanse the body of spiritual pollutants. For pollutions that affect sexual health, apply the water to the genitalia and wash downward. Some also ingest a small amount of it if they are sick or suffering the effects of pollution or curse.[15]

You can also heat spirit water to produce steam that can be used for cleansing. Place the water on the floor between the legs of the person being cleansed and let the steam rise up the body when the water is heated. You can also use it as a spiritual cleansing bath. One typical bath involves combining vodka and whole milk and pouring spirit water into the mixture. (Never pour anything directly into spirit water, or it loses its power.)[16] Then pour the mixture over your head and allow it to run down your body. Wash yourself from top to bottom, and let the air dry you (drying yourself with a towel or cloth will remove the blessing aspect of the milk).

There are several ways to make spirit water. Here are just a few.

Energy Manipulation

Begin by placing a bowl of water before you and, in a meditative state, visualize your energy field as a sphere that surrounds your body. Feel the sensation of energy flowing up and down your body. Hold out your hands and, while visualizing the natural flow of energy that falls from the heavens and onto the earth, pull and collect that energy into your hands. Concentrate the energy in your hands until it feels hot or electrical, then transfer it into the water. Alternatively, you can collect the energy in your mouth and transfer it by blowing into the water.

Make a prayer to your spirits or gods, and ask them to pass through the water to bless, activate, and empower it to be used for cleansing and healing. Sarangerel recommends using natural spring water, as this is easier to bless and empower than treated water. She also notes that you can create more powerful spirit water by using water from nine different springs, as nine is a sacred number (3 x 3).[17]

Sacred Herbs

This method employs sacred herbs and therefore can be much more powerful. As with smoke cleansing, I recommended using either herbs your ancestors used, and/or herbs that grow naturally in your area. When making spirit water, always use an odd number of herbs. I use juniper (commonly used by Mongols), Asian thyme (commonly used by Manchus), and marsh labrador (commonly used by the Amur).

Heat some water until it boils and place the herbs in it. As the water continues boiling, make a prayer to your spirits or gods, and ask them to pass through the water to bless, activate, and empower it to be used for cleansing and healing. Just as using water from nine different springs can make your spirit water more powerful, using nine herbs that are sacred in your culture or land can increase its power when made in this way.[18]

Indirect Methods

There are also several indirect ways to make spirit water. One common way is to use an activated shamanic mirror. As the mirror is already a spirit house and, in some ways, a portal to the spirit world, you can pray to the mirror and blow across it or dip it into the water for its spirits to pass through.[19] Another way is to incorporate water into a larger shamanic ceremony. Any water that has been involved in a shamanic working is considered to have been blessed by the spirits. But it's still a good idea to pray over it for good measure.[20]

Cleansing Baths

Given the relative scarcity of water in North Asia, baths were historically not as common there as in other places. In fact, it is strictly taboo
to bathe in a natural body of water or to wash anything in it, especially
anything soiled with feces, blood, or urine. It is also taboo to urinate
or defecate within ten meters of a body of water. When nomads needed
water, they had to remove it from its natural source and store it in large
jugs or barrels. Only then could it be used for purposes like washing.

Nevertheless, baths were discovered to be a good form of spiritual
cleansing in North Asia. As in many Asian cultures, water and liquids
like milk were seen as an essence of life that could repel harmful spirits
and pollution associated with death. We saw in chapter 3 how water
was used to repel ghosts and evil spirits, including sky vampires. One
way to temporarily prevent pollution from entering your home (if you
suspect traces of pollution) is to splash spirit water or water that has
been blessed at the threshold before entering. When you enter, close
the door behind you without looking back.[21] Some also splash cold
water onto their hands and faces to repel pollution temporarily.[22]

Another bath that is sometimes used for both cleansing and blessing
involves combining a pinch of powdered juniper (or other cleansing herb)
with a pinch of salt and a pinch of dirt that was stepped on by a horse
(preferably a white one) and placing the mixture into a bowl of milk. The
milk is meant for blessing, the juniper and salt are for cleansing and puri-
fying, and the horse-dirt is for raising a person's windhorse (see chapter
2). Occasionally water and vodka are mixed in as well, but be sure the
mixture contains an odd number of nonliquid ingredients. Perform this
cleansing bath in the same way as the one described above. I learned this
method from a Darkhad shaman during my first visit to Mongolia.[23]

Soul-Calling

When people appear to have lost vitality or to have unusually bad luck
or difficulties in their everyday lives, it may be a sign that a piece of
their soul has been detached. This type of soul loss can be triggered

by spiritual attachments, pollution, trauma, near-death experiences, or even everyday events like falling, getting hurt, or being startled. They will first use divination to confirm the condition and determine the best remedy for it. Unfortunately, you can't perform these ceremonies for yourself, only for others. So if you believe you require one, find someone you trust to perform it for you.

Below are descriptions of two simple soul-calling ceremonies—one Mongolian and one Manchu. The Mongolian ceremony is considered too dangerous for non-shamans to perform given its trance aspect, but the Manchu ceremony is commonly performed by non-shamans, perhaps because trance is not involved and its fire aspect makes it spiritually safer. In both methods, smoke cleansing is conducted before the ceremony begins.

Mongolian Ceremony

The Mongolian ceremony relies somewhat heavily on using patients' personal effects, specifically their belts. Patients hold their belts in their hands, along with a bowl of sweets that they enjoy to lure back the lost soul part. If the patients are not present, shamans use their clothes to act in their place and set the belt and bowl on top of them. They then engage in shamanic trance and call in their spirits, followed by a specific prayer that is meant to call out to the lost soul part, encouraging it to return, to retrace its steps back if it's lost. They emphasize how much it is needed and loved, and may also ask their own spirits to help guide it back into the person's body. Sarangerel notes that, before she begins any type of soul calling, she finds a way to startle the client to loosen the soul body so the retrieved soul part can be reintegrated easily.[24]

While this is happening, patients move their arms in a clockwise motion while chanting *hurai* in the same manner used to call for blessings (see above). If shamans have successfully summoned the lost soul part, they check to see whether it has landed in the patient, in the bowl of sweets, or even in one of their tools, in which case, they transfer it directly into the patient. If the soul-calling was unsuccessful, they may repeat the ceremony or even journey in the spirit world to find the lost part.[25]

Manchu Ceremony

The Manchu ceremony is similar, in that the preparations and prayers are almost the same. The key difference lies in the tools used. While Mongols use belts and clothing to represent patients, Manchus use a chain of paper dolls holding hands, which they create by cutting folded red paper.

Paper-cutting and paper dolls are significant in Manchu culture, including in Manchu shamanic practice, and they are often used to represent people or souls in ceremonies. At other times, they serve as spirit representations and/or as depictions of ancient stories or legends. The color of the paper is significant because red represents blood or life energy. You can find simple tutorials for making paper doll chains online.

Once you have cleansed and blessed the paper-doll chain, pray over it using a soul-calling prayer that states the patient's name and astrological information. During the Qing Dynasty, Manchus started writing these prayers and this information directly on the dolls, then tossing them into a fire, sometimes with sacred herbs like Daurian rhododendron as an offering. Sometimes the prayer was repeated or accompanied by a chant like: "Come over! Return to us!"

While this ceremony is better if patients are present, that is technically not necessary, as the paper dolls provide a direct link between them and the missing soul part. When the dolls are finished burning, some mix a pinch of the ash in water and have clients drink it, especially if they believe that the lost soul part landed in the doll's ashes, which can potentially act as a retrieval container. Some simply toss the ashes outside toward the north.

Fire Magic

Fire is the ultimate cleanser and purifier. In ancient times, people sometimes applied it directly to their own (or others') bodies for purification and sometimes engaged in lighter practices like walking through or over fire, as well as heavier practices like walking on hot coals or even pressing red-hot metal (typically a blacksmith's tool) directly to the skin.

Today, several forms of fire cleansing are performed that do not risk physical harm. One involves praying over and lighting three matches, then holding them near the body part or area where pollution is suspected until the matches burn out. How brightly the flames burn indicates how strong or effective the cleansing was. For a stronger cleansing, repeat this process twice, up to a total of nine matches.[26]

Another modern adaptation is to heat a knife or blade until it is red-hot, then make a prayer to the spirits to empower the blade to remove spiritual pollution. When the red-hot blade is moved over the skin and around the body, it cuts away spiritual pollution. When finished, cool the blade in water, then wash it with spirit water.[27]

During the Mongol Empire, anyone who was granted an audience with the great Khan had to pass between two flaming torches meant to cleanse them spiritually before they appeared before him. This practice can also be done with herbs in a way that incorporates smoke cleansing. Have the person pass between two piles of burning or smoking herbs, then allow the herbs to burn out naturally. If you don't use charcoal or some other lighting agent, the herbs should burn out quickly.

The Daur Mongols also used fire to protect infant boys, incorporating an appeal to the goddess *Umay/Ome Barkan*. Prepare a picture of the goddess Umay on a piece of paper. You can draw this or simply use a picture of a female figure. Make sure you pray to the goddess, however, so that the picture represents her in ritual use. Then obtain a small arrow—this can be toy-sized, but should include a metal (ideally iron) arrowhead and feathers.

When you are ready to begin, light a ritual fire and sprinkle some rock salt on it, then place the picture or representation of Umay into the fire and pray for her to inhabit and bless the fire with protective powers. Next, pass the miniature arrow through the fire (ideally three or any odd number of times), while praying that it take on the fire's ability to protect. Place the arrow in the infant's bed, generally under the pillow, to act as a protective talisman.[28] This ritual is not used for infant girls, but there are ways to protect children in general, including girls.

Manchu Fire Ceremony

The purpose of this ceremony is not only to worship fire, but also to feed and strengthen the household fire spirit so it can bless and protect the family bloodline. All North Asian shamanic traditions perform fire ceremonies in some form, although they may use different materials and invoke different spirits or deities. Here, I attempt to recreate a Manchu fire ceremony, the original practice of which is likely kept hidden within specific village traditions. This adaptation incorporates Manchu cosmological practices, spirits that were inspired by the Mongol method, and prayers that were inspired by Amur prayers.

Most Turkic, Mongolic, and Siberian Tungus fire ceremonies required shamanic trance. In fact, Amur tribes required that shamans travel to the realm of fire in the spirit world. Because the spirits invoked here are "domestic" spirits in the Manchu pantheon (specifically Omosi Mama), this is a "domestic" ceremony that is not meant to incorporate trance. While the original Jurchen-Manchu ceremony may have incorporated trance, fire ceremonies survived into the Qing Dynasty with the trance aspect removed, since Qing emperors outlawed trance work. Because my recreated version does not incorporate trance, it is considered safe for non-shamans to perform.

Before beginning, calm your mind using breathing exercises, visualization, or meditation—whatever method works for you. You don't want to be performing a fire ceremony if you are agitated, angry, or depressed.

For this ceremony, you will need:

- Chopped wood for the fire; small twigs for an indoor fire

- Rock salt, roughly grain-size

- An image of Omosi Mama (a picture or a single paper doll cut from red paper) that has been prayed to beforehand to make it a spiritual representation of the goddess

- Nonmeat offerings—vodka or liquor, milk, tea, biscuits, dried fruit, or tobacco— that have been divided into altar offerings and fire offerings.[29]

- Cooked meat offerings with no trace of blood, both fatty and non-fatty pieces.[30] Mongols and Central Asians traditionally use sheep; Manchus use pork or beef; Dukha and northern Tungus use reindeer; Amurs use pork, beef, or fish (salmon, sturgeon, etc.)

- Small Tibetan prayer flags—five flags of different colors (red, green, blue, yellow, and white) strung together.[31]

- Several handfuls of cleansing and offering herbs

- Several bundles of incense sticks (optional)

Set up the firewood in a fireproof dish in front of your altar or sacred space, or in a fire pit if you are working outside. I advise against using a cast iron or black cauldron, as black invites death in North Asian cultures and you don't want these influences to affect your household fire. The wood can be arranged to form a cone or stacked. In Mongolia, the wood pieces are traditionally stacked in layers of three to represent the three worlds. Cleanse yourself and the area where the fire will be lit with herbal smoke.

Traditionally, you can carry some fire from your hearth (if you have one) to the place where the fire ceremony will be performed using a paper lantern. If you don't have a hearth, stove, or fireplace, you can light the lantern in the kitchen and then transfer the fire to the ceremony site. If you don't have a lantern, you can use a match or candle. If working outside, you can throw the lantern directly into the fire pit. If working indoors, be sure to snuff out the lantern after the fire has been lit.

Start by throwing the salt into the fire while chanting this prayer:

I banish all negativity from this place! I summon
  forth all that is good to this place!
This fire is now awakened! Welcome Tuwa
  Mama, the hearth fire spirit!

> *You, who are descended from the stars and*
> *brought down by Tuwayalha.*
> *Please forgive me and do not punish me for*
> *any offences I have committed.*
> *I am but a small, silly, stupid person, bowing*
> *to you in your splendor.*
> *I welcome your brilliance and thank you*
> *for keeping our lineage strong!*

When finished, toss the picture of Omosi Mama into the fire. As the picture burns, chant this prayer:

> *I welcome Fere Fodo Omosi Mama, and*
> *greet your presence in the flames.*
> *You, who connect the three worlds together,*
> *connecting us with Heaven and the ancestors.*
> *You, with both the gentleness of the willow*
> *and the rage of infernos,*
> *Who in your balance, manage the hearth and*
> *keep this world's fires strong.*
> *Please forgive me for any wrongs I have committed,*
> *For I am but a small, silly, stupid person,*
> *bowing to you in your magnificence.*
> *I light incense of sacred herbs, may this sacred*
> *smoke please you and feed the ancestors.*
> *I give you offerings of milk, cookies, pork, (and/*
> *or other offerings prepared).*
> *Your servant, [state your name and your*
> *birth/astrological animal],*
> *Kindly begs for your blessings and protection on my house,*
> *And strengthen our humble fire so that my line remains strong.*

Prepare the offerings that will go into the fire in order—first the cloth, then the meat offerings, then the nonmeat offerings. The cleansing and offering herbs should be last.

Now that both the hearth fire spirit and the fire aspect of Omosi Mama have been invoked, place the offerings into the fire one by one, in the order given above. Try to face north when doing this. The flammable offerings (cloth, meats, food, vodka, tobacco, etc.) can be placed directly into the fire, but the nonflammable liquid offerings (milk, tea, etc.) must be poured along the side of the stove, dish, or pit, and not directly into it. As you do this, say:

Fere Fodo Omosi Mama, Goddess of Life and Fire on Earth,
May the strength you give our fire nourish us
    with blessings, warmth, and light,
And protect us from the darkness that seeks to harm our lineage.
Let our offerings burn to you.
Our offerings are small, but may their oils and smokes please you.
Please forgive us for any trespasses we make, for
    we are small, silly, stupid humans.
We are learning. We will keep learning for the rest of our lives.

Great fire spirit, burning with strength and passion,
Your sparks, your scorching blue, your bed of iron and stone.
We thank you for providing us light, food, and
    the continuation of our lineage.
Thanks to you, we have lived well and will continue to honor you.
Forgive us for any offences we have committed,
    for we are small, silly, stupid humans.
I have tried to obey all the laws and follow
    everything I have been taught.
But I am a small person who is still learning.
Please keep us in your warm embrace, and
    protect us against the darkness.
Guardian of our bloodline, please keep our household strong.
And adorn us with your blessings.
We are still learning; please continue to bless our destiny.
May our lines long live.

Let the fire burn out by itself. For the ceremony to be successful, you must not put the fire out before it finishes burning. Do not use water or dirt to hasten this, or the fire will be offended.

While the fire burns, Manchus sometimes light several bundles of incense sticks from it and celebrate or dance while twirling the incense bundles in their hands, though this is not necessary. Close the ceremony as you normally would, and respectfully dispose of any leftover offerings in the usual way (see the prayer ritual on page 219).

Because fire is sacred, there are several taboos that you must respect when performing this ceremony:

- Never offer blood, or uncooked or half-cooked meat into the fire.

- Never offer nonflammable offerings like milk or tea directly into the fire. Pour them to the side of the stove, dish or pit.

- While you can use a poker to shift wood or burning offerings, never poke it, directly into the fire, as this shows disrespect. Do not poke sharp blades into the fire; if necessary, use the flat or dull side first.

- Never throw dirt or garbage into the fire.

- Avoid pointing your feet directly at the fire.

- Avoid quarrels and arguments while near the fire.

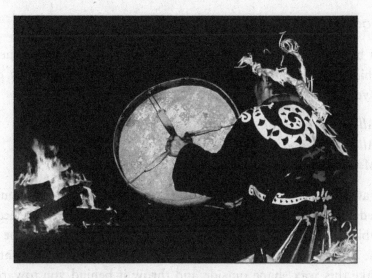

Figure 27. Ulchi shaman Grandfather Misha Duvan (1903–1997) performing a fire ritual.

Folk Magic for Children

Infants have high spiritual sensitivity and can sense spirits and energies that adults typically cannot. Since infants are only recently born into the physical world, they still have remnant connections to the spirit world that don't fade until their toddler years. Unfortunately, this makes them vulnerable to spiritual sicknesses, as frightening entities can easily attach to them.

Although these spiritual afflictions are quite easy to remove, if they are not removed, they can cause spiritual trauma into adulthood. Signs of these ailments can include unexplained illnesses, difficulty sleeping, general uneasiness, nervousness or fear, and imaginary friends who don't provide comfort. The most common sign of these sicknesses occurs when a child cries at night for no apparent reason. Many families perform folk magic whenever their children cry for no reason. Below are two methods for removing children's spiritual ailments— one Mongol, one Manchu—as well as instructions for making a protective talisman commonly used to guard children while sleeping.

Mongol Healing Ceremony

Fill a bowl half full of water and set it aside. Melt some wax next to the child's head (you can use a candle for this). As the wax melts, chant a prayer like:

> *All that is harmful, go away!*
> *All that is good, come forth!*
> *May the higher powers bless you!*

Repeat this prayer an odd number of times. When done, pour the melted wax into the bowl of water, as close to the baby's head as possible (so the baby can hear the splash). The wax will take the form of the attachment or entity that is frightening the child and absorb it. Take this wax shape outside and throw it behind you toward the northeast, then return inside without looking back.[32] Some sources say you should break this wax piece in half.

Manchu Healing Ceremony

This method involves using a red paper-doll chain like the one used in the Manchu soul-calling ceremony above. Pray over the dolls to draw out whatever evil may be bothering the child, repeating the child's name and astrological information. The paper dolls act as a substitute for the child to which the entity can attach itself. Light a fire in a pan and place it next to the bed while the child is sleeping. Then place the dolls under the pan. After the fire has burned out, if the dolls are scorched, it means that whatever was bothering the child was absorbed by the dolls and burned away. The burn marks may also form the shape of whatever was disturbing the child. Take the doll remnants and ashes outside, toss them toward the north, and return inside without looking back. Be sure never to leave the fire unattended.

Children's Bundles

Many Mongols today hang a small figure of a fox made of sheep-wool felt over their babies' cribs. The practice comes from a folk legend that tells how a fox spirit once came across a sleeping child whose parents were some distance away doing household chores and chopping wood. The fox woke the child, who was initially delighted to see it. But the fox was mischievous and deceived the baby, saying that the parents had abandoned it. When the baby cried loudly, the fox tried to reassure it, but the parents heard the cries and came running, causing the fox to flee. The baby stopped crying when it saw its parents, but whenever it fell asleep, the fox came back to play tricks. One day, the father saw the fox as it fled, and decided he would try to stop it from returning. To prevent this, the father cut a figure of a fox from sheep-wool felt harvested from the family's flock and hung it above the baby's bed. The next time the fox came, it saw that there was already another fox there, so it left to find another victim.

Over time, this felt figure became a common protection talisman used to ensure that children were kept safe from harmful spirits and could enjoy peaceful sleep. It was eventually incorporated in another type of talisman called "children's bundles" (*teeg* or *huudiin teeg*), which consist of a string of triangular pouches, each of a different color, that are usually stuffed with wool, but may also contain herbs and/or horsehair. These pouches are shaped like wide isosceles triangles pointing downward and usually have tassels and other objects or charms attached to them, like tiger bells, cowrie shells, or coins. According to Sarangerel, they traditionally consist of three pouches (blue for the Upper World, green for the Middle World, and red for the Lower World) with an additional yellow pouch if the baby is a girl.[33]

Today, these bundles are also often made with five pouches of blue, white, yellow, green, and red, which indicates Buddhist elemental influence. Even non-spiritual families sometimes purchase them to hang over their babies' cribs as toys. In a nod to the original legend, there is usually a sheep-wool felt fox tied at the bottom of the bundles that serves as both a toy and a protective talisman. These bundles can usually be purchased from Mongolian vendors, but are sometimes made by a shaman or family member.

Final Thoughts on Shamanic Ceremonies

This chapter has focused on simple blessings, protection, and cleansings, most of which can be performed by shamans and non-shamans alike. They are the primary practices of North Asian shamanic workers. For more information on practices like these, consult my book *North Asian Magic: Spellcraft from Manchuria, Mongolia, and Siberia,* which organizes practices by intention rather than type, although there are areas of overlap, as certain practices are ubiquitous.

For those that are interested in using shamanic rituals and ceremonies for more specific or focused purposes—like romance, prosperity, or success in business—I suggest using *serjim* ceremonies, which incorporate trance as well as offerings (typically alcohol), but can be customized for specific intentions. Rather than giving offerings in a purely devotional sense, these ceremonies use them to "pay" for specific requests. Alcohol serjims are generally classified as "cold" or "hot," depending on whether or not they use fire. There are also serjims that incorporate milk, tea, grains, and even salt and sand. You can find instructions for different types of serjims in my *North Asian Magic,* as well as in Sarangerel's *Chosen by the Spirits.*

Conclusion:
The Journey Continues

In this book, I have attempted to provide a comprehensive, yet easily comprehensible, view of the different shamanic traditions found across North Asia. While each of these traditions is unique, we have seen that they are also quite similar in many ways, since they arose from the same sources and have since intertwined with each other.

Throughout this writing process, I have asked myself: What right do I have to be writing this book? I am, after all, still in the middle of my own journey—a journey that started when I began exploring the roots of my own Manchu ancestry. During the Qing Dynasty, many Manchus intermarried with Mongols to form political alliances, and my own ancestors were no exception. I strongly suspect that the Mongols with whom my Manchu ancestors intermarried were Khorchin Mongols, given the strong historical relationship between these two peoples. I may even have found hints of Daur or other Inner Mongolian progenitors as well. I am still looking for my appropriate initiatory teacher, however—perhaps a Manchu, perhaps a Khorchin, or perhaps someone from another group altogether.

Once I enter that stage of my journey, I suspect I will become so focused on that specific tradition that I may no longer be able to take the broad comprehensive view that this book required. This is a book that I would have found very valuable many years ago, and I hope that others will find value in the wide-ranging research presented here. But

I know in my heart that by writing this book, I am now closing one chapter of my spiritual journey and embarking on the next phase.

When writing, I also had to consider the effects this book might have. Everything in life carries karmic debt. On one hand, I wanted to provide Western and American audiences with a new awareness and perception of North Asian traditions. I wanted the knowledge I share here to broaden the scope of my readers' spirituality and enrich their own spiritual experience. On the other hand, the potential cultural appropriation this knowledge might enable could have disastrous spiritual effects.

Shamanism is a very deep and profound form of spirituality. Some of the beliefs and practices I describe here only in general detail are not intended to be approached casually. After all, "playing" at being a shaman can invite all sorts of harmful entities and energies into your life. If you abuse the knowledge and practices discussed here, both you and I will suffer the karmic consequences. My traditional shaman friends frequently reminded and warned me that I have a responsibility to protect our ancestral traditions from those who seek to learn about them without giving them proper respect. Any inappropriate use of these traditions will endanger not only them but me as well.

That said, those who do not come from a shamanic culture can still engage in safe practices that can help guide both them and their communities to spiritual and physical health. While I have been critical of Western core shamanism, I admit that it can give people a starting point from which they can approach the practices found in true shamanic cultures. For those who pursue core shamanism, however, I urge you to explore a traditional cultural lineage as well and follow its rules and guidelines exactly.

If you come from a culture that has deep unbroken lineages, that is the best path you can take. If you come from a culture that has broken or lost lineages, you can still learn, initiate, and train from another culture's spiritual heritage—*if* their elders accept you and *if* you follow their rules and taboos. It is not cultural appropriation if a culture's elders have accepted you and you abide by their rules and taboos. And by respectfully learning from the elders of a living tradition, you can come to understand the depth of your own spiritual power in connection with your own ancestral and local land spirits, in addition to connecting with that tradition's deities.

For those engaged in Western witchcraft traditions, many of which have been reconstructed over the last century, you likely already understand that, while many of those practices and beliefs are drawn from traditional ancient sources, they were repurposed piecemeal into modern frameworks. But even if there is no direct connection between modern Celtic, Norse, Hellenic, or other practices and more ancient ones, you can still use traditional shamanic techniques from other cultures to help enhance your understanding of your own beliefs. You can even work to establish a new lineage if you choose to, provided that you received those teachings respectfully from a traditional elder.

Within the witchcraft community, there are many who inappropriately refer to themselves as "shamanic witches" when they do not actually incorporate shamanic beliefs and concepts into their practice. And there are also many who claim they are practicing "Celtic shamanism" or "Norse shamanism." In nearly all cases, these are actually core shamanism techniques overlaid with Celtic and Norse themes and deities. I urge you to realize that these modern reconstructions are not ancient lineages. Above all, please don't take any themes or spirits from this book or from any living shamanic cultural lineage, mix them with core shamanism, and call it true Mongolian/Siberian shamanism. To do so when those cultural traditions are still alive is both offensive and dangerous.

For those from non-shamanic communities who study traditional shamanism today, this can open a path by which your souls (or your descendants' souls) can become honored ancestral spirits. If you choose this path as an ancestral spirit, you can identify descendants to act as human conduits and work with them intimately for their lifetime, perhaps even developing shamanic trance work after one or more generations. In theory, this is how shamanic lineages are born, but it is only after several generations that anyone can tell whether a specific non-shamanic practice or lineage has become shamanism. This is one of the main reasons why traditional shamans choose to teach outsiders. And perhaps, indirectly, that is why I have written this book.

Practitioners in shamanic cultures do not feel the need to prose-lytize. Rather they hope that, by teaching those who are spiritually minded and talented, they can open their paths to create their own multigenerational "shamanic lineage" using their own ancestral and cultural spirits. Aside from building positive karma, they receive no real benefit by doing this. But at the end of the day, remember that the purpose of shamanism is coexistence and balance. In our increasingly volatile global environment, we all need more harmony and balance. I hope spiritual practitioners of all shamanic, animistic, and magical faiths will rise to the occasion.

Acknowledgments

This book's journey would not have been possible without a team of people who provided material, as well as technical and emotional support in the creative process.

First, I want to give special thanks to the Darkhad Mongol shamans Aminaa Batmunkh, Huyagaa Byambajav, and their elder who allowed them to share their knowledge at Mother Tree Shamanism Teachings. I am also deeply indebted to the late Jan Van Ysslestyne, researcher of Ulchi-Manchu shamanism; I wish she'd had the chance to see this book. I also want to thank Jan's assistant Ron Teeples, who has been extremely helpful providing insight and context to the Ulchi, as well as to Jan's research and photo materials. Thanks as well to Marguerite Garner, researcher of Khorchin Mongol culture and spirituality; to Nicholas Breeze Wood, editor of *Sacred Hoop* magazine; to Amalia Rubin, whose research and expertise in Mongolian and Tibetan traditions were invaluable; and to the Asian American spiritual community, most notably to Korean Mudang shaman Jennifer Kim, Chaweon Koo, and Fei Lu, who inspired me to create this resource for and on behalf of Asian Americans.

I also want to express my gratitude to the members of the Western Pagan and witchcraft communities, who have been not only supportive of my journey, but also curious, respectful, and highly encouraging. Particular thanks go to the hosts of "That Witch Life" Podcast (Courtney Weber, Kanani Soleil, and Hilary Whitmore) as well as to many others—including, but not limited to, Elizabeth LaBarca, Langston Kahn, Jennifer

Blue June, Chiron Armand, Vanessa Sinclair, Eddie Massey, and Nikki Kirby—for actively inviting me to promote my work.

And of course, this book would not have been possible without the support and approval of members of the traditional shamanic community, who have told me that this is a great way to build bridges between our traditions and the West.

And of course, I am deeply grateful to my family, who always want the best for me.

And greatest gratitude for my partner, Charles Li, who has been my bedrock of emotional support during this entire process.

Finally, I want to thank Judika Illes, who has been asking me to write this book since the first day we met. Without her and the team at Weiser Books, it would not have happened.

Bibliography

Balogh, Mátyás. "Khorchin Shamans 4." Situgen Blog, May 27, 2009. *situgen.blogspot.com/*.

Balzer, Marjorie Mandelstam. "Yakut." Encyclopedia of World Cultures. *Encyclopedia.com*.

Banzarov, Dorji, et al. "The Black Faith, or Shamanism among the Mongols." *Mongolian Studies*, vol. 7, Mongolia Society, 1981, pp. 53–91.

Batmunkh, Aminaa, with Isaac Wortley and Olena Hladkova. "Practical Shamanism of Nomads 6-Month Course." *Mother Tree Shamanism Teachings*. Online course. September 2020–March 2021.

Bulgakova, Tatiana. *Nanai Shamanic Culture in Indigenous Discourse*. Fürstenberg/Havel, Germany: Verlag der Kulturstiftung Sibirien, 2013.

Buyandelger, Manduhai. *Tragic Spirits: Shamanism, Memory, and Gender in Contemporary Mongolia*. Chicago: University of Chicago Press, 2013.

Crossley, Pamela Kyle. *The Manchus*. Oxford, UK: Blackwell Publishers, 1997.

Czaplicka, M. A. *Shamanism in Siberia*. London: Forgotten Books, 2007.

Delaby, Laurence. "Yakut Religion." Encyclopedia of Religion. *Encyclopedia.com*.

Dmitrieva, Oksana. "Religious Beliefs of the Yakut People in the Wedding Ceremonial Poetry (Algys)." *Karadeniz Uluslararası Bilimsel Dergi*, Kültür Ajans Tanıtım ve Organizasyon, 19, 2013.

Elliott, Mark C. *The Manchu Way: The Eight Banners and Ethnic Identity in Late Imperial China*. Stanford University Press, 2009.

Fu, Yuguang. *Shamanic and Mythic Cultures of Ethnic Peoples in Northern China I*. Routledge, 2021.

──────. *Shamanic and Mythic Cultures of Ethnic Peoples in Northern China II*. Routledge, 2021.

Garner, Marguerite. *Shamans and Healers of Inner Mongolia*. Facebook Video Series. June-July 2020.

Garrett, Stephen. "The Shamanic Empire and the Heavenly Astute Khan: Analysis of the Shamanic Empire of the Early Qing, Its Role in Inner Asian Hegemony, the Nature of Shamanic Khanship, and Implications for Manchu Identity." MA thesis: University of Hawai'i at Manoa, 2020.

Grimaldi, Susan. *Drums of the Ancestors: Manchu and Mongol Shamanism*. Film. Mill Valley, CA: Foundation for Shamanic Studies, 1995.

──────. "In Search of Traditional Shamans: Daur of Inner Mongolia, China, and the Tsaatan Reindeer People of Mongolia." *Journal of the Foundation for Shamanic Studies*, December 2011.

Grimaldi, Susan, and John Lawrence. *Siqingua, Daur Shaman of Inner Mongolia, China*. Film. 2013. *cultureunplugged.com*.

Hays, Jeffrey. "Evenki and Even." *Facts and Details*, 2008, *factsanddetails.com*.

Hoppal, Mihaly. "Nature Worship in Siberian Shamanism." *Eesti Rahvaluule: Indeks*, *folklore.ee*.

Humphrey, Caroline, with Urgunge Onon. *Shamans and Elders: Experience, Knowledge, and Power among the Daur Mongols*. Oxford, UK: Oxford University Press, 1996.

Kenin-Lopsan, Mongus 1993. *Magic of Tuvian Shamans*. Kyzyl, Russia: Novosty Tuva.

Liu, Taiping. "Manchu traditional customs do not burn paper and insert 'Foduo' on the grave during the Qingming Festival." *Zhihu*, March 21, 2020, *zhuanlan.zhihu.com*.

Moss, Robert. "The Nishan Shaman Brings Back a Soul from the Land of the Dead." *The Robert Moss BLOG*, February 23, 2020, *mossdreams.blogspot.com*.

Noll, Richard, and Kun Shi. "Chuonnasuan (Meng Jin Fu): The Last Shaman of the Oroqen of Northeast China." *Journal of Korean Religions*, 6, 2004, pp.135–162.

Popov, A. "Consecration Ritual for a Blacksmith Novice among the Yakuts." *The Journal of American Folklore*, vol. 46, no. 181, University of Illinois Press, 1933, pp. 257–71.

Purev, Otgony, et al. *Mongolian Shamanism*. Ulaanbaatar, Mongolia: Fifth Edition, Munkhiin Useg, 2012.

Sa, Minna. "The Inheritance and Change of the Contemporary Daur Shaman." *MDPI Religions*, 10.1, 2019: 52.

Shi, David. *North Asian Magic: Spellcraft from Manchuria, Mongolia, and Siberia*. Forestville, CA: The Yronwode Institution for the Preservation and Popularization of Indigenous Ethnomagicology (YIPPIE), 2016.

Stewart, Julie Ann (Sarangerel). *Chosen by the Spirits*. Rochester, VT: Destiny Books, 2001.

—————. *Riding Windhorses: A Journey into the Heart of Mongolian Shamanism*. Rochester, VT: Destiny Books, 2000.

Stutley, Margaret. *Shamanism: An Introduction*. London: Routledge, 2003.

Tkacz, Virlana, et al. *Siberian Shamanism: The Shanar Ritual of the Buryats*. Rochester, VT: Inner Traditions, 2015.

Turner, Kevin. *Sky Shamans of Mongolia: Meetings with Remarkable Healers*. Berkeley, CA: North Atlantic Books, 2016.

Van Deusen, Kira. "New Legends in the Rebirth of Khakass Shamanic Culture." *Anthropology of East Europe Review*, vol. 16, no. 2, October 2000, pp. 55–61.

—————. *The Flying Tiger: Women Shamans and Storytellers of the Amur*. Quebec, Canada: McGill-Queen's University Press, 2001.

Van Ysslestyne, J. *Spirits from the Edge of the World*. Seattle, WA: Pathfinder Communications, 2018.

—————. "The Art of Classical Siberian Shamanism." *Pathfinder Counseling*. Online course. 2021.

Wood, Nicholas Breeze. "A Little Shamanic Background." *Sacred Hoop* (1993). Online at *sacredhoop.org*.

—————. "Free Guide to Shamanism." *Sacred Hoop*, 2017. Online at *sacredhoop.org*.

Zabiyako, Andrey P., Anna A. Zabiyako, and Eugenia A. Zavadskaya. *Reindeer Trail: History and Culture of the Amur Evenks*. Blagoveschensk, Russia: Amur State University Publishing, 2017.

Zamaraeva, Yulia, Vladimir Luzan, Svetlana Metlyaeva, et al. "Religion of the Evenki: History and Modern Times." Krasnoyarsk, Russia: *Journal of Siberian Federal University*. Humanities and Social Sciences, 2019, pp. 853–871.

Zorbas, Konstantinos. "The Origins and Reinvention of Shamanic Retaliation in a Siberian City (Tuva Republic, Russia)." *Journal of Anthropological Research*, vol. 71, no. 3, The University of Chicago Press, 2015, pp. 401–22.

Endnotes

Chapter 1

1. Nicholas Breeze Wood, "A Little Shamanic Background," *Sacred Hoop* (1993): 2. *sacredhoop.org*.

2. Wood, "*A Little Shamanic Background*," 2.

3. Dorji Banzarov, "The Black Faith, or Shamanism among the Mongols" *Mongolian Studies*, vol. 7, 1981, 11–31.

4. Jan Van Ysslestyne, *Spirits from the Edge of the World* (Seattle, WA: Pathfinder Communications, 2018), 29.

5. Van Ysslestyne, *Spirits from the Edge of the World*, 336–337.

6. Kevin Turner, *Sky Shamans of Mongolia* (Berkeley, CA: North Atlantic Books, 2016), 16.

7. Van Ysslestyne, *Spirits from the Edge of the World*, 234.

Chapter 2

1. Yuguang Fu, *Shamanic and Mythic Cultures of Ethnic Peoples in Northern China II* (Routledge, 2021), 70.

2. Jan Van Ysslestyne, *Spirits from the Edge of the World* (Seattle, WA: Pathfinder Communications, 2018), 10–17.

3. Julie Ann Stewart (Sarangerel), *Riding Windhorses: A Journey into the Heart of Mongolian Shamanism* (Rochester, VT: Destiny Books, 2000), 31–32.

4. Sarangerel, *Riding Windhorses,* 32–33.

5. Van Ysslestyne, *Spirits from the Edge of the World,* 10.

6. Sarangerel, *Riding Windhorses,* 28.

7. In her book *Chosen by the Spirits,* Sarangerel gives a Buryat prayer that also refers to an additional seventy-seven tengers who dwell in the north and an additional ninety-nine tengers who dwell in the south. Julie Ann Stewart (Sarangerel), *Chosen by the Spirits* (Rochester, VT: Destiny Books, 2001), 208.

8. Aminaa Batmunkh with Isaac Wortley and Olena Hladkiva, "Practical Shamanism of Nomads," *Mother Tree Shamanism Teachings* online course.

9. Ibid.

10. Otgony Purev et al., *Mongolian Shamanism* (Ulaanbaatar, Mongolia: Fifth Edition, Munkhiin Useg, 2012), 115–116.

11. Andrey Zabiyako et al., *Reindeer Trail: History and Culture of the Amur Evenks* (Blagoveschensk, Russia: Amur State University Publishing, 2017), 146.

12. Purev, *Mongolian Shamanism,* 126–127.

13. Marguerite Garner, *Shamans and Healers of Inner Mongolia* (Facebook Video Series, June–July 2020).

14. Sarangerel, *Chosen by the Spirits,* 83.

15. Sarangerel, *Riding Windhorses,* 58.

16. Caroline Humphrey and Urgunge Onon, *Shamans and Elders: Experience, Knowledge, and Power among the Daur Mongols* (Oxford, UK: Oxford University Press, 1996), 213.

17. Yuguang Fu, *Shamanic and Mythic Cultures of Ethnic Peoples in Northern China I* (Routledge, 2021), 16.

18. Fu, *Shamanic and Mythic Cultures of Ethnic Peoples in Northern China I*, 17.

19. Sarangerel, *Chosen by the Spirits*, 29.

20. Batmunkh, "Practical Shamanism of Nomads."

21. Zabiyako, *Reindeer Trail: History and Culture of the Amur Evenks*, 207.

22. Ibid., 141.

23. Batmunkh, "Practical Shamanism of Nomads."

24. Purev, *Mongolian Shamanism*, 130.

25. Sarangerel, *Riding Windhorses*, 53–54.

26. Van Ysslestyne, *Spirits from the Edge of the World*, 101.

Chapter 3

1. Yuguang Fu, *Shamanic and Mythic Cultures of Ethnic Peoples in Northern China II* (Routledge, 2021), 65–92.

2. Andrey Zabiyako et al., *Reindeer Trail: History and Culture of the Amur Evenks* (Blagoveschensk, Russia: Amur State University Publishing, 2017), 148–149.

3. Julie Ann Stewart (Sarangerel), *Chosen by the Spirits* (Rochester, VT: Destiny Books, 2001), 218.

4. Julie Ann Stewart (Sarangerel), *Riding Windhorses: A Journey into the Heart of Mongolian Shamanism* (Rochester, VT: Destiny Books, 2000), 147.

5. Jan Van Ysslestyne, *Spirits from the Edge of the World* (Seattle, WA: Pathfinder Communications, 2018), 31.

6. Van Ysslestyne, *Spirits from the Edge of the World*, 28.

7. Sarangerel, *Riding Windhorses*, 25. Sarangerel describes the sun and moon as the eyes of Tenger on earth, but also describes the sun as a female deity (always staying close to the family) and the moon as a male deity (often goes away to hunt or wage war).

8. Van Ysslestyne, *Spirits from the Edge of the World*, 25.

9. Ibid., 32–33.

10. Ibid., 67, 47.

11. Sarangerel, *Riding Windhorses*, 55.

12. Sarangerel equates Umay with Omosi Mama, the Manchu goddess of life, though in Manchu belief Omosi Mama resides in the Lower World. Sarangerel, *Chosen by the Spirits*, 229.

13. Among the Daur Mongols, a goddess-centered spiritual movement emerged known as the *Niang-Niang* cult, whose main goddess is Omi Niangniang/Barkan (equivalent to Umay, Fodo Mama, and Omosi Mama). Caroline Humphrey and Urgunge Onon, *Shamans and Elders: Experience, Knowledge, and Power among the Daur Mongols* (Oxford, UK: Oxford University Press, 1996), 286–287.

14. Sarangerel, *Chosen by the Spirits*, 230.

15. Van Ysslestyne, *Spirits from the Edge of the World*, 57.

16. Humphrey and Onon, *Shamans and Elders*, 323.

17. Aminaa Batmunkh with Isaac Wortley and Olena Hladkiva, "Practical Shamanism of Nomads," *Mother Tree Shamanism Teachings* online course. The lus are the same as the nagas in Buddhist and Hindu beliefs, and therefore generally appear in serpentine/snake-like form. In Turkic and Mongolian initiation ceremonies, the ancestral shamanic spirits are bonded with lus savdag spirits, so they can carry the ancestral spirits to the shaman. Shamans who are considered to be "fortified by lus" are known to be much more powerful in divination and magic. The

families of those who offend a lus may suffer dire consequences, however.

18. Van Ysslestyne, *Spirits from the Edge of the World*, 57–58. The kuljamu lived in stone houses/caves, wore clothing, and used tools like axes and knives. Van Ysslestyne believes they are the same species as the yeti in the Himalayas and the Sasquatch/Ci'tonga in North America. She has interviewed Ulchi shamans who have working relationships with kuljamu through wooden spirit dolls with conical heads.

19. Ibid., 67.

20. Sarangerel, *Riding Windhorses*, 57–58. Sarangerel suggests that the Mongolian Alma spirits may be the equivalent to the Kuljamu, as she suggests they may also correspond to the yeti and sasquatch.

21. Zabiyako, *Reindeer Trail: History and Culture of the Amur Evenks*, 146.

22. In the War of Heaven, Yeruri sought to cover the land in snow and ice, but the heavenly spirits thwarted him by bringing fire from the sun and stars down to the Middle World, thereby weakening Yeruri. This is one of the reasons why Manchus worship fire. Fu, *Shamanic and Mythic Cultures of Ethnic Peoples in Northern China II*, 71–72.

23. Batmunkh, "Practical Shamanism of Nomads."

24. Sarangerel, *Riding Windhorses*, 58.

25. Van Ysslestyne, *Spirits from the Edge of the World*, 35–39.

26. Kevin Turner briefly mentioned several classes of demons/troublesome spirits in his interviews with Mongolian shamans in *Sky Shamans of Mongolia* (Berkeley, CA: North Atlantic Books, 2016), 118.

27. Laurence Delaby, "Yakut Religion" (Encyclopedia of Religion, *encyclopedia.com*.)

28. The Islamification of Central Asian Turkic peoples may have contributed to this negative portrayal as well. The belief in Erlik even spread to Hungarian/Magyar Paganism, where he is known as Ordog, who was identified with the devil after Christianization.

29. Omosi Mama figures most prominently in the Nisan Shaman legend. She personally guaranteed that Nisan would be a great shamaness, sending her own disciple to train her.

30. Omosi Mama is one of the few ancient goddesses that Manchus who still practice shamanism pray to and venerate. Sometimes she is combined with Fodo Mama through the title Fere Fodo Omosi Mama. Her worshippers often employ a sacred rope with knots and anklebones tied to it, usually tying the rope from the altar to the spirit tree or pole to represent the goddess connecting the physical and spiritual worlds. Stephen Garrett, "The Shamanic Empire and the Heavenly Astute Khan: Analysis of the Shamanic Empire of the Early Qing, Its Role in Inner Asian Hegemony, The Nature of Shamanic Khanship, and Implications for Manchu Identity" (MA thesis: University of Hawai'i at Manoa, 2020), 117–118.

31. Sarangerel, *Chosen by the Spirits*, 229.

32. Fu, *Shamanic and Mythic Cultures of Ethnic Peoples in Northern China I*, 83.

33. Different Evenk groups refer to the fire spirit as either *toyo onin, toyo ono,* or *golomta,* also depicted in the form of an old woman. The Oroqen knew the fire spirit as Tuowo Bukan. The Manchus similarly believe in the sacred importance of fire for the protection of the family health and originally referred to the fire spirit as *Tuwa Enduri, Tuwa Emu,* or *Tuwa Mama.* Following the Manchu conquest of China, this belief merged with the Chinese kitchen god Zhaowang-ye. While the kitchen god in Chinese tradition was considered to be a messenger, the Manchu version of this god took on a more fiery aspect and was treated more as a devotional figure.

34. Nicholas Breeze Wood, "The Shamanic Blacksmith Spirit" (*Sacred Hoop* Free Articles, 3Worlds Shamanism website), *3worlds.co.uk.*

35. In Khovsgol, there is a cave sacred to Dayan Deerh that is accessible only by horseback, where Buryat shamans and worshippers continue to venerate him and conduct ceremonies. My Darkhad friends tell me that the ancient black shamans placed a curse on their lineages that forbids Darkhad shamans from going there. It is said that, if Darkhad shamans even set foot in the cave, they will meet a tragic death very soon.

36. Sarangerel, *Riding Windhorses*, 61.

37. Sarangerel, *Chosen by the Spirits*, 231.

38. Ibid., 231–232.

39. Garrett, "The Shamanic Empire and the Heavenly Astute Khan," 94.

40. Ibid., 116.

41. Ibid., 116.

42. Sarangerel, *Riding Windhorses*, 31–34.

43. Humphrey and Onon, *Shamans and Elders*, 189.

44. Sarangerel, *Riding Windhorses*, 73.

Chapter 4

1. I list the nine degrees here, but for deeper explanation, see Julie Ann Stewart (Sarangerel), *Chosen by the Spirits* (Rochester, VT: Destiny Books, 2001) and *The Different Types of Shamans* (Circle of Tengerism, website is no longer active). See also Virlana Tkacz, *Siberian Shamanism: The Shanar Ritual of the Buryats* (Rochester, VT: Inner Traditions, 2015).

2. Sarangerel, *Chosen by the Spirits*, 233–236.

3. Jan Van Ysslestyne, "The Art of Classical Siberian Shamanism" (*Pathfinder Counseling,* Online Course), *www.2pathfinder counseling.com.*

4. Van Ysslestyne, *Spirits from the Edge of the World* (Seattle, WA: Pathfinder Communications, 2018), 99–100.

5. Ibid., 112–113.

6. Ibid., 195.

7. Kevin Turner, *Sky Shamans of Mongolia* (Berkeley, CA: North Atlantic Books, 2016), 129–130.

8. Sarangerel, *Other Spiritual Callings: Bariyachi-Midwives* (Circle of Tengerism, website is no longer active).

9. Aminaa Batmunkh with Isaac Wortley and Olena Hladkiva, "Practical Shamanism of Nomads," *Mother Tree Shamanism Teachings* online course.

10. Marguerite Garner, *Shamans and Healers of Inner Mongolia* (Facebook Video Series, June–July 2020).

11. Sarangerel, *Other Spiritual Callings: Otoshi-Healers.*

12. Caroline Humphrey and Urgunge Onon, *Shamans and Elders: Experience, Knowledge, and Power among the Daur Mongols* (Oxford, UK: Oxford University Press, 1996), 287–288.

13. Sarangerel, *Chosen by the Spirits,* 164.

14. Batmunkh, "Practical Shamanism of Nomads."

Chapter 5

1. Dorji Banzarov, "The Black Faith, or Shamanism among the Mongols," *Mongolian Studies,* vol. 7 1981, 11.

2. A. Zakharov "Central-Asian Origin of the Ancestors of the First Americans," *First Americans,* 11, 2003, 139–144.

3. M. Kenin-Lopsan, *Magic of Tuvian Shamans* (Kyzyl, Russia: Mongus, 1993), 1–5.

4. Margaret Stutley, *Shamanism: An Introduction* (Routledge, 2003), 91.

5. Konstantinos Zorbas, "The Origins and Reinvention of Shamanic Retaliation in a Siberian City (Tuva Republic, Russia)" (University of Chicago Press: *Journal of Anthropological Research*, vol. 71, no. 3), 409.

6. Ibid., 408.

7. Marjorie Mandelstam Balzer, "Yakut," (Encyclopedia of World Cultures. *Encyclopedia.com)*

8. Laurence Delaby, "Yakut Religion," (Encyclopedia of Religion. *Encyclopedia.com.)*

9. A. Popov, "Consecration Ritual for a Blacksmith Novice among the Yakuts" (University of Illinois Press: *The Journal of American Folklore*, vol. 46, no. 181, 1933), 257.

10. M. A. Czaplicka, *Shamanism in Siberia* (London: Forgotten Books, 2007), 60.

11. Ibid., 50.

12. Oksana Dmitrieva, "Religious Beliefs of the Yakut People in the Wedding Ceremonial Poetry (Algys)," (Yakutsk, Russia: *Karadeniz Uluslararası Bilimsel Dergi*, Kültür Ajans Tanıtım ve Organizasyon, 2013), 2.

13. Popov, "Consecration Ritual for a Blacksmith Novice among the Yakuts," 261.

14. Kira Van Deusen, "New Legends in the Rebirth of Khakass Shamanic Culture," (*Anthropology of East Europe Review*, vol. 16, no. 2, October 2000), 56.

Chapter 6

1. Amalia Rubin, guest speaker, "Practical Shamanism of Nomads," *Mother Tree Shamanism* Teachings online course.

2. Ibid.

3. Anonymous Darkhad shaman, personal communications.

4. Rubin, "Practical Shamanism of Nomads."

5. Ibid.

6. Anonymous Darkhad shaman, personal communications.

7. To learn more about the Darkhad tradition of Mongolian shamanism, see Purev, *Mongolian Shamanism* (Authors Unlimited, 2006) or look into the Mother Tree Shamanism Teachings group, which presents classes and intense studies on practical nomadic shamanic concepts led by a traditional Darkhad shaman.

8. Kevin Turner, *Sky Shamans of Mongolia* (Berkeley, CA: North Atlantic Books, 2016), 73.

9. Julie Ann Stewart (Sarangerel), *The Different Types of Shamans* (Circle of Tengerism, website is no longer active).

10. Ibid.

11. Julie Ann Stewart (Sarangerel), *Becoming a Shaman* (Circle of Tengerism, website is no longer active). In the first stage, new shamans are required to run around a group of birch trees with the community representatives and children while in trance and drumming. Then they must successfully climb up and down a very tall tree that symbolizes the World Tree while in trance.

12. Caroline Humphrey and Urgunge Onon, *Shamans and Elders: Experience, Knowledge, and Power among the Daur Mongols* (Oxford, UK: Oxford University Press, 1996), 286–301.

13. Minna Sa, "The Inheritance and Change of the Contemporary Daur Shaman" (*MDPI Religions* 10.1, 2019, 52), 4.

14. Sa, "The Inheritance and Change of the Contemporary Daur Shaman," 5.

15. Ibid., 6.

16. Ibid., 5.

17. Ibid., 7, 9.

18. Susan Grimaldi. *Siqingua, Daur Shaman of Inner Mongolia, China*. (Film. 2013).

19. Susan Grimaldi, *Drums of the Ancestors: Manchu and Mongol Shamanism* (Mill Valley, CA: Foundation for Shamanic Studies, 1995).

20. Mátyás Balogh, *Khorchin Shamans 4* Siitugen Blog, 2009, *situgen. blogspot.com/).*

21. Grimaldi, *Drums of the Ancestors: Manchu and Mongol Shamanism.*

22. Marguerite Garner, *Shamans and Healers of Inner Mongolia* (Facebook Video Series, June–July 2020).

23. Ibid.

24. Balogh, *Khorchin Shamans 3* (Situgen Blog, 2009, *situgen. blogspot.com/).*

25. Rubin, "Practical Shamanism of Nomads."

Chapter 7

1. Kira Van Deusen, *The Flying Tiger: Women Shamans and Storytellers of the Amur* (Quebec, Canada: McGill-Queen's University Press, 2001), 228.

2. Mark Elliott, *The Manchu Way: The Eight Banners and Ethnic Identity in Late Imperial China* (Stanford University Press, 2009), 47–48.

3. Pamela Crossley, *The Manchus* (Oxford, UK: Blackwell Publishers, 1997), 18.

4. Crossley, *The Manchus*, 17.

5. Ibid., 38.

6. Stephen Garrett, "The Shamanic Empire and the Heavenly Astute Khan: Analysis of the Shamanic Empire of the Early Qing, Its Role in Inner Asian Hegemony, the Nature of Shamanic Khanship, and Implications for Manchu Identity," (MA Thesis, University of Hawai'i at Manoa, 2020), 49.

7. Andrey Zabiyako, *Reindeer Trail: History and Culture of the Amur Evenks* (Blagoveschensk, Russia: Amur State University Publishing, 2017), 131–147.

8. Ibid., 190.

9. Ibid., 172.

10. Ibid., 149–154.

11. Ibid., 11.

12. Ibid., 193.

13. Ibid., 203–207.

14. Ibid., 208.

15. Ibid., 210.

16. Minna Sa, "The Inheritance and Change of the Contemporary Daur Shaman" (*MDPI Religions* 10.1, 2019, 52), 9.

17. Richard Noll and Kun Shi, "Chuonnasuan (Meng Jin Fu): The Last Shaman of the Oroqen of Northeast China" (*Journal of Korean Religions*, 6:135–162, 2004), 8.

18. Ibid., 12.

19. Ibid., 12.

20. Ibid., 6–8.

21. Ibid., 9.

22. Ibid., 10–11.

23. Ibid., 3.

24. Ibid., 11.

25. Ibid., 8–9.

26. Ibid., 12–13.

27. Jan Van Ysslestyne, *Spirits from the Edge of the World* (Seattle, WA: Pathfinder Communications, 2018), 211–217.

28. Ibid., 19.

29. Ibid., 20–21.

30. Ibid., 47.

31. Tatiana Bulgakova, *Nanai Shamanic Culture in Indigenous Discourse* (Fürstenberg/Havel, DE: Verlag der Kulturstiftung Sibirien, 2013), 13–15.

32. Jan Van Ysslestyne, *The Art of Classical Siberian Shamanism* (Pathfinder Counseling, Online course)

33. Van Ysslestyne, *Spirits from the Edge of the World*, 251–252.

34. Yuguang Fu, *Shamanic and Mythic Cultures of Ethnic Peoples in Northern China II* (Routledge, 2021), 70.

35. Garrett, "The Shamanic Empire And The Heavenly Astute Khan," 65–66.

36. Ibid., 86.

37. Ibid., 105.

38. Ibid., chapter 1.

39. Ibid., 88–100.

40. Ibid., 167–168.

41. Ibid., 122–125.

Chapter 8

1. Otgony Purev et al., *Mongolian Shamanism* (Ulaanbaatar, Mongolia: Fifth Edition, Munkhiin Useg, 2012), 196–199.

2. Nicholas Breeze Wood, "Free Guide to Shamanism," *(Sacred Hoop*, 2017. Online at *sacredhoop.org)*, 40.

3. Jan Van Ysslestyne, *Spirits from the Edge of the World* (Seattle, WA: Pathfinder Communications, 2018), 256.

4. Purev, *Mongolian Shamanism*, 183.

5. Julie Ann Stewart (Sarangerel), *Riding Windhorses: A Journey into the Heart of Mongolian Shamanism* (Rochester, VT: Destiny Books, 2000), 85.

6. Aminaa Batmunkh with Isaac Wortley and Olena Hladkiva, "Practical Shamanism of Nomads," *Mother Tree Shamanism* Teachings online course.

7. Julie Ann Stewart (Sarangerel), *Chosen by the Spirits* (Rochester, VT: Destiny Books, 2001), 235.

8. Susan Grimaldi, *Drums of the Ancestors: Manchu and Mongol Shamanism* (Mill Valley, CA: Foundation for Shamanic Studies, 1995).

9. Remember the Khorchin folk legend of the ancient battle between a shaman and a buddhist monk, in which the shaman's skirt was ripped to shreds. Grimaldi, *Drums of the Ancestors: Manchu and Mongol Shamanism*.

10. Van Ysslestyne, *Spirits from the Edge of the World*, 249.

11. Marguerite Garner, *Shamans and Healers of Inner Mongolia* (Facebook Video Series, June–July 2020).

12. Virlana Tkacz et al., *Siberian Shamanism: The Shanar Ritual of the Buryats* (Rochester, VT: Inner Traditions, 2015), 48.

13. Sarangerel, *Chosen by the Spirits*, 156.

14. Van Ysslestyne, *Spirits from the Edge of the World*, 244.

15. Ibid., 248, and Batmunkh, "Practical Shamanism of Nomads."

16. Van Ysslestyne, *Spirits from the Edge of the World*, 248, and Sarangerel, *Chosen by the Spirits*, 156.

17. Batmunkh, "Practical Shamanism of Nomads."

18. Ibid.

19. Sarangerel, *Chosen by the Spirits*, 163–166.

20. Van Ysslestyne, *Spirits from the Edge of the World*, 248, and Sarangerel, *Chosen by the Spirits*, 258–260.

21. Sarangerel, *Chosen by the Spirits*, 156–157.

22. Purev, *Mongolian Shamanism*, 228–229.

23. Nicholas Breeze Wood, "Tiger Bells" (*Sacred Hoop* Free Articles, 3Worlds Shamanism website), *3worlds.co.uk*.

24. Van Ysslestyne, *Spirits from the Edge of the World*, 251–253.

25. Sarangerel, *Chosen by the Spirits*, 168–169.

26. Yuguang Fu, *Shamanic and Mythic Cultures of Ethnic Peoples in Northern China II* (Routledge, 2021), 8.

27. Tkacz, *Siberian Shamanism: The Shanar Ritual of the Buryats*, 43–44.

28. Van Ysslestyne, *Spirits from the Edge of the World*, 142.

29. Sarangerel, *Riding Windhorses*, 40–42.

30. Van Ysslestyne, *Spirits from the Edge of the World*, 142.

31. Sarangerel, *Riding Windhorses*, 145.

32. Batmunkh, "Practical Shamanism of Nomads."

33. Sarangerel, *Riding Windhorses*, 59–62.

34. *Evenk Udaganka Shaman* (Documentary available on YouTube).

35. Van Ysslestyne, *Spirits from the Edge of the World*, 260–269.

Chapter 9

1. Aminaa Batmunkh with Isaac Wortley and Olena Hladkiva, "Practical Shamanism of Nomads," *Mother Tree Shamanism Teachings* online course.

2. Yuguang Fu, *Shamanic and Mythic Cultures of Ethnic Peoples in Northern China II* (Routledge, 2021), 19.

3. David Shi, *North Asian Magic: Spellcraft from Manchuria, Mongolia, and Siberia* (Forestville, CA: The Yronwode Institution for the Preservation and Popularization of Indigenous Ethnomagicology (YIPPIE), 2016), 33.

4. Fu, *Shamanic and Mythic Cultures of Ethnic Peoples in Northern China II*, 8.

5. Batmunkh, "Practical Shamanism of Nomads."

6. Mudang Shaman Jennifer Kim, personal communications.

7. Batmunkh, "Practical Shamanism of Nomads."

8. Among Mongols, all sections of a prayer end with the word s*hoog* repeated three times. This is a sacred word used to call shamanic spirits and to calm them when they arrive. Batmunkh, "Practical Shamanism of Nomads."

9. Julie Ann Stewart (Sarangerel), *Riding Windhorses: A Journey into the Heart of Mongolian Shamanism* (Rochester, VT: Destiny Books, 2000), 16.

10. Nicholas Breeze Wood, "Free Guide to Shamanism" (*Sacred Hoop*, 2017). Online at *sacredhoop.org*, 28–33.

11. *Practical Shamanism of Nomads*, Mother Tree Shamanism Teachings.

12. Julie Ann Stewart (Sarangerel), *Chosen by the Spirits* (Rochester, VT: Destiny Books, 2001), 175.

13. Ibid., 176.

14. Ibid., 177.

15. Ibid., 55–56.

16. *Practical Shamanism of Nomads*, Mother Tree Shamanism Teachings.

17. Sarangerel, *Riding Windhorses*, 88.

18. Ibid., 177.

19. Shi, *North Asian Magic*, 49.

20. *Practical Shamanism of Nomads*, Mother Tree Shamanism Teachings.

21. Ibid.

22. Sarangerel, *Chosen by the Spirits*, 182.

23. Anonymous Darkhad shaman, personal communications.

24. Sarangerel, *Riding Windhorses*, 114.

25. *Practical Shamanism of Nomads*, Mother Tree Shamanism Teachings.

26. Sarangerel, *Chosen by the Spirits*, 183.

27. Anonymous Darkhad shaman, personal communications.

28. Shi, *North Asian Magic*, 57.

29. If working outside or without an altar, set liquid offerings and cleansing herbs aside to be sprinkled, as in a prayer ceremony.

30. Although it is now taboo to offer blood to fire, there is evidence of blood thrown into fire in ancient times. Notably, in the ritual alliance between Jianzhou Jurchen chief Wanggao and the Gorlos Mongols, black ox blood was sprinkled into a fire. All northern shamans now agree that fire is offended by blood, so it is strictly taboo. Yuguang Fu, *Shamanic and Mythic Cultures of Ethnic Peoples in Northern China I*. (Routledge, 2021), 31.

31. Five flags of different colors (red, green, blue, yellow, and white) that are strung together, each blessed with Tibetan windhorse blessing prayers. In Tibetan Buddhism, old flags are disposed of by burning so that the prayers are carried into heaven. The same principle applies here. This is a reflection of Tibetan Buddhist influence on Manchu beliefs. Mongols similarly use five pieces of cloth of the same colors. Batmunkh, "Practical Shamanism of Nomads."

32. Ibid.

33. Sarangerel, *Chosen by the Spirits*, 176–177.

About the Author

Charles Li

David Shi is a shamanic worker and folk magic practitioner who engages in traditional North Asian forms of shamanism. He is primarily of Manchurian descent but can also trace his ancestry to Mongolian, Han Chinese, Korean, as well as trace amounts of Tungus Siberian and ancient Central Asian Turkic heritage. David's practices are deeply rooted in spirit work in which ancestral and land spirits are called upon to empower all workings. He has appeared at conferences and festivals throughout the United States and is always aiming to introduce Westerners to Eastern spiritualities and helping fellow Asian Americans connect to their spiritual roots. He currently resides in New York City. Follow him on Instagram @davidjshi311.

To Our Readers

Weiser Books, an imprint of Red Wheel/Weiser, publishes books across the entire spectrum of occult, esoteric, speculative, and New Age subjects. Our mission is to publish quality books that will make a difference in people's lives without advocating any one particular path or field of study. We value the integrity, originality, and depth of knowledge of our authors.

Our readers are our most important resource, and we appreciate your input, suggestions, and ideas about what you would like to see published.

Visit our website at *www.redwheelweiser.com*, where you can learn about our upcoming books and free downloads, and also find links to sign up for our newsletter and exclusive offers.

You can also contact us at *info@rwwbooks.com* or at

Red Wheel/Weiser, LLC
65 Parker Street, Suite 7
Newburyport, MA 01950